D1613064

SECRET SIGHTS

Unknown Celtic Ireland

SECRET SIGHTS

Unknown Celtic Ireland

ROB VANCE

Gill & Macmillan

Gill & Macmillan Ltd
Hume Avenue, Park West, Dublin 12
with associated companies throughout the world
www.gillmacmillan.ie
© Rob Vance 2003
0 7171 3664 7
Design and print origination by Fergal Norris, Outburst Design
Colour reproduction by Ultragraphics Ltd, Dublin
Printed by ColourBooks Ltd, Dublin

This book is typeset in Arrus BT Roman 10 on 15.

The paper used in this book comes from the wood pulp of managed forests. For every tree felled, at least one tree is planted, thereby renewing natural resources.

A CIP catalogue record for this book is available from the British Library.

1 3 5 4 2

Illustrations on the following pages were taken from
Treasures of the National Museum of Ireland: Irish Antiquities
edited by Patrick F. Wallace and Raghnall Ó Floinn (Gill & Macmillan 2002)
and are reproduced by kind permission of the National Museum:
2 (bottom), 9 (bottom), 12, 24, 29 (top), 40 (bottom), 41 (top and bottom),
44, 54 (right), 55, 60, 81 (bottom), 109, 116 (top), 147.

For Clodagh, Beatrice and Jocelyn

This book is a guide to the legend, archaeology and
history that underlies modern Ireland.
It is a guide to the past and a possible template for future inquiry.

Contents

The Province of Leinster 58

COUNTY DUBLIN 60

COUNTY KILDARE 67

COUNTY WICKLOW 73

COUNTY WEXFORD 79

COUNTY LOUTH 83

COUNTY LONGFORD 85

COUNTY WESTMEATH 91

COUNTY MEATH 99

COUNTY KILKENNY 106

COUNTY CARLOW 110

COUNTY LAOIS 114

COUNTY OFFALY 117

COUNTY LEITRIM 121

*Carnsore Point,
Co. Wexford, an
eerie site, venerated
since pre-Christian
times.*

Preface

Born and educated in Dublin, it always puzzled me how Early Ireland did not really feature in the history taught in this country.

Christian Ireland was, however, freely available. It had high crosses, manuscripts, saints and scholars, but even though the metalwork and stonework were artistically brilliant, they were overlaid with Christian iconography to the extent that the Celtic element only appeared as the medium for the message.

This book, therefore, is about that mysterious place, what the general public calls, 'Celtic Ireland', a region remote in time and space, and surreal in its dynastic and mythological complexity. The pages contain descriptions of structures existing millennia before the Celts, extracts from mythology mostly transcribed by Christian monks, and is written in English, which began replacing Gaelic as the dominant language some three hundred years ago. The book describes the various sinews that go to make up the body Celtic, and offers appraised speculation as to custom, ritual and belief.

The Office of Public Works and the State Heritage Service, *Dúchas*, have preserved and imaginatively rebuilt many sites that could otherwise have been either demolished by developers or quietly forgotten, to be reused as stones for a field boundary. They have done so with good taste and great care, and some of their sites are described in the text. But the sites so displayed are perhaps a neutered version of what was there, shorn of its pagan roughness, tidied and made clean for the visitor.

The less well-known locations are not so easily emasculated, not readily tamed, not anything, just *there*, in their primal and often broken state. But in that condition of nature, they are accessible to our senses and our imagination in a way that sometimes allows uninterrupted experience and personal interpretation. My intention is to show, through pictures and description, that many of these *liminal* spaces exist in Ireland, metaphorical gaps in time and space where mythology and imagination combine to repair the temporal gap of twenty centuries, and the perpetual rasping of the weather.

Of these enigmatic 'religious' sites, early Christian and pagan, usually in remote parts of the countryside, many retain what a religious person would describe as 'presence', that indefinable sense of recent inhabitation by something extra-sensory. This phenomenon, the perceived absorption by the individual of the atmosphere of a locale, may be a subjective fiction but, nevertheless, some sites appear to have a tangible and palpable quality of that

presence, often benign, sometimes less so. In choosing the sites, I realised that many are practically unknown, appearing only in the great manuscripts. And while a few have an elaborate and detailed history, others have scant reference anywhere. Most of the locations chosen for this book, however, have a particular property, a *numinosity*, a capacity to fire the imagination with vivid pictures from their ancient past.

This work is not a substitution for archaeological or historical scholarship. It is, hopefully, complementary to the painstaking work by experts in many different fields, and may encourage more interest and further reflection. It is somewhat of a compendium, with jigsaw-shaped pieces of information about many things which, if taken together, may illuminate little-known areas of this island's early history.

There are many diverse areas of study associated with the complex and convoluted history of this island: archaeology, linguistics, mythology, social history, economic history and other more esoteric disciplines. In addition, certain of the locations chosen for this book are from 3000 BC, thus moving these structures beyond the Celts and beyond any recorded history. It moves them into a different imaginative register, a landscape where speculation about astronomic and electromagnetic functions takes root and produces exotic growth. In general, I have kept to the common or garden variety of supposition and inference, rather than the exotic blooms of wider speculation.

In choosing a 'time frame' for this book, I have encompassed the earliest known structures and a small number of early mediaeval sites. My time frame starts in the Neolithic age of 3500 BC and travels forward to the Christian period, covering some ancient structures dedicated to ancestors or gods, forward to the beginnings of early Christian Ireland. These monastic sites are still *relatively* old structures, but almost 'brand-new'

when compared to the ancient tombs and observatories of Newgrange and similar locations.

The search for sites that are 'Celtic' is problematic in respect of actual evidence that the people who inhabited these sites came from a European Celtic homeland in sufficient numbers to warrant Ireland being called a 'Celtic' country. Nevertheless, Ireland remains the only country in Western Europe where something in a tangible form remains of the European Celts. What we do have is an amalgam of many things that are undoubtedly Celtic, such as the Early Christian manuscripts, although they have stylistic similarities to other traditions of Northern Europe and their 'Celtic' style is almost a revival of European La Tène decoration of several centuries earlier. We also have a language, *Irish*, spoken passionately by cultured and educated people who have businesses, raise families, make TV programmes, lecture in universities, and participate in what appears to be an alternative culture, almost an underground and somewhat subversive linguistic alternative to the karaoke suburbanism of 21st-century Ireland.

In Co. Kildare, a massive dike and inner ditch encircles the isolated Dún Aillinne, enclosing over 34 acres. This extensive hillfort, once a seasonal seat of the kings of Leinster, has no approach road and access is through fields and over fences. It has been partly excavated but remains largely unknown, its rough pasture hiding the burnt remains of a ritual structure of great complexity, suggesting an immense timber circular arena with tiered seating. Over 2,000 years ago, the great pagan festival of *Bealtaine* was held here, with complex and bloody rituals enacted within the amphitheatre.

Now, sheep graze the uneven grassland and foxes hunt for rabbit in the honeycombed ramparts.

This book is about such places.

Opposite page: The great Mound of Rathcroghan, at Cruachain Ai, a vast site in Roscommon, traditionally the home of the warrior queen Maeve and burial ground of the kings of Connacht.

*Rathangan,
Co. Kildare, the
residence of the Uí
Fhailghe dynasty of
Leinster as early as
the 6th century.
Their kings, who fell
through war and
assassination, are
recorded in poignant
verse from the period:*

The fort over
against the
oak-wood,
it was Bruidge's, it
was Cathal's,
it was Aed's, it was
Ailill's,
it was Conaig's, it
was Cuilene's, and
it was Mael
Duin's. The fort
remains after each
king in turn, as for
the hosts, they
sleep in the clay.

[Byrne, 2001]

Acknowledgments

Special thanks are due to Brendan Walsh, friend and solicitor, who started the whole ball rolling by introducing me to Jonathan Williams, now my agent, whose patience and good humour is matched by his attention to detail. Ann Cole, now in Colorado, sent many books and gave valuable early direction, and Maura, Susan, Lucy and Paddy McGilligan offered help and assistance; I appreciate their good wishes. History began for me at Avoca School and without Dr John de Courcy Ireland I would never have understood or enjoyed it so much. My daughter Clodagh gave her support and my younger daughter BiBi was a treat to be with as always.

Repro 35 processed the transparencies and made the superb digital transfers and thanks are due to Paddy and Frank Deery and particularly Jim Butler. Gill & Macmillan are better than the Coombe Hospital for anxious and expectant authors; my thanks to Fergal Tobin, Deirdre Rennison Kunz and the staff involved.

Writing and photographing a book such as this takes a lot of time. It couldn't happen without someone sensible and thrifty, willing to subsidise and support the work in progress. To my wife Sheila I offer my heartfelt thanks for her valuable contribution.

Finally, this photographer rarely works alone and, for the majority of the pictures, my son Jocelyn was both assistant and companion. I could not have asked for better company.

Author's Note

Finding the locations

Ordnance Survey references are principally from the half-inch map series; the remainder are from either the Discovery series (a new set of maps of astonishing detail, based on aerial photography) or from the Ordnance Survey of Northern Ireland. The references are arranged as follows: map number, quadrant, top numerical reference and side numerical reference.

Photographic information

The majority of the pictures were shot on Canon cameras, A1 and AE1, using FD lenses from 20 to 300 mm. Some additional pictures were shot on Pentax 6x7 and Rollieflex 6x6. Fujichrome Velvia 50 ASA was generally used.

*Opposite page:
Silhouette of the
Punchestown
standing stone, a
burial marker of the
Bronze Age.*

Introduction

Becoming a Celtic Land

Towards an Irish Identity

The word 'Celtic' is a useful metaphor for describing music, art, a volatile temperament, and the identity of a people. It has been used as a symbol by a celebrated Scottish soccer club, and by champion boxer Steve Collins ['The Celtic Warrior']. Descriptions of an eloquent people with a ready wit and perhaps a certain reckless bravery are not new, and are found in portrayals of the Gauls by Diodorus in the 1st century BC and Elizabethan descriptions of the Irish in the 16th century. Such ascribed 'Celtic' traits may well be romantic, in that they become embedded in the cultural imagination rather than describing character as such, but nevertheless they descend to us today without any indication that they have been diluted — by several millennia, countless Vikings, Normans, Palatines, Huguenots and the many other incomers who have created this island race.

Celtic Ireland

It would appear that the various tribal groups that ultimately became what we term 'Celts' began to migrate toward Western Europe from their putative homelands somewhere between the Caspian and the Black Sea, perhaps around 1500 BC. They were not an homogenous group but one of a series of races, broadly Eastern in origin, that brought a more advanced society into contact with the pre-existing European 'Urnfield' culture. This culture, agrarian and mainly concentrated in central Europe, was characterised by the placing of cremated remains in [usually] upturned funerary vessels. Similar burial practices appear in Ireland, and a type of urn known as 'Beaker' appears at sites across Ireland around 2000 BC, with concentrations along the River Bann, and the glacial kame ridges

Standing stone,
Co. Mayo, possibly
the grave of a
warrior or the
border of a
territory. These
stones were often
the focus of ritual
and ceremony,
c. 2000 BC.

of the midlands. Ultimately, these proto-Celtic peoples produced an art-form in the shape of gold lunulae, torcs, bronze pins and other metalwork items of the highest quality in design and manufacture. Their work, that of the late Bronze Age, is suggestive of a prosperous and artistic society, trading and exchanging ideas and artefacts, albeit on a modest scale, across much of Europe.

The horse-mounted Indo-Europeans probably subjugated the Urnfield peoples of the Danube and Rhine valleys and from them formed a new hybrid classification, later to be known as Keltoi. What these peoples did share was probably certain core language elements, and their linguistic inheritance forms a deep root in French, Italian, Armenian, Welsh, Brittonic and Gaelic. By the end of the 3rd century

Bronze shield,
Lough Gur, Co.
Limerick,
c. 700 BC.

BC, these vibrant 'barbarians' had sacked Rome, plundered the Oracle at Delphi and some at least had probably reached the shores of Britain and Ireland.

But from the point of view of empirical history, Celts only became recognised as a classification in relatively recent times. Prior to the 19th century, most of pre-Roman Europe was seen as barbarian and therefore not worthy of study. In Ireland at that time, Celts as a distinct race did not exist in the historical imagination. It was assumed, in a naïve though accurate way, that Ireland had been inhabited since the distant past by an unknown race of venerable antiquity. This was reasonably legitimate, in that every land and territory has antecedent inhabitants, of which a proportion remain, and a proportion become dominant.

Those described as Celts first enter the European narrative through writers like Aristotle, Strabo and, in particular, Julius Caesar, who encountered them as a series of tribes living across western Europe, from the Alps to the Baltic. They were known under various names, Belgae, Aquatani, Sequani, Tectosages and many others. They did not share similar looks, nor did their customs and beliefs form a common discourse. Tacitus, writing in the 1st century AD, described at least three different types of insular Celts; the Scotii, having 'reddish hair and large limbs', the Cymrii of 'small stature with dark hair', and the inhabitants of what is now south-west England being 'of tall stature, fair and ruddy, terrible for the fierceness of their eyes, fond of quarrelling and of overbearing insolence' [Cunliffe, 1986]. There is little evidence to suggest independent, large-scale emigration from Europe to Ireland of any of these tribes, but plenty to recommend commercial intercourse and small-scale settlement from Britannia.

In the early decades of the 20th century it was assumed, in southern Ireland at least, that we alone were truly 'Celtic' and that the arrivals and additions from the mediaeval period onwards were therefore of a foreign race. The theory that Ireland was an unsullied and isolated Christian and Celtic land until the arrival of 'foreigners' proved useful to both xenophobes and detractors alike, and Irish history written from the 1930s onwards tended to delete the benefits of so-called 'foreigners', thereby fostering the romantic illusion of the 'dreaming Celt' happy in his pious devotions and rural simplicity.

Artistic and Social Contacts

The evidence would suggest, however, that rather than a Celtic invasion from Gaulish Europe reaching Ireland in the centuries preceding the Christian era, there was continuous artistic and social contact across the sea between Ireland and Celtic Britain of much greater significance and subsequent effect. Tribal groups such as the Dumnonnii, Setantii, Belgae and Brigantii all have antecedents in Celtic Britain and succeeding tribal territories identified in Ireland. The earliest, possibly European 'Celtic' evidence in Ireland is from the 3rd century BC with subsequent arrivals, perhaps refugees from Caesar's Gaul or Britain, intermittently arriving during the following three hundred years. Archaeological excavation is suggesting that settlers from Britannia, perhaps responding to Germanic arrivals, continued to arrive in Ireland as late as the 5th century AD and established themselves on existing hillforts. It is perhaps coincidental that Irish history, in terms of written and Christian record, begins around this period. While there is a popular conception that the people of Ireland as a whole have retained more of a Celtic 'flavour' than the other inhabitants of these islands, it remains largely linguistic or anecdotal, for hard evidence in the form of archaeological remains are meagre for the insular Celts in general and for Ireland in particular.

Pagan female goddess from Cathedral Hill, Armagh.

Irish Celtic life was archaic by the standards of the early European Christian period, and this island, as so often in her history, was beyond many of the developments that occurred on mainland Europe and specifically those obtained through contact with the Roman empire. There probably were limited trading contacts with intrepid merchants from the Romano-British world as evidenced by the pottery shards found at a possible Roman-Irish trading-post at Loughshinny in Co. Dublin and also by the Romano-British burial at Stonyford, Co. Kilkenny. The ancient kingdom of Ossory, based around Gowran in Co. Kilkenny would appear to have been especially busy in the period around the fall of Roman Britain. At Lagore in Co. Meath, a lake Crannóg of the *Sil nAedo Slaine* [seed of Aed of Slane] the dominant ruling family of Brega in the 6th century, was found to have numerous small items dating from the earlier Roman period.

Base of Castledermot high cross, c. *9th century.*

Though in general Ireland and the Irish Celts remained isolated from mainstream developments elsewhere in Europe, Celts from Gaul and possibly Ireland were hired by the Romans, Egyptians and Syrians as mercenaries — a large hoard of Roman coins found at Limerick could have been payment for such work. Recent identification by Professor Barry Raftery of a horse-bit found in Transylvania, but of Irish derivation, lends credence to an Irish-Celtic mercenary hypothesis. Later records show Irish kings coming to the aid of Anglo-Saxon families at war, usually as a result of intermarriage and subsequent alliances.

Language in Early Ireland

The Celtic languages of Wales, Scotland and Ireland, while suggesting the past, can but infer the distant society from which they descend. The early mythic stories relate to an heroic society, perhaps removed by several centuries from the period in which they were transcribed. Nevertheless, the mythological tales written down for the first time in history by the monks of the early Christian period contain many observations of everyday life, with details of

weaponry, modes of transport and accommodation.

Writing, as an example of a progressive society, does not appear in Ireland until Christian times, although the rudimentary Ogham script was used for memorials in lands around the Irish Sea. Ogham, a series of horizontal strikes across a vertical monolith, was granite shorthand generally used for fallen warriors and others deemed worthy, and gives an indication of the families and dynasties that were connected across the Irish Sea. Many of the Ogham stones found in South Wales probably relate to the *Deisi*, an Irish tribe based in Wales but originally from Waterford.

The cultivated language of Irish Gaelic was the language of the *Fili*, the learned class of poets and seers who were highly respected and venerated. The Celtic oral tradition was probably *not* an ignorance of the written word, but more likely an attempt to retain the wisdom and knowledge embodied in that tradition for the use of a sacred elite and their patrons. As long as it remained oral, it could only be learnt and used by a trained patrician caste. Nevertheless, it is from this trained and educated class that the mythology, genealogy, history and traditions of the early Irish race descended.

The Ogham stone from Kilmalkedar, Co. Kerry.

Early Irish Art

Early monastic Ireland was recognisably 'Celtic' in its art and decorated manuscripts. The monks and priests, largely drawn from princely families, appear to have been aware of many artistic sources and probably had secular craftsmen doing some of the work as well as themselves. This can be seen in the differing degrees of literacy found on some examples of metalwork. They commissioned high crosses for the monasteries and copies of the gospels to assist in conversion and education. Their extravagant

Stones with Christian motifs in the hermitage of St Berraherb, Glen of Aherlow, Co. Tipperary.

became Christian. Early Christian Ireland is itself a 'transitional space', somewhere 'in between', where the ancient gods appear to have not quite departed but have been transmuted into other more amenable deities. We can observe through the manuscripts, the high crosses and the metalwork how the Celtic involvement with nature and its vibrancy becomes sublimated into Christian art and representation. This period of Irish history has left us some of the finest illuminated manuscripts in Europe, evocative nature poetry and a unique artistic tradition in stone and precious metals.

European Celtic Beginnings

In 1846, Halstatt was a small lakeside village in Austria which was fortunate to have a keen amateur archaeologist, George Ramsaeur, as director of the nearby state salt mine. He discovered an extensive pre-historic cemetery containing over 2,500 graves and, through his careful excavation, changed the perception of the

calligraphy, containing Eastern, European and La Tène influences followed in several examples — the eastern habit of not portraying any divinity in a realistic way — and this custom, allied with the Celtic predilection for abstract and swirling patterns, produced the 'carpet pages'. These elaborate and spectacular pages show the Celtic artists at their best, combining animals, abstract patterns, foliage and Christian symbolism into an interlacing design of incredible detail and complexity [Arnold, 1969].

The lands occupied by the monasteries were part of the local lord's demesne land and, quite often, we find an impressive ringfort nearby, identified by Stout [1997] in particular as probably the residence of the local landowner. Several monasteries follow this pattern and it would appear that the monasteries were usually sited in close proximity to the [Lord] Tighearna's [often] tri-vallate ringfort. Many of the priests may have been druids who 'converted' and several of the saints [Brigid, Molaise] were pre-Christian deities who, through a variety of methods,

The 'Alphabet' stone of Kilmalkedar church, Co. Kerry, founded in the 7th century.

hitherto unknown 'Celts' and their society. The graves contained a recurring series of pots, implements and weapons, and other evidence of continuous occupation. This was to suggest for the first time in the case of these pre-historic peoples, that they were a recognisable ethnic 'grouping', such as 'Slav', 'Teutonic' or as was now claimed, 'Celtic'. Prior to these discoveries, descriptions of the Celts were from Classical sources, with Caesar's *Gallic Wars* and the commentaries of Strabo portraying them as barbarians.

The Halstatt cemetery changed the way Europeans saw their early ancestors and, for the first time, a picture of a sophisticated, metalworking, hierarchical society began to emerge from what had been a fog of pre-history. Interestingly, there was quite a contrast between the remains of miners and their simple artefacts found at the site, and the cemetery on the hill above, where a rich and bejewelled aristocracy were laid to rest. The Halstatt period of *c.* 800 BC to *c.* 500 BC in turn elides into the first recognisably Celtic cognitive and artistic

category, La Tène. Its name comes from a village to the western side of the Alps, beside Switzerland's Lake Neuchâtel. There, members of a wealthy and stable Celtic settlement made ongoing votive offerings comparable with their status. As pressure from the east increased, possibly from Scythian and Sumerian tribes, the 'Celtic' tribes began a more rapid incursion into Europe. Unexplained events, however, perhaps climatic or social, saw the destruction of the initial south-east German Halstatt culture, possibly due to population increase with a concurrent though perhaps unrelated decline of activity in Ireland. By *c.* 450 BC, however, the *Keltoi* were the dominant tribal grouping in north-east France, the Middle Rhine and Hungary [Cunliffe, 1986]. In Ireland, the Halstatt and La Tène designations often refer to items of a later date, suggesting a slower acceptance or later arrival on this island of cultural motifs and styles. No Halstatt settlement has been recognised in Ireland, but

Anglo-Saxon map of the 10th century, showing Ireland in the bottom left corner [Knights Engravings of Old England, *1845*].

Between the ramparts of Longfordpass, Co. Tipperary, a triple-banked ringfort of the Iron Age.

Part of the ancient **Slighe Mhor** *chariot road as it nears the village of Glasson, Co. Westmeath.*

several European Halstatt-style swords have been recovered from the River Bann, and may have been votive deposits. At a slightly earlier time, there were Halstatt-style swords being made in the north of Ireland [*c.* 1200 BC] and these [Ballintober type] were similar to European models, being slashing swords rather than the later stabbing variety. Cunliffe [2001] suggests the continuation of trading patterns established for generations, if not millennia, as being responsible for the numbers of Halstatt swords found in Ireland.

The La Tène Celtic Period in Ireland

La Tène in Ireland was a continuation of Bronze Age traditions and some imported ideas, and it is difficult to show any clear arrival of newcomers from the archaeological evidence. Immigration probably took place from Europe and Britain,

but it may have been fleeing refugees or established trading or marital contacts rather than an invasion. There were trading contacts between Wales and Ireland, and an Irish tribe, the *Deisi* from Waterford, who, after raiding the coast for several years, established a permanent base at Dyfed, in South Wales. Other Irish Celts from Antrim established a kingdom in the Scottish isles, *Dalriada*, which continued as a viable trans-maritime tribal territory until the Viking raids of the 9th and 10th century rendered undefended settlements and coastal communities uninhabitable.

During this period, techniques in metalworking were adapted from Europe and Irish La Tène metalwork, while stylistically similar to material from Celtic Britain and Gaul, is of local manufacture. Geographically, it is to be found in the northern part of the country, and so far, no La Tène material has been found in Munster. This may coincide with Ulidian influence over the northern part of the island. An 'invasion' and the presumed disruption and upheaval that such would entail does not show in the archaeological record. The coming of Christianity from the 5th century onwards brought a revival of the La Tène artistic tradition in Ireland. Most of the artefacts described as Celtic come from this period and although the style of engraving and illumination is centuries later than comparable work on the European continent, it is of an equivalent standard.

In manuscripts, religious metalwork and stonework decoration, the artists and craftsmen brought an exuberance of style to their creations. For a people presumed to be illiterate, the Irish manuscripts, especially the 8th century *Book of Kells,* are wonders of early calligraphy and illumination. A small and unknown 9th century treasure, the *Stowe Missal*, contains instructions as to the celebration of the Mass, together with a mystical treatise on the meaning of the sacraments and, additionally, should prayer prove ineffectual, three spells [O'Neill, 1984].

European Language Development

The languages of those Indo-Europeans, of which today's Gaelic is a descendant, contained elements of many Asiatic languages including *Sanskrit*, *Tocharian* [a Chinese dialect] and *Iranian*. The Tocharian *ser* for sister, *cu* for hound and *yakwe* for horse have linguistic similarities to

the Old Irish *suir, cu* and *echach* respectively [Mallory, 1989]. The peoples who spoke the Indo-European languages and a smattering of dialects such as Hittite, now completely lost, were themselves scattered and mostly nomadic. The scholarship of early Christian monks created Irish as a written language, adapting as they did, Roman script to the transcription and classification of the existing oral tradition.

It must be said, however, that in doing so, they neutered many of the sexual connotations inherent in the language and especially those relating to the hero and those of a supernatural aspect. The most common name for a hero in the [Christianised] Irish texts is *laech* which is a Latin loan word *laicus* meaning a 'layman' who bears arms. The ancient Celtic words, however, which refer to the hero have quite a virile and active root. *Nia*, for example, forms the root for *nith* [combat], the Welsh *nwyd* [ardour and passion] and several early Germanic words for hostility and hatred. The same root provides the Gaelic *niah* [vivacity and energy], Welsh *nwyf* [excitement] and perhaps the Gaelic *noeh* [holy]. The hero thus is conceived as one imbued with virility, numinosity and the defence of the tribe [Sjoestedt, 1982].

Twelfth-century Romanesque heads from Dysart O'Dea, Co. Clare.

The 11th-century Stowe Missal Shrine, *showing the revival of earlier Celtic styles but with the beginnings of Romanesque representational art.*

SECRET SIGHTS — *Unknown Celtic Ireland*

The word 'Celtic' is applied almost exclusively to the majority of the people of Ireland, and as regards language, it is a romantic appellation. It would be as accurate as calling the inhabitants of Britain 'Anglo-Saxon', if by that suggestion we imply they actually speak the language of the tribal group they are descended from. There is a linguistic argument as to whether one can claim to be a true 'Celt' while the discourse of the Irish Republic as expressed through law, politics, and popular culture is conducted almost exclusively through the English language. If it is true to say that language is a defining element of identity, then in the case of a postulated 'Celtic' people of Ireland it must be the undeniable and enduring core of nationality and thereby true nationalism. However, despite the pervasive nature of English as a world-wide language, and our adjacent and intertwined relationship, Ireland still has in small but vibrant areas one of the real and tangible aspects of what it is to be Celtic: a *native language*. This language, Gaelic, spoken on a daily basis by over 75,000 people, is the descendant of the language spoken by the first 'Irish' Celts of *c.* 300 BC, and is one of a series of tongues that perhaps originated within a Indo-European homeland some 2,500 years ago. Although the majority of European languages could be said to have Indo-European origins, Gaelic is unique in that it was never directly influenced by Latin, nor did it blend with other and later European linguistic developments. It remains the most quintessentially 'Celtic' thing about Ireland.

Toponymy

The counties and townlands of Ireland are patterned with Gaelic names for the physical geography, often with epic or mythic connotations. The people who did the naming are elusive, mysterious and romantic, and their descriptive names for the Irish landscape often have a poetic quality, resonant with the imagery of a vanished race of gods, goddesses and warriors. These designations, many dating from

the early historic period and in some cases of much older origin, give an indication as to usage and settlement. Frequently onomatopoeic and sometimes alliterative, the names given to pasture-land, mountains, lakes and rivers are part mythology, part folk-tradition and barely within recorded history.

The rath of an Aire, or noble, straddles a hill on the Virginia–Cavan road.

Early Arrivals

How and when Celts came to Ireland is still an area of debate and controversy and the archaeological record is thin compared to Europe. We have yet to discover any princely burials similar to Hochdorf in Bavaria, where a Celtic prince was laid to rest in a vaulted chamber complete with chariot, bronze funeral bier, weapons and vats of wine. Likewise, our hilltop sites have not yielded evidence of settled communities, such as the *oppida* or prototype towns which European Celtic tribes occupied in the Iron Age. The ringfort, a widely distributed Iron Age rural dwelling usually occupied by a single family, is the Irish parallel to the European *einzelhofe* or dispersed individual farmstead. These circular enclosures, varying in size and complexity according to the status of the occupier, are often to be found in clusters, within

Opposite page: The River Boyne, taking its name from the goddess Bo-Ann, winds through Co. Meath at Dunmoe Castle.

a 'visual territory' of mutual support. In many cases, there is evidence to suggest a tribal or family grouping, often with a tri-vallate ringfort of considerable size being the residence of the *Tighearna* or Lord [Stout, 1997].

The Beaker Folk

The first Celtic or, more accurately, *Gaelic*-speaking immigrants who arrived on these shores were probably Beaker Folk of the 2nd millennium BC. These indigenous peoples, classed in Europe as *Urnfield* communities [from their habit of burying their dead in pots or urns] did not appear to have great contrasts in wealth within their communities. Their cord-impressed urns are found at sites in many different parts of Europe, and the larger Urnfield burial sites suggest a more permanent settlement with the probable cultivation of crops and the lineaments of a settled agrarian society. Most of their burials excavated in Europe contain simple beads, and it is only as we move toward the Halstatt horizon, *c.* 600 BC, that some graves appear with more elaborate funerary goods and artefacts. These Urnfield peoples did not appear to use the horse for transport, and it is undecided as to whether it was domesticated in Ireland at this period. In Europe, the Indo-Europeans interbred with existing Urnfield peoples and produced a new classification: *Keltoi*, the Celts.

Naming the Land

Many of the Celtic myths of origin may be retrospective explanations of how this happened and why. But whoever the first Gaelic-speaking settlers were, and wherever they originated, they brought the facility of naming with them, and their attributions and those of subsequent 'Celts' remain to this day, frequently beneath an

C. 700 BC gold collar from Borrisnoe, Co. Tipperary. This ceremonial 'necklace' was carefully folded, before being deposited in the bog.

anglicised veneer. In many cases, it is only through an interpretation of the landscape as text that we can glimpse the past beneath the contemporary surface. Just as archaeology strips away the topsoil to reveal burials or the remains of ritual structures, so a basic sympathy towards topography allows us to prise away the later crust and imagine the wandering of heroes, the battlefield of millennia ago and perhaps the ordinary lives of farming people. Within place-names we can recapture some of the meaning that our ancestors gave their land, and if naming and meaning are similar, then perhaps the names convey the true nature of the place, its entity and its underlying reality.

Some of the sites have both an archaeological record and references within the great mythological tales. These tales, transcribed sometime around the 11th century but perhaps from earlier sources, are historically too late to give direct evidence of belief and behaviour of the early Celts, but taken with the Roman commentaries of Livy, Caesar and others can give a viewpoint on manners and possible belief systems. Within the tales, some of which relate to the *Tuatha Dé Danann* (a divine race reputedly in Ireland before the Celts), wonderful and probably hugely exaggerated descriptions of the palaces of monarchs were written to flatter and enhance the 'owners' of the tales, while in others, elaborate genealogies detail the descent of Irish kings from the 3rd century BC down to the 8th century AD. The most important of the early manuscripts is the *Lebor na hUidre* [*Book of the Dun Cow*] containing a version of the *Táin Bó Cuailigne*, the oldest vernacular tale in Europe. This tale of Iron-Age barbarity and splendour is probably set in an Ireland of the first centuries

AD, but offers a glimpse of a Celtic heroic age that may have continued up to the beginning of the Christian period.

Mystery and Imagination

But the power of the sites named within the texts and their sometimes inaccessible and remote locations lies primarily in their ability to engender the imaginative space, to turn our 'inner eye' away from the techno-society of today towards the archaic and libidinous world of Europe's Celtic forebears. When we walk upon ground that was revered by the Celts, we enter a world that is both sacred and profane, where the sacral power is not exclusively male, nor entirely moral.

The places within Ireland where the early Celts lived and died are mysterious and enigmatic. They do not, like an archaeological site in Asia Minor, have great stone lions guarding an entrance to a lost city. Frequently they appear as circular undulations in a wide field, with nothing to suggest their former importance. These material remains of history are to be found in every county of Ireland sometimes juxtaposed with the ruined estate walls of an 18th-century Arcadia. Both decay at the same rate, are part of the history of this island and can lay claim to Irishness in their own way. To qualify as a true native of Ireland has always been a somewhat slender category, defined in more recent historical times by religious belief, or the etymology of a surname. And yet to some degree, all of the peoples who have come to inhabit this island arrived from elsewhere, the peoples established before them asserting either a primacy of territorial ownership, or accepting subjugation and probable slavery. Each succeeding tribal grouping that came to the island brought their own peculiarities of ceremony and belief from their homeland, and that homeland was always some part of the greater European continent. The axe-making

Twelfth-century Romanesque Celtic head from Clonfert Cathedral, Co. Galway.

aboriginals, who existed on this island before the tomb builders arrived, left little trace.

Mistress of the Beasts

Likewise, various types of burial chamber, ritual circle, barrow, rath and hillfort all appear to be 'Celtic', but may not be remotely connected to those distant *proto*-Europeans to whom we attribute the Irish language and much of the cultural inheritance of this country. Much of what is claimed as 'Celtic' existed a thousand years before any 'Celt' set foot on this island. The Celts, however, incorporated the pre-

The great mound of Newgrange in the Boyne Valley, Co. Meath, constructed before 3000 BC.

existing structures into their own narratives and the ancient burial grounds are often the 'womb' from where heroes are both born and sometimes conceived. As an example, the mythological tale of *Dechtire* [probably a primordial mother-goddess], having had a child die, is seduced by the great god *Lug* in the *Brugh na Bóinne* [the Megalithic tomb at Newgrange], and after aborting the child because of accusations of incest, becomes pregnant again with the same child. Setanta, the result of this conception, is thus re-born for the third time, re-living and replicating the triple divinity common to European Gaulish tradition, and replicated within later Christianity. Thus incoming Celts embedded themselves into a pre-existing narrative by being symbolically re-born from earth-based structures that were objects of veneration for the race they displaced.

The acceptance of the earth as being essentially female, in its fecundity and nurturing aspect, is fundamental to any understanding of the beliefs and perceptions of the Celtic world. Hills and valleys especially were seen by the Celts and their predecessors as the dwelling place of the Great Earth Mother, *Áine, the smiling one* and in Co. Kerry, her twin mountains, the 'Breasts of Anu' retain their nipple-like cairns to this day. Female designations occur regularly in the landscape, and *Cailleach*, a Gaelic term used to describe a female enchantress whether wicked or benign, represents both a vanished Christian nunnery, *Calliaghstown* in Westmeath, and in the neighbouring county of Meath, *Sliabh na*

Cailliach [the Hill of the Hag], where a 4,000-year-old burial ground straddles a series of low hills.

Society in Ancient Ireland

Most of the Celtic people were farming folk, living in simple circular huts within a larger circular enclosure, tending their animals, bringing up children, and probably staying out of the way of the powerful aristocracy that controlled their local *tuath* or principality. The farming folk were part of a complex and multi-layered society, and the more powerful and wealthy families vied with each other in clothes, jewellery, slaves and imported luxuries. Ireland was not unique in that respect, and graves of the differing Celtic periods both in Ireland and Europe show widely differing levels of adornment and burial ritual. Very few *structures* anywhere in Europe can be called 'Celtic', but on this island, however, the great stone forts of Staigue in Kerry, and the Grianan of Aileach in Donegal still display the power and confidence of

their builders. Considerable skill was required in the construction of these multi-layered stone-walled citadels, and Dún Aengus, a ceremonial and ritual site on the edge of a 92 m [300 ft] cliff on Inishmore, one of the Aran Islands, has additional stone *Cheveaux de Friese* to hinder landward attackers. The Friesians from whom such defences are named first developed the idea of sharpened stakes to inhibit cavalry during the 2nd–3rd century BC, and the use of stone in a similar way occurs at several forts on the Iberian peninsula. Current theory is that these structures, and Eamhain Mhaca in particular, are not Celtic, in the sense of being constructed by any outside ethnic group, but 'Irish' in that they developed within Ireland and do not have European precedents from which they were cultivated.

The builders of Ireland's earliest and most famous structures, those of Newgrange, Knowth and Dowth in the Boyne valley were not Celtic as we understand the term, but their art, their enigmatic rock scribings, carefully inscribed spirals, whorls and lozenges have been incorporated into the canon of 'Celtic Art'. In some ways they are *proto*-Celtic, in that their structures have become part of the Celtic

The goddess of Fourknocks, Co. Meath, perhaps wearing a lunulae necklace, c. 2000 BC.

Solar and lunar symbolism inside the pre-historic Mound of the Hostages, Tara, Co. Meath.

SECRET SIGHTS — *Unknown Celtic Ireland*

narrative, appearing in later myth and legend as being the place of entrance to the underworld and the residence of the *Sidhe*, with the celebrated triple spiral motif of Newgrange now forming a popular corporate logo and symbol of a prosperous and confident modern Ireland.

Climatic Change

In slightly more recent times there remains the well described 'Enigma of the Irish Iron Age' [Raftery, 1994]; a gap in the historical narrative, a lack of evidence in the archaeological record that suggests some social trauma, some dramatic upset to society in the last centuries BC. The artistic and well-provided society of Eamhain Mhaca, a ritual and habitation site outside Armagh, declines rapidly around that time, material content declines within the archaeological record in the hillforts and burial sites, and a silence descends upon the developing insular cultural discourse. Around that period there was a northern climatic decline of 2–3 degrees Celsius, recorded in core pollen samples taken from Ballinderry Bog, and such a temperature drop would be sufficient to reduce the grain crop and render low-lying land boggy and unusable. The negative impact of a reduction in food supplies, a worsening climate and possible raids from the [now] iron-using Halstatt Celts may have led to a serious decline in the fragile 'economy' of late Bronze Age Ireland. Combined evidence would suggest a deteriorating climate, the introduction of a harder metal, iron, and the subsequent collapse of the Irish Bronze 'market' brought a stage of relative prosperity to a close.

Indications from Europe would also suggest that migration around this time was undertaken by entire communities, possibly due to overpopulation and depletion of resources, or the presence of predatory tribes or disease. The timber palace/temple and related buildings of Eamhain Mhaca were deliberately burned to the ground in the last years preceding Christianity, and abandoned. This was the case also in Switzerland when the Helvetii migrated *en masse* from the area around Lake Lucerne in *c.* 200 BC, burning down their great log houses as they did so.

The climate appears to have improved from *c.* 250 AD onwards and agriculture begins to show a more advanced methodology and, as the Irish Christian period begins, we find increased evidence of arable farming, especially in the vicinity of monastic settlements. The ringforts which formed the 'homestead' of this period had an average landholding of around 32 ha. and when forming a clan or family group, were usually no more than 1 km [0.6 miles] apart for defence and security. Areas that have historically-attested borders and conflicts appear to have more *high-status* ringforts than other quieter districts, presumably due to the presence of additional 'warrior caste' individuals and their men-at-arms.

Many questions remain as to why ringforts are numerous in some areas and scarce in others. There are obvious relationships between soil productivity, population growth and subsequent social alliances, perhaps reflecting a stable, if stratified society. Forest growth and clearance for tillage may account for the 'cluster' groupings of ringforts in some areas, although difficult local politics may have contributed to the need for solidarity among the pioneers.

Aristocratic, Hierarchical and Independent

If we take the 3rd or 4th century BC as a starting point for 'immigrant' arrivals, then around this period a series of peoples, possibly speaking a similar language to the natives but with a different style of art and different qualities of organisation, began to arrive in Ireland in numbers that are still the subject of argument.

Opposite page: Early Christian cross, Glencolmcille. This rugged Christian symbol stands in the glen at one of the spots visited every year on the 'pattern' conducted on St Colmcille's feast day, 9 June. It may have been a glave-slab and shows a Latin cross with wedge-shaped terminals [Richardson and Scarry, 1990].

They may have met resistance from earlier proto-Celtic races already established on the island.

Although the social organisation of Irish society from the 1st or 2nd centuries AD can only be implied from later and documented developments, a quality of leadership would definitely have been required for the 1st century construction of the strategic embankments (*The Duncla*, the *Black Pigs Dyke* and others) between Bundoran in Donegal and Strangford in Co. Down, suggesting a 'border' for the territory of the emergent tribal grouping of the *Ulaidh*, centred in what is now Co. Armagh.

The society that was developing by the 2nd century AD was certainly monarchical and aristocratic in character, with elaborate and strictly defined grades of people, comprising both free and unfree. Each separate community [*tuath*] was largely self-sufficient, growing its own food, spinning its own wool and erecting its own houses from the woods within the tribal principality. The political organisation of early Ireland was highly decentralised, consisting as it did of these numerous separate states of various sizes and degrees of independence. Each was ruled by its own king or princely family. These numerous families accepted, in theory at any rate, the primacy of the *Ard-Rí*, or High King of a loose nation-wide confederacy. The reality, however, was that it was a title more of honour than jurisdiction. The later advantage of these fragmentary states, as successive invaders were to discover, was that there was no central administration to overcome, no pivotal ruling family to overthrow, only continuous and relentless local resistance, so that Ireland, while relatively easy to occupy, was singularly difficult to conquer. The *tuath* was the political unit of the loose confederacy that was early Ireland. They had an average size of about 272 sq. km [170 sq. miles], and by the early Christian period, Ireland contained about 200 of these

principalities. Estimates of the population of Ireland in the late Bronze Age to early Iron Age [100 BC–100 AD] would suggest around 500,000 in total, allowing a possible average *tuath* to contain about 5,000 people.

These principalities were each ruled by a local royal family, the *Derbfine*, the 'true' family of that state, perhaps the descendants of the first Celts who settled therein. The [King] *Rí tuaithí* was elected from that royal *derbfine*, but other *derbfine*, that is free non-royal family groups, could vote. The elected king was not an absolute monarch. He had to govern the *tuath* according to the laws of old, observe the *geasa*, or taboos and generally hold himself responsible for all that befell the peoples within his jurisdiction. There were other groups within the *tuath* — poets, bards, druids, brehons and a class called *aire*, or nobility. The *aire* comprised several different grades of landowner, some of whom were related to the ruling royal family. They frequently married into the *bo-aires* [cattle baron], a rich cattle-owning class, not aristocrats as such, who only rented their land from the ruling elite.

An Early Legal System

But if Ireland did not have a political authority or a controlling family, it did have an alternative set of national unities, perhaps more valuable and rewarding to that society. While England and Wales had numerous and contradictory law codes, someone from the *tuath* of Desmond in the south-west was subject to the same laws about offences to the person and property as a person from *Tír Conaill* in Ulster. The Brehon Laws were unique in Europe. They were not derived from Roman law, but from the *Brehons*, or professional jurists, who spent long years studying and committing the code to memory. It was a form of common law, the result of immemorial custom and experience and also the decisions, rulings and opinions of the jurists.

Opposite page: Part of the Black Pigs Dyke, *near Granard, Co. Longford, c. 100 BC.*

It is not until the later 12th century, and work such as the Cross of Cong, that we see a three-dimensional modelling of animal heads of a style similar to Europe of five centuries earlier. The monks who worked on the manuscripts were, obviously, Christian, but we might ask ourselves by how much? And how far did they accept the monotheistic viewpoint, the denial of sacred life to animals and nature in general? To judge by the interpellation of Celtic motifs around the Gospel text in the 9th-century *Book of Kells,* for example, would suggest that Pantheism was still there, scampering around the margins of the text as the belief it represented moved slowly to the periphery of society.

Mythology

It is of course impossible to specify exactly what the beliefs and practices of these early peoples were, and archaeologists are one group who are reluctant to do so. It is beyond speculation to infer from the archaeological record alone specific ritual or religious observance, but the European Celtic record — more abundant, more detailed — may prove a guide. It is, however, fortunate that we have the mythological tales and their vivid descriptions of Iron Age Ireland, relating to a society perhaps as early as the centuries preceding Christianity. These tales are a *fantastic* view of ancient society — part-dream, part-propaganda and part-sacred cosmology. At that historical time, it is probable that the knowledge of the tribe (outside of everyday functions) was a circumscribed and closed system, whereby cosmogony and genealogy were intertwined and irreducible. There would appear to be little understanding that things could be different, and the individuals who essentially controlled everyone's lives also 'owned' the access to reasoning, debate, and probably time itself, through their ownership of the laws, religion, and the sacred mythology of the tribe. Having access to language was the same as access to thinking itself.

We have a record of these decisions and rulings in the manuscript collections, showing us that the Brehon Laws applied to every conceivable event and transaction that involved the individual, his kin, his neighbour and his land.

Nature as Soul

Celtic society was also intertwined with nature, seeing it is as a sacred presence, engendering things with spirit, and creating the life of the tribe anew. It also was an essential part of the 'economy', whereby barter and fines for wrongdoing were calculated primarily in terms of cattle and the value of certain types of wolf-dog, hawk and slave. Numerous gold and bronze ornaments from Iron Age Gaul show the prominence that animal form took in representation and use, but in Irish terms, the animal form is primarily limited to the superb and masterful illustrations in the early Gospels.

Head of a pagan Celtic deity from Cathedral Hill, Armagh.

As an Iron Age *narrative*, the Irish mythological texts are unique in Europe. They pre-date other, similar stories by at least 300 years and are a warmer and less brooding chronicle than the later tales. They are the written versions of an oral tradition that may go back centuries before Christianity and are vivid and dramatic, moving from a tender and poignant description of lovers to a scene as brutal and savage as anything from contemporary cinema. Some of the tales are pure storytelling, written to enhance the status of the owner or claimed heroic descendant of a protagonist. But the action of the tales, the sudden violence, the rapid and dramatic plot manoeuvres, all bring to mind the games of children, wherein reality, imagination, superhuman powers and rapid changes in mood form an everyday part of play. Others tales are mythic, in that the people within the tales are themselves part-god and part-human.

The Psychology of Myth

Many of the tales were stories of the divine origins of the tribe and the Setantii of Western Britain and Meath cannot realistically be separated from the mythic hero Setanta, who may have been their personal god. There is the also the dynamic part of myth, the mechanism whereby it works its 'magic'. A true myth interacts with an ancient and perhaps instinctive part of our unconscious, and exerts a subterranean pressure on the perceptions we have of reality. It intertwines with our language and through association, metaphor and metonym, alters the linguistic 'screen' through which we classify experience. In Ireland, perhaps like no other country in Europe, ancient myth continues to exert a deep undertow, and when encountered, pulls our consciousness about like an unexpected squall, sending us in a strange direction, and bringing us to a new perspective. Myth slips through a gap in our imagination, creating a space that cannot be illuminated with the techno-scientist viewpoint of modern society.

It is the space where poetry begins, where desire may roam, and where play, whether that of child or adult, takes its form.

I think most people can all recall the sense of deep rapport with an aesthetic experience, perhaps a poem, a novel or a piece of cinema. In those moments we encounter the sense of being 'lost' in a written or visual text. We also 'split' ourselves, in that we are both in the 'ritual space' of the cinema, and in the story, yet also in 'ourselves'. In these moments of rapt attention, when an aesthetic experience takes us out of ourselves and traps us within its text, we experience the motive force of mythology, with its binding and integrating energy.

But there is a surreal quality to the Irish mythological tales, as the reader's mind is bent like heated bronze to the shape of a Celtic wordsmith's last. They are similar to a dream, as the emotions within the myth are condensed and displaced onto other figures, and deities appear and take human form. The tales are probably the nearest thing to a narrative of the pre-Christian unconscious mind. The hypothesis being that mythology, like a dream, is not essentially *created* to entertain or instruct, but is a spontaneous eruption from a people of their sublimated wishes and desires; a pre-historic society alternating between prohibition and license, love and revenge.

But that inner space, the locale wherein mythic narrative is created, still exists within us. It is perhaps the gravitational core, the rotating hub of all religious belief. It is the 'eye' that sees beyond what is tangible reality, and is the locus of our artistic endeavours. Perhaps what we inherit from our distant forbears is the ability to perceive in the place-name *Doire*, the expansive oakwoods of Celtic Ireland, to imagine the voices of the poets, and to discern, however faintly, a presence from the mythical world.

The Province
of Ulster

The mound covering the burnt remains of the great palace of Eamhain Mhaca, the 'capital' of Ulster in the 1st century BC.

Ulster has always been a separate 'place' in mythology and geography. It is traditionally the coldest part of Ireland and in winter, the darkest. In legend it is the abode of the 'Cailleach', the winter hag of death and dormant life; physically, it is separated from the rest of Ireland by the drumlin belt in counties Monaghan and Cavan, and by the extensive waterways of Lough Erne. It has three mountain ranges, the Antrim Plateau in the east, the Sperrins in the centre of the province and the Donegal Mountains in the west.

Because of its physical isolation from the rest of the island, its early chronicles record a natural exchange of language, commerce and occasionally war, across the narrow channel to what is now Scotland. The earliest hunter-gatherers, regarding the north channel as a barrier or a causeway, depending on politics or commercial advantage, used the tidal streams of

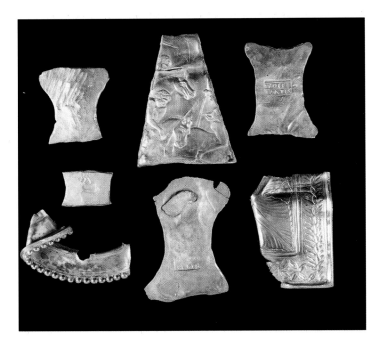

Roman silver ingots, 4th century AD. Perhaps a pirate hoard left behind by a raider returning from Britain.

Megalithic tombs from *c.* 4000 BC along the Antrim coast have similarities with tombs elsewhere in Ireland, but earlier theories suggesting a common origin have been superseded by more likely cultural influence from trading or marriage. These were primal agriculturists, siting their monuments to the dead along the fertile lowlands of the river valleys, and it was they who probably began the first forest clearances, and the pollen diagrams from deep bog studies show elm and oak declining, being replaced by familiar farmland weeds, dock, nettle and ribwort [Mitchell, 1976].

The Ulster pottery of 2300–1800 BC, the 'Irish Bowl Tradition' [Waddell and others], shows an definite Irish origin, but the remains of the pottery is found in a westward cultural, and perhaps physical, diffusion. As the pottery was probably made by the women of the community, perhaps as an individual, her skills would travel as she moved with marriage or other social change. Later Urnfield culture was to travel the opposite direction, bringing a 'collared urn', already widespread across England and Wales, to scattered settlements mainly on the eastern seaboard of Ireland. The early mythology speaks of great kidnapping raids carried out by both the *Cruithin of Dalriada* [Scotland] and the Gaels of Ireland. Perhaps the potter and her clay were part of the booty. The broken pieces of these urns, decorated by 'impressing' a rope into the damp clay before firing, have been found in neolithic and early Bronze Age graves across Ulster.

the greater Irish sea as a natural and tangible causeway. Ulster's inhabitants, part-Gaelic, part-*Cruithin* [Pict], fought, traded and married within the maritime autonomy of the seas surrounding their northerly territory. This ultimately provided a cultural interface with other pre-Celtic tribes and population groups across the relatively short passage between Galloway in Scotland and Co. Down. Galloway, an Anglicisation, similar to Galway, meaning 'foreigner from Gaul' has provided much archaeological evidence of cultural and commercial interchange across the north channel at this time.

Early Settlement

Human settlement in Ireland began in Ulster sometime around 7000 BC, when hunter-gatherers, living along the coast near the present-day Larne, manufactured porcellanite axe-heads from nearby deposits. Piles of discarded, imperfect items formed debris near their workshops and 'Larnian' axes with a high degree of finish have been found in Scotland, England and further afield in continental Europe.

Woodland

Prior to the 17th century, the great woods of *The Fews* and *Killultagh*, covering hundreds of square kilometres between what is now Dundalk and Armagh, prevented any ingress to Ulster's central plain. These vast woodlands provided timber for houses, abundant game for the chase and a secure and impenetrable defence against marauders. The woods of *Killetra* and *Glenconkeyne* formed a forest of some 500 sq. km [313 sq. miles] around the south shore of Lough Neagh, providing the O'Neills of Dungannon with similar cover and provisions up to the 17th century. In the centre of what would have been the great woods, there is the deserted and little-visited inauguration site of the northern Uí Néill, the dominant family of Ulster from around the 7th century until the late-Medieval period. Their equine ritual of enthronement, whereby the king symbolically mated with a white horse, was described in Hindu Vedic manuscripts of 1000 BC detailing symbolic mating of king and tribe, man and beast.

The 'Division' of Ireland

Early mediaeval historians suggested that Celtic Ireland was divided into two halves, *Leth Moga Nuadat* or 'Mug Nuadat's half' and *Leth Cuinn*, 'Conn's half'. These divisions referred to the descendants of Conn and Mug Nuadat, who reputedly divided the country between them prior to the 7th century. The southern half was dominated by the race of Eogan, the *Eoghanacht*, based in Cashel [Tipperary] and the northern by the dynasty known as Uí Néill, the descendants of Niall, a fifth-century king of Tara. We may therefore, with some reservations, infer from [mainly] later records that from the sixth century onwards there were two dominant Gaelic dynasties, one southern and one northern.

The 'Ulaidh', Lords of Eamhain Mhaca

Ulster is the country of the *Ulster Cycle*, a barbaric, sexual and poignant collection of mythology and folktale, first collected in the 8th century, and perhaps hundreds of years older and it is the part of Ireland where her patron saint, Patrick, spent several years as a swineherd on

Slemish Mountain, brought there by the man whose god he would ultimately replace. Prior to this rudimentary and broadly *political* division, a concept of Ulster existed from the 4th century AD as 'Coiced Ulaidh', the kingdom of the Ulaidh. These peoples, one of the early arrivals to Ireland, probably subjugated the Pretanii or Cruithin of Dal nAraidi, whose trans-maritime tribal territory extended to the western isles of Scotland. Their apex of power, possibly around the 1st or 2nd centuries AD, was based at Eamhain Mhaca, an extensive ritual and habitation site in Armagh, and there exists the remains of a series of earthworks from Donegal to South Down, the *Black Pigs Dyke*, the *Dorsey* and others, probably erected to prevent attacks or cattle raids from the south. As O'Rahilly and others have suggested, sometime in the 5th century, the Uí Néill forced themselves northwards into the Ulidian kingdom, as traditions from that time refer repeatedly to warfare and incursions from the south, culminating in the destruction and burning of Eamhain Mhaca.

Ulster, therefore, would appear to be a derivation of the old Gaelic tribe of the 'Ulaidh' who,

Crowned Irish king, seated, with shield, sword and spear; a dog on each side. From the high cross at Durrow, Co. Offaly [Joyce, 1913].

according to the mediaeval chroniclers, were dominant over much of the north of the island from around 200 BC to 350 AD. The Ulidian territorial claim of *Ó Drobais go Boinn*, from the River Drowes in Donegal to the Boyne in Co. Louth probably coincided with their dominance. They were probably La Tène Celts from Britain and their superior arms and tactics enabled them to conquer the tribes whose land they wanted [Byrne, 1973]. Their conflicts with the tribal grouping called *Fir Ól nEcmacht* of Connacht form the underlying conflict to the *Táin Bó Cuailigne* although they probably shared suzerainty with the another dominant group, the *Airgealla* of mid-Ulster at this time. The intense rivalry and feuding with the *Connachta* [the grouping of tribes west of the Shannon] may be traced to an event, first written about in the 8th-century *Táin Bó Cuailigne* when Fergus takes 3,000 warriors into exile in Connacht after a treacherous murder.

Ultimately, southern pressure drove the tribe of the Ulaidh eastward toward Co. Down, where they evolved into four separate groupings, *Dal Fiatach* [in the diocese of Down], *Uí Echach Coba* [in the diocese of Dromore], the *Dal nAriade* around Belfast Lough and *Dal Riata* in Northern Antrim. Even as the Uí Néill began to claim the high-kingship from this period onwards, the Ulaidh regained and exercised a reduced jurisdiction east of the Bann. Ulster, then, could be said to have had an independent existence from the earliest times, in the sense of their being a territory in or around the north-east corner of Ireland, containing a group of people of Irish, Scottish and later Norse blood, with a distinct and independent viewpoint to the rest of Ireland. Perhaps the contemporary separatist character of Ulster has its origins in contesting remote and incomplete southern claims of sovereignty.

The recorded designation of this northern province was first defined in official edicts of 1603 and 1610, as an English administrative area of nine counties. This 'province' was a derivation from the ancient Gaelic kingdom, of different geographic area, but similar political independence. In the centuries preceding the arrival of the Normans, a trans-maritime kingdom developed across the north channel between the present-day Antrim and the Western Scottish isles. It was dominated by the MacDonnells, a part-Scottish, part-Irish clan, with their main castle at Dundonnell in Antrim.

Early Christian Ulster

Ulster has a long tradition of association with St Patrick and the saint's reputed burial place is at Saul, in Co. Down. This county also had one of the most important monasteries in Ireland, Bangor, founded by St Comgall in the 6th century. He was its abbot for over 50 years, under the patronage of the Dal Fiatach. It was in this monastery under its Ulidian patrons that the *Táin Bó Cuailigne*, probably the oldest vernacular tale in Europe, was first written down as a dynastic struggle between the Ulaidh and the Connachta. It was from this monastery that St Columbanus set forth for barbarian Europe, founding monastic settlements in France at Annegray, Luxeuil and Fontaine, before founding what was to become the most famous Irish monastic settlement at Bobbio in Italy in 614 AD.

The northern coastal settlements were harassed and plundered successively by Viking raids from 795 AD onwards until the attackers were defeated by the northern kings and their armies in 811 and 825 AD, being finally destroyed by the Uí Néill in 866 AD. Before that, however, the Vikings had destroyed and desecrated the shrine of St Comgall at Bangor, and the Irish tribes, noting the lack of divine retribution, began to follow suit. The damage caused by these raiders left the monasteries bereft of scriptoria, as

capable monks fled to Europe, taking both manuscripts and the skill of illumination with them.

Identity

Ulster is the only one of the provinces whose designation has enduring historical meaning. It is the only one in which 'I'm an Ulsterman', is a badge of tribal and religious identity, unlike Leinster, Connacht and Munster. Ulster was in fact the last place to remain independent of English domination, but since 1912, the name has stood for vehement opposition to any notion of a united Ireland. Ulster today is a place apart. It is going through a process of relearning its own identity, sometimes with great pain and little advance. The ancient historical and cultural sites are owned by all, claimed by some, and subject to fable and misrepresentation. The land itself is Ireland in every respect. Its valleys and hills have the same Celtic underlay as the rest of the island, with an added twang of Scots gallic, and the red pillar box of the royal mail.

Ulster Counties and Sites

County Antrim *Aon-treibh*

The Gaelic name suggests a single monastic habitation, the tower of which is situated outside the county town with a round tower known locally as 'the Steeple'. The county forms part of Dal Riada, a territory which had its origins with the expulsion of the Ulaidh from Eamhain Mhaca in what is now Armagh. These possibly Belgic peoples were driven northwards by the Uí Néill in the fourth century. They settled in the Glens of Antrim, but found their needs and numbers exceeded the productive capacity of these small river valleys. Sometime around St Patrick's era, their chieftain, Fergus mac Erc, sailed to Scotland with his best warriors and after a bloody campaign, established a foothold in the land of the Cruithin for his expanding but impoverished community. Dunseverick [*Dún Sobairche* fort of the primrose] between White Park Bay and Benbane Head, was the castle or *dún* of the Dal Riada tribal group and was the

Dunseverick, The Fort of the Primrose, and terminus of the Slighe Mhidluachra, the northern chariot route from Tara, Co. Meath.

terminus of the *Slighe Mhidluachra*, the great chariot-route which began at Tara. It appears in several stories in the manuscript collections *The Fate of the Children of Uisneach* suggesting that Dunseverick was the landing spot for Deirdre of the Sorrows, a beauty who eloped with the brother of a king with tragic results.

Up to perhaps the Early Christian period, Antrim had areas that were heavily wooded to judge by the 'derry' [*doire* oakwood] place-names along eastern Lough Neagh and evidence would suggest extensive woodland of hazel and alder along the slopes of the Glens of Antrim. These areas of fertile and productive farmland became the developing contact point for commerce and cultural intercourse across the north channel from the earliest known presence of humankind on this island up to the present day.

As in most counties, modern motorways and high speed roads have replaced the older slighe, or trackways which connected royal sites and later ecclesiastical foundations. Occasionally, modern highways run parallel to the older routes, one of which ran south-west from the harbour of Larne. This modern, thriving port got its name from Lathar, the daughter of a pre-Christian king *Ugaine Mór*, who possibly had connections with tribal groups in nearby Scotland. This routeway probably joined up with the *Slighe Mhidluachra*, the main northern route from the citadel of Eamhain Mhaca which ran through the wooded territory of the *Dál Fiatach*, a tribute-paying tribal group who established a bruden or hostelry at Bruslee [the bruden on the slighe], where the A8 now branches off toward Newtownabbey.

Ballinderry [*Baile na Doire* the farm of the oakwood], west of Lisburn, was probably on the edge of the forest that stretched from the inlet at Belfast, around the shore of Lough Neagh as far south as Armagh. Glengormley, a suburb between Newtownabbey and Belfast, is a corruption of *Clann Ghormlaith*, a tribal territorial designation which seems to suggest an association with Queen Gormlaith, the wife of King Niall Caille of Tara in the 9th century. The county's most famous 'son' was of course St Patrick, whose time as swineherd to a chieftain, Miliucc, really began Ireland's fruitful association with Christianity. Patrick, or Succetus as he was then, was brought to Ireland at the age of 16 and spent his time in slavery on Slemish Mountain, west of Ballymena, whose Gaelic name *Sliabh Mis* means the mountain of *Mis*, a local pagan goddess. Perhaps seven years of close acquaintance with the *Dea Regina* of the mountain brought his spiritual nature to maturity.

Ballymacaldrack
Grave of Leader of Early Farmers

This part of Ulster also holds an important early grave, a 3000 BC court-cairn on Long Mountain near Dunloy. In this grave, pottery remains showed impressions of small spelt wheat, a cereal unknown outside Denmark at this time. The evidence of wheat would suggest the arrival from northern Europe of Beaker peoples using the Irish Sea in a north-south route, bringing new farming techniques and resultant cultural change. The chamber also had a long passage behind the main burial area, with pits that may have been used for cremation. This would be unusual as cremation usually took place outside the mound [Harbison, 1992]. Later gold artefacts from the area bear a striking resemblance to cultural styles established in Denmark and Bohemia at this time, suggesting that around the second millennium BC, European prospectors and farmers discovered the island that lay west of Britain. Sometime around 1300 BC, the people of Ballyalbanagh con-structed a causeway of oak beams to enable them to cross a [presumably] particularly wet and dangerous bog. This *togher* or causeway was made by laying beams lengthways in the direction of

Opposite page [top]: A porcellanite axe and chisel from c. 5000 BC. This incredibly hard stone probably cleared the first forests and engraved the great megalithic art of a later period.

travel and then placing other, shorter cut planks across the 'floor' of the trackway. The width of this early road was over 2 m, much wider than required for a footpath, although there is no evidence that any type of wheeled transport was used. Other bogs have produced crude types of block wheels, a type suitable for perhaps an ox-cart and made by cutting semi-circles from the trunks of large trees and dowelling them together.

Luriegethan
Mountain Fortress
OSNI SHEET 1 32.58

This inland fortress has similarities to other defended sites in southern Ireland, especially those along the Munster coastline. Luriegethan occupies a 'hill-peninsula' between the Glenariff and Ballyemon rivers, about 1.5 km [1 mile] from the sea at Cushendall. The fort has rows of ditches dug across the narrow 'neck' of the hill and looks like the Baily Lighthouse promontory fort at Dublin, where a settlement was created in the early centuries of the Christian era. Peter Harbison has suggested that Luriegethan may be a fort of the Venetii, a maritime people defeated by Caesar in the Battle of Morbihan in 55 BC. The Venetii were not agriculturalists and the other promontory forts which are similar to this example are usually sited near to harbours, presumably for trade and commerce. The dating of these promontory forts varies across all the known sites and some have given perhaps unreliable dates in the late centuries BC.

Tievebulliagh
Early Axe Factory

This mountain lies inland from Cushendall and is the site of one of the earliest examples of entrepreneurship in these islands. Sometime around 5000 BC, porcellanite, a hard, bluish form of flint was discovered by early prospectors who established a 'factory', manufacturing axes of durability and sharpness that were used to clear forests for farmland, and engrave and chisel the

Below: Luriegethan mountain, site of a promontory fortress, possibly of the Venetii, Celts who fled from Brittany after their defeat by Caesar in 55 BC. To the distant right of the picture can be seen the tip of Tievebulliagh, where axes were manufactured around 5000 BC.

remarkable art of megalithic Ireland. Axes from Tievebulliagh and another 'factory' on Rathlin Island have been discovered across Scotland and the English midlands. The artisans who manufactured and bartered these implements were also cultural emissaries, in that their engraving process and ability to translate concepts into tangible 'art' enabled ideas and symbols to travel across physical and imaginative distances, establishing a conceptual language in a pre-literate, scattered society. The sharpness of the axes and their usefulness in agriculture and perhaps war enabled the owners to 'move ahead', to outlive and outsurvive their competitors and enemies. The 'cromlech' marked on the OS map 2 beside this site may be a burial mound of the later prospectors.

Beaker people of 2000 BC constructed this 200 m diameter ritual circle at Ballynahatty, Co. Down, around an already existing burial mound.

County Down *An Dún*
The Fort

Intrepid voyagers of the 2nd or 3rd millennium BC, peering from Scotland across the north channel would have seen the Mourne Mountains without any difficulty. Their journey, possibly in boats of hide stretched across a timber frame, would have taken less than half a day in fair weather. They were probably the earliest settlers in this part of the island, and their burial sites and collared-urn pottery predominate in the south of the county. The present county was the site where a hoard of Bronze Age woodworking tools was found in the last century. This important find at Glastry showed that there was a differentiation of trades and crafts and that specialisation was carried out by skilled wood and metal workers.

An important part of Co. Down is the southern area known as 'Lecale'. This area, stretching from an inlet on Strangford Lough to Clough on the Blackstaff River, was an area rich in natural resources from the Mesolithic period. The marshes between the Quoile and Blackstaff rivers provided a natural boundary to the area and provided a year-round supply of birds and marine life for the early hunter-gatherers that settled there.

This county formed part of Ulidia, which was a territory of the tribal grouping known as Ulaidh, who were possibly earlier settlers than those later called Celts. The Ulaidh were an important northern tribe who were eventually pushed back by the Uí Néill of Connacht during their drive to become the dominant dynasty of ancient Ulster. The Ulaidh may also have had later Viking connections as the *ster* part of 'Ulster' is an early Norwegian word meaning 'stead' — hence Ulster as *Homestead of the Ulaidh*.

Ballynahatty
The Giant's Ring Ritual Site
OS 5J.327.677

This circular earthwork, 183 m [600 ft] in diameter, was probably constructed by Beaker peoples of *c.* 2000 BC. It is an impressive monument, with high rolling ramparts giving a sense of theatre to the site. At its centre are the remains of a burial chamber of about 1,000 years earlier, which may have contained the remains of someone of importance to the community. Whether this was the case or not cannot be stated with accuracy, but it would seem reasonable to suggest a relationship between the sacred relics within the mound and the congregational nature of the site. The open nature of the earthwork is a marked contrast to the earlier 'closed' internal and dark ritual spaces that existed in previous centuries. Barry Cunliffe [Oxford, 2001] has suggested that the move to open and accessible monuments suggests a move away from the chthonic/secret 'cave' systems of belief to open/'sky'/public participation.

The earthwork forms part of a series of prehistoric monuments in the area which included an oval timber structure of 90 m [295 ft] in diameter with a raised interior platform upon which bodies of important

Ballynoe stone circle, Co. Down, dating to the Bronze Age and earlier.

individuals could have been placed for defleshing by carrion birds or the elements [Waddell, 2000].

Ballynoe
Stone Circle
OS 9J.481.404

This 33 m [108 ft] in diameter stone circle surrounds a half-buried cairn, which contained two cremated burials when excavated in 1937. The site is approached by a long *boreen* [small cow-path] which meanders between tall hedges of yellow gorse and old field boundaries suggesting frequent visitations through the centuries.

Bangor Monastery
Important Monastic Site

The remains of this monastery, founded by St Comgall in the 6th century, sits on the south side of Belfast Lough. He was the son of a warrior and had himself been in battle before entering the church. This combination of soldier and saint, combined with a formidable intellect, was to ensure the success of his foundation. It became a distinguished seat of learning and produced the *Antiphonary of Bangor*, a commentary on the hymns of the early Irish church and also provided the resources and collating skills that resulted in the later *Annals of Ulster*. It was in this monastery, described by St Bernard of Clairvaux

A scribe of the 9th century copying a manuscript [Knights Engravings of Old England, 1845].

as 'a place truly sacred, the nursery of saints' that St Columbanus of Luxeuil and Bobbio was trained. The monastic school was run by a monk called *Sinlan Moccu Min* on Cranny Island in Strangford Lough, and historical studies, Latin and Greek were part of the curriculum. One of the earliest Gaelic epic poems, *The Voyage of Bran*, was first written down at Bangor. By the 9th century, Bangor had become a thriving *proto-town* and port with over 4,000 inhabitants recorded by the *Annals of Ulster*. It was ideally placed for travel to Dalriada, Britannia and points south, and arriving wine ships from Gaul returned to the continent with hides, fleeces and tallow. The inhabitants of Bangor included craftworkers, farm workers, their families and the monks themselves. Despite several Viking attacks, the settlement survived in reduced form until *c.* 1127, when it was destroyed by Irish warlords in a retributive attack, after an industrious but interfering bishop attempted to reform their matrimonial arrangements — he was forbidding them to have their usual mistresses and numerous children outside Christian marriage.

Downpatrick
Dún Phadraigh Ancient Fortress
OS 9J.483.445

This site, associated with St Patrick through later tradition, was anciently *Dún Lethglaise*, perhaps meaning the 'fort by the stream' and referred to as a residence of the MacDunlevys, the principal family of the area. They [*MacDuinnsleibhe*] 'became' MacDunlevys after 1137, when the descendants of Donn Sleibhe mac Eochada [d. 1091] called themselves by his name to demonstrate they were *rigdamnaí*, a royal family. Opposite and below the cathedral is a massive ringfort surrounded by a fosse. Originally a drumlin, this royal seat of the Ulaidh was highly defensible due to its relationship to the River Quoile. A deep ditch cut around the base of this *dún* was flooded for most of the year and gave

extra security to the inhabitants who reputedly included Cealtair, *the huge grey warrior*, a famous Ulster hero of perhaps the 6th century. He was the son of Uthecar Hornskin and appears in several of the early epic tales, being one of the Ulster warriors afflicted with a strange enervating sickness during the *Táin Bó Cuailigne*. Perhaps his ancestors were the original owners of the gold neck ring from *c.* 1000 BC, discovered in the locality along with earlier cordoned urn pottery similar to that found at Knockast, Co. Westmeath [Waddell, 2000].

On 1 February 1177, the Norman adventurer John de Courcy launched a surprise attack on the dún and defeated the MacDunlevys. Eighty-three years later, Brian O'Neill, accompanied by the O'Cahans of Inishowen and several Connacht chieftains, joined in an attempt to oust these invaders and attacked de Courcy and his knights. In a violent and bloody clash they were defeated by the archers and armour of their opponents. Brian and 23 leaders of the Ulster nobility were killed, leaving de Courcy in control of east Ulster. The MacDunlevys never recovered their lands and by 1280 they were to be found in service as physicians with the Ua Domhnaill [O'Donel] of Tír Conaill. Like the O'Clerys of Uí Fiachrach, another 'ex'-royal family, the ancient MacDuinnsleibhe family, established since at least the 5th century as kings of Dal Fiatach, were forced to find service and position with other, more powerful monarchies.

Goward
Dolmen
OS 9J.224.310
This massive 'cloghmore' or great stone is from *c.* 3000 BC and its enormous 50 ton capstone has

The massive sloping rampart of the Dún of the MacDunlevys at Downpatrick.

Goward Dolmen, dating from c. 3000 BC.

shifted sideways due to weight. These stone arrangements were probably the earliest structures on the island and may have had a function related to time, in that they would have established, in a hard and durable form, a sense of before, after and duration. This monument to the long-vanished tribe for whom it served as tomb and symbol stands in a silent grove of young sycamores, approximately 3.2 km [2 miles] north-east of Hilltown.

Moira

Maigh Rath [The Fort of the Plain]
Ancient Battle Site
OS 5J.157.618

In 627 AD, Congal Claen, king of the Dal nAraidi of east Ulster became king of the Ulaidh, a composition of population groups united in their antagonism toward the Uí Néill and their territorial desires. The Uí Néill had, at the

Convention of Druim Ceatt some 50 years previously, agreed to an alliance between the kings of Dalriata in western Scotland and themselves and thereby isolated the Dal nAraide population group in the middle between the two groups. Domhnall Brecc, king of Dalriata decided to break this alliance with the Uí Néill and joined Congal Claen to strike at the Uí Néill king, Domnall mac Aedo. The result was a four-day pitched battle between foot-soldiers, horsemen and chariots fought near the present village of Moira. Among the casualties was Cenn Faelad mac Ailella who received such a severe head injury that the 'brain of forgetting' was struck out of him. He was later cured by the Abbot Bricin at Toomregon [see Cavan entry]. During excavations for the extension to the M1 outside the village, mass graves of men and horses were uncovered in 1972. The motorway cut through two townlands, Carnalbanagh ['field of the slaughter'] and Aughnafosker ['Scotsman's grave'], referring to the warriors from Dalriata in western Scotland who had fallen in the battle. These townlands in the demesne of Berwick Hall, near Moira railway station, are traditionally held to be the site of the battle.

St Adamnan was probably an eye-witness to the battle and in his *Life of St Columba* he describes: 'The snorting and neighing of their steeds, bounding under the chariots, supporting and commanding the battle in every direction.' He further decried the battle for putting Colmcille's Iona community under Dal Riata control without the benefit of Uí Néill influence and power [Edel, 2001].

Adamnan's description suggests, however, that chariots were still in use in the Early Christian period and the literary texts use *carpat* as one of several words for chariot. *Corb* was also used, in the context of a personal name Corb-mac, 'he who is born of a chariot'. They were usually made by a *culmaire*, or *saor denma carpait*, a 'freeman who makes a chariot'. The body of the chariot is described as being of wicker, fixed to a frame of solid wooden bars, often of holly, as were the shafts and axles. St Brendan tells Jarlath of Tuam, 'Let a new chariot be built for thee: and whenever

the two shafts shall break, then shall thy resurrection be'. Presumably he was calculating a lengthy time before redemption. There were several versions of the vehicle, with either one or two horses, depending on the status of the owner and the purpose — domestic or aggressive. They also came with a driver, *ara*, who would deliver the warrior into combat, then await the outcome nearby. Should the warrior need assistance, the *ara* would drive into the fray and rescue his *Cairpthech* for another day.

Movilla
Ancient Pagan Site
This mainly Mediaeval site was founded in the 6th century by St Finnian on what had been a pagan site of importance. The Druidic religion was often centred around groves of trees and many Irish tribes had a sacred tree as their centre of worship and identity. The Irish name for this site *Magh Bile* would suggest 'Plain of the Great Tree' [Joyce, 1883].

Struell
An tSruthail [The Stream]
OS 1 S5J.504.744
These holy wells are fed from underground water and have a reputation for curing eye ailments. Throughout the Early Christian period and up to Mediaeval times there were two bath houses, one for males and the other for females. In the year 1260 a fierce conflict occurred here between a force led by the O'Neills and O'Connors against the English of Co. Down in which the Irish were defeated.

County Armagh *Ard Mhaca*
The Hill of the Goddess Mhaca

Rampart of the 'Dorsey', a vast cattle 'kraal', perhaps forming part of a boundary between pre-Christian Ulster and the rest of the island.

This county is believed to have come into existence as a result of the push northwards of the Uí Néill in the 4–5th centuries AD. The dominant tribal grouping, the Ulaidh, were pushed northwards, first to an area around Lough Neagh, and then into Down and south Antrim. It is a county famous for its apple trees and has a physical geography similar to its neighbouring counties of Cavan and Fermanagh. The miniature 'city' of Armagh is the site of St Patrick's church, built within the royal rath of Daire who presented it to Patrick. To acknowledge the gift, Patrick consecrated the place by walking *dessil*, sunwise, from left to right around the site, followed in procession by his followers and ecclesiastics [Joyce, 1913]. Despite being raided by the Vikings over 10 times between 832 and 943, the city had established a university as early as 1162 and no-one could hold a masters position in any Irish monastic school who was not an alumnus of

Armagh. It was endowed by the high-king, Rory O'Conor to provide for the numbers of students coming to the great school from both Ireland and Scotland. The county also contains Eamhain Mhaca, the ancient capital of the Ulaidh, and the area within 2 sq. km [1.25 sq. miles] of the principal mound contains over 45 sites from the pre-Christian period. Two of these are 4000 BC burial mounds and the rest comprise ring-barrows, linear earthworks, a hillfort, an artificial lake and many other archaeological sites suggesting a complex habitation and ritual site, developing and flowering from about 1300 BC until the 5th century AD [Waddell, 2000].

The Dorsey
Great Wall of Ireland

OS 8H.94.19

Sometime around 150 BC, the rulers of Eamhain Mhaca decided to construct a series of earthworks to prevent incursions from the south of the island. They relied on natural obstacles, such as lakes, rivers and woods, building their ramparts between these natural barricades. Although we cannot know whether the barriers relate to specific historic incidents, it may well be that the arrival on the island of 'Celts', perhaps highly mobile warrior bands intent on taking land, cattle, slaves and anything else they could grab, prompted the erection of such defences.

The rampart is in places invisible, known only to farmers and archaeologists. Local folklore suggests that huge numbers of cattle were corralled within the Dorsey in ancient times, as quantities of cattle bones and skulls have been accidentally unearthed during land and bog reclamation. One almost levelled portion of the rampart, the east gate (perhaps an elaborate skewed entrance), crosses the old coach road to Armagh, itself archaic, in that it formed part of the Slighe Mhidluachra, the route from Tara to Eamhain Mhaca.

This writer was invited by Mr Samuel Burns, a local farmer, to examine a series of rectangular post-holes, some 18 ins sq., discovered at a depth of 8–10 ins when topsoil was removed to facilitate the construction of a bungalow driveway. The holes were considerably darker than the surrounding soil and appeared to form an regular line running obliquely from where a high and intact part of the embankment could be seen. This standing part of the Dorsey consisted of a massive 6 m-high [20 ft] rampart with a deep ditch on its southern side, enclosed by a high bulwark collapsed at both ends. This has formed a unique mini-ecosphere, filled with ferns of differing emerald greens, butterflies, dragonflies, bluebells and bog myrtle, hidden from the world for centuries, resplendent in its primitive beauty, verdant and dark.

Comparing the Dorsey to parts of the *Black Pigs Dyke* may appear extremely speculative, but similarities do appear in the impressive size and quality of the ditches and banks and the sense of

Stained-glass panel of the Red Hand, from St Columb's Cathedral, Derry city. The hand has traditionally been the symbol of an independent Ulster. It is part of the O'Neill coat-of-arms, with an accompanying motto, 'Lámh dearg Éirinn' [Red hand (of) Ireland], suggesting an O'Neill ancestor claimed Ulster by being the first to lay a hand on its soil.

an overall purpose. Taking the *Black Pigs Dyke*, the Dorsey and Eamhain Mhaca together, one develops a sense of an identity based on trade and relatively peaceful co-operation coming into contact with a more aggressive and warlike western neighbour, and being without the manpower or resolve to defeat them or adequately defend the Ulaidian territory.

Eamhain Mhaca
Site of Palace and Warrior Camp
DISCOVERY SERIES 28B.45.85

This great Iron Age earthwork was the seat of power of the Ulaidh until the 5th century AD. Legend would suggest it was founded by a princess, Mhaca, who died after giving birth to twins following a horse-race. Mhaca is probably related to the Gaulish Epona, also a horse-goddess, and in Wales the same goddess was known as Rhiannon 'the great queen'. A second tale relates to the fortress being constructed in a manner similar to a brooch or neck-pin [*eomhuin* being the original form of eamhain] worn by the goddess Mhaca, and the fortress does resemble Celtic brooches of the La Tène style, which date from the much later 9th century. This impressive fort was the seat of Conchobar mac Nessa and, like King Hrothgar in the saga of Beowulf, was surrounded by warriors and beautiful women, a 'court' where stories, entertainment and intrigue was the order of the day. It was the place where Cú Chulainn, the greatest of the Ulster heroes, shows his valour as a hero by arriving with a stag tied to his chariot, a flock of captive birds flying above it and the heads of three enemies within. In this display he shows similarities to Conall Cearnach [see Ballyconnell] as a lord of the animals.

Although the earliest occupation dates are from around 800 BC and these refer to simple huts frequently replaced, a Halstatt sword chape [part of the sheath] was also found. This sword may have been part of the equipment of arrivals from northern Britain or Scotland due to climatic deterioration caused by the Icelandic volcano Mount Hekla, which erupted around 1150 BC, causing a dust-veil across much of northern Europe. The Ulaidh were therefore Celtic, of an early variety and from Britain or Scotland [Waddell, 2000].

The grassy remains of the great citadel of Eamhain Mhaca are still impressive. The cairn that crowns the summit of Navan Fort appears as a burial mound and was thought to be so until excavation by archaeologist Dudley Waterman between 1965 and 1972. Instead, the charred post-holes of an immense 37.3 m [122 ft] in diameter timber-and-thatch 'teepee' was discovered beneath the stones, with indications that a huge piece of timber, perhaps 13 m [43 ft] high, stood in the centre. There was no indication of habitation within the remains of this huge structure and the conclusion would be that it was ceremonial and ritual in function and use. It was carefully and deliberately filled with stone and burnt in a systematic and ritualised way. Perhaps the constant intrusions from Connacht combined with a crop failure or plague may have precipitated the intentional destruction of the Ulaidh palace.

Haughey's Fort
Workshop and Warrior Home
This neighbouring site is roughly contemporary with Eamhain Mhaca but was perhaps used by artisans or servants of the lords of the hill, as pieces of coarse pottery [some with a capacity of 16 litres (3.5 gallons)] were found to contain carbonised residue suggesting tanning of hides. Other small finds included pieces of gold wire, bronze pins, various timber artefacts and the skulls of large hounds with a possible shoulder height of 65 cm, suggesting the breeding of special animals for hunting or gifts to other noble families. Evidence from mediaeval excavations in Dublin, however, have shown that a large breed

of dog was used for cheap food for the poor, but in early times there was a *geasa*, a tabu, on the Irish nobility eating dogs. According to the *Book of Leinster* there was also a *rigthech* or 'royal house' at Eamhain Mhaca, a special residence for old and retired warriors who were looked after when their fighting days were over. They were under the command of another warrior and when the Ulidians were threatened by the forces of Maeve of Connacht the king called Irgalach, son of Mac Lauach, to bring them to order and to advise him how to defeat the Connachta.

The King's Stables
Ritual Water Site

This curious sunken pond was a ceremonial depository for the population group of Navan Fort. The leaders of the Ulaidh appear to have used this pond as an entrance to the underworld, using it for ritual and certainly for the deposition of important objects. It would have had a depth of around 4 m [13 ft] of water and the small area excavated delivered animal bones, part of a male skull and pottery moulds for leaf-shaped bronze swords. It may resemble Shad Lake, near the ritual and habitation site of Cruachain in Connacht, in function and usage.

Nuada

[Anglican Cathedral, Armagh]
Iron-Age Idol

This mysterious stone idol was removed from a rath near Eamhain Mhaca in the 19th century for unknown reasons and is of the early centuries AD, or possibly earlier. The figure appears to clutch a wound, or wounded arm. He may be Nuada Airgetlamh [Nuada of the Silver Arm] one of the primal gods of Ireland. He was a leader, possibly mythological, of the Tuatha Dé Danann [the people of the god Danu], and was wounded during the battle of Magh Tuiread by a *Fir Bolg* warrior called Sreng [the Fir Bolg were probably 'Belgae' from north Gaul]. He lost an arm in the encounter and had a silversmith make

a copy, thereby enabling him to remain unblemished and a king.

This fearsome 1.5 m totem, perhaps an interface between humanity and a darker more brutal side of our nature, now sits with some enigmatic companions in the chapter room of the Anglican Cathedral on Armagh Hill.

County Monaghan *Muineachain*
The Little Hills

This county is remarkable for the number of small hills [drumlins] which form a continuous chain between the lakelands of Fermanagh and Slieve Gullion in Armagh. Many of its low hills are crowned by raths and several have [or had] a wide ramp between their banks, presumably for ease of defence. This feature, different to the more usual slim bank between ramparts, is more predominant in Monaghan and Cavan examples. This Ulster county is a landscape of neat hedgerows and prosperous local industry, especially in the food and food-processing areas. It was historically an important route into the north and the Channen Rock, between

Possibly the god Nuada, a pagan entity of the Ulaidh, the ancient people of Ulster.

The 'Worm Ditch', behind Scotshouse village, part of the Black Pigs Dyke, a rambling linear earthwork that parallels the existing Ulster/Republic of Ireland border in places.

Carrickmacross and Dundalk, was traditionally the northern boundary of the Pale, the earthen-banked defence that ran from Dundalk to Dalkey during the 14th and 15th centuries. A monastery was founded where the town is now situated during the Early Christian period but was plundered in 830 AD and again 931 AD.

Black Pigs Dyke
Great Wall of Ireland
OS 8 50.22

[East of Redhills Village] This is part of the fortification that runs from the Drowes River in Donegal to the sea at Dundalk. It was part of a series of earthworks designed to keep out the rustlers and raiders of the south and to retain the integrity of the Ulaidh territory. The two sections of this 'Great Wall of Ireland' run for approximately

C. 2200 BC gold discs from Tedavnet, Co. Monaghan, possibly 'badges' to be worn as marks of distinction.

2 and 3 kms [1.3 and 1.9 miles] respectively. The first, about 2½ km [1.5 miles] from Treehog Crossroads and over a ditch into a field is reasonably visible, about 1 m above ground running in an east-west direction. It disappears under the L24 and re-appears 2 km [1.3 miles] further east on the Scotshouse-Ballinageeragh road.

Clones
Celtic Christian Site
OS 8H.50.26

The town grew up around St Tighernach's monastery, founded in the 6th century, and has seen its fortunes ebb and flow according to its relationship to the border with Northern Ireland and the price differentials between essential commodities. There is a high cross in the centre of the town which crisply depicts biblical scenes and has geometric patterns on the lower parts of the shaft. A later abbot of Clones, John O'Carbry, was responsible for commissioning the restoration of the *Domhnach Airgid* (the Silver Church) in 1350. This book shrine has gone through several restorations and therefore contains art styles from the 7th to the 14th century. This particular shrine has a certain 'numinous' quality to its appearance, suggesting centuries of veneration and prayer associated with its use. There is a close relationship between the scrollwork of the base and the decoration in the *Book of Durrow*, and the Domhnach is a good example of how artistic ideas were becoming more developed through commercial and social intercourse between the monasteries of England and Ireland.

Clones was also the location for the finding of a 21.5 cm gold dress fastener, dating to *c.* 800 BC, which was used to close a garment by slipping through two buttonholes. The surface is decorated with concentric circles freely scattered around the curve and has a pleasing balance between the symmetry of the paired halves and the practised randomness of the decoration. The size and elaborate decoration of such an item would suggest its usage was restricted to ceremonial occasions only.

Tedavnet
Pagan and Celtic Christian Site
This small village 7.2 km [4½ miles] to the north-west on the Monaghan to Clogher road is the site of an early nunnery founded by St Damhnat in the 6th century. Her name is also commemorated at Calldavnet (*Coill Damhnat* Damhnat's Wood), on the slopes of Sliabh Beagh. Tedavnet was also where two gold sun-wheel discs were found in the 19th century.

The Domhnach Airgid, *by tradition given by St Patrick to St Macartan and remodelled by the abbot of Clones, John O'Carbry, in the 14th century.*

These 11.6 cm in diameter discs were created sometime around 1800 BC and were made by cutting a circle from a sheet of beaten gold and punching a variety of ridges, chevrons and dots from the reverse side. The design suggests a sun-wheel, divided into quarters with a star intersection at the centre. Small 'button-holes' would suggest that these were for wearing as a decoration on clothing, perhaps as a badge of distinction.

County Cavan *An Cabhan*
The Hollow
The county is the most southerly of the province of Ulster and has a varied geography, from mountains [Cuilcagh 667 m (2,188 ft)] to numerous lakes and waterways. The River Erne passes through its centre and spreads itself into a green and blue kaleidoscope of water, sky and land. The county is interspersed with streams, marshes and rivers and offered early settlers ideal defensive situations for their numerous ringforts and burial tombs, many of which are unmarked and undisturbed.

Before buttons were invented, these gold dress-fasteners of c. 800 BC, found near Clones, Co. Monaghan, were used to fasten the clothes of the Bronze-Age nobility.

As a county, or even an area, Cavan was relatively undeveloped until the Iron Age and the early centuries AD. It does, however, have a high proportion of beehive querns, the circular stone cereal-grinders first introduced into Britain in the 4th or 5th century BC. The majority of Irish examples are between 28 cm to 36 cm in diameter and worked by having two stones [usually decorated] which rotated upon each other, crushing the cereal within. Their concentration in Cavan would suggest an improvement in arable farming, but no contemporary settlement has been found at their locations. Another possible explanation is that they were used for specific grinding and for the preparation of grain for alcohol; perhaps the skills required were relatively rare and possessed by certain people who only lived in certain areas. Cavan's earliest monument is the court-cairn at Cohaw, near Cootehill, a double court-tomb with two chambers, back-to-back. Ancient Cavan lay at the outer limits of Connacht power and was inaccessible from the south due to its topography of hills, lakes and bogs. It formed a natural and formidable part of early Ulster's defences. Pressure from expanding population groups to the west of the present county resulted in the establishment of farming communities within small defended settlements during the Early Christian period and the church at Drumlane near Milltown dates from that time. The town of Cavan itself was originally the site of the Mediaeval castle and friary of the O'Reillys, of which there are now no remains. Their original seat was on Tullymongan Hill outside the town and on another hill, Shantemon, they were inaugurated as kings of East Breffni. On the northern slope of the hill are 'Finn Mac Cool's Fingers', a row of standing stones which may represent the inauguration site.

Ballyconnell

Beal Atha Conaill [The Great Horned God]
[N87 Belturbet to Swanlinbar] Conall Cearnach,
a foster-brother of Cú Chulainn the famous hero, was a legendary Ulster warrior and defender of the Ulaidh people before the Christian era began. He was believed to have defended the ford at Ballyconnell against invaders from Connacht and the village takes its name from him. Conall Cearnach was eventually killed by the Connachtmen and buried in a place called Ballyheady. This townland [5 km (3 miles) south on R205] is a concentration of standing stones, megalithic tombs and burial mounds. The old road from Connacht to Ulster passes through this relatively unknown burial and ritual site, probably used as a warning to approaching strangers that the dead were watching and their land lay ahead. It was quite usual to have a cemetery and ritual landscape at the boundary of a tribal area, keeping the dead at arm's length and warning off potential foes.

During archaeological excavations at one of the sites in Ballyheady, bodies from the Bronze Age of *c.* 100 BC were found.

Opposite page: The standing stone at Kilnavert, part of the extensive ritual site south of Ballyconnell, Co. Cavan, containing megalithic tombs, standing stones and burial mounds. The entire site is probably positioned for visual impact, along the strategic road into Ulster from the west.

A Gaulish deity, Esus [Knights Engravings of Old England, 1845].

Cernunnos

As well as being a warrior, Cearnach may have been something else entirely, an authentic deity from continental Europe transposed to Irish soil centuries before Christianity. He appears in the manuscript, *Táin Bó Fraoich* [*c.* 8th century rendition] where he accompanies Fraoich to Europe to recover his wife and cattle who have been kidnapped. Cearnach is attacked by the guardian serpent of a fortress near the Alps which attaches itself to his belt for the duration of the battle. Neither harms the other [*ní dergini nechtar de olc fria chéile*] and Cearnach returns unhurt to Ireland. This repeats a motif associated with the Celtic god Cernunnos who is often shown with a serpent as a belt. Another representation of Cernunnos on the Gundestrup Cauldron [Denmark] shows him wearing a torc and holding a ram-headed serpent in his left hand, with a stag at his right side. He also is the god of the forest and all the animals are subject to him, a rhetorical theme found in the story of St Cíarán of Saighir. It is worth bearing in mind that the four evangelists, Matthew, Mark, Luke and John, are each shown with an animal and are each associated with particular animals.

Another of the 'legendary' pre-Celtic peoples of Ireland, the warlike Formorians, were also known as gobarchind [goat headed] and had Cernunnos/Cearnach as their tribal divinity. It would suggest either direct arrivals from Gaul, or cultural adaptation from existing or later arrivals.

Drumeague
Ritual Site

This site, *Maodog's ridge*, was the site of an important find in 1885 when a farmer discovered a three-headed idol, now known as the Corleck Tricephalos, on his land. This tri-faced and sombre sandstone head is perforated at the base and may have been mounted on a plinth or column. There is also a perforation in one mouth, similar to other head-idols in Czechoslovakia and continental Europe where tri-faced heads appear in the three-dimensional arts of the continental Celts [MacCana, 1997].

The area may have been a 'head-shrine' and this idol, possibly Lugh, may have represented the resident deity. The original head is in the National Museum, Dublin and a copy may be seen in the Cavan county museum.

Toomregon
7th-Century Medical Techniques
OS DISCOVERY SERIES 27A.15.28

Four kilometres [2¹/₂ miles] south of Ballyconnell in the townland of Mullynagolman are the remains of the monastery of Toomregon where schools of medicine, law and poetry were in existence in the 7th century. A surgeon, St Bricin, is commemorated by the Toomregon stone, a large, carved, limestone triangle depicting what could be an operation taking place on a chieftain's head. It appears more likely to be the lintel from a round tower, or other doorcase, perhaps suggesting hell or damnation. According to the manuscripts, a young chief, Cenn Faelad, had his skull fractured by a sword blow in the ferocious and bloody battle of Moira [Co. Down] in *c.* 637 AD. As a result of this head wound, he lost the facility of memory and was brought to the Abbot Bricin who used the technique of trepanning, an operation which involved drilling through the skull, to remove the damaged bone and part of the brain also. The young chieftain recovered, but with a different attitude and approach to life. He renounced the role of warrior and became instead a scholar and jurist, whose 'new name' was Cenn Faelad *the Learned*, later to write *Uraicept na nEces*, a primer for poets and several legal commentaries on the Brehon Laws.

The Corleck Idol, a three-faced representation of a deity, possibly the Celtic god, Lugh.

He finally founded a school of law at Derryloran in Co. Tyrone [Joyce, 1913].

Other sources suggest this may be an allegory for the first transcription of the *The Brehon Laws* from oral to written form which is reputed to have taken place around this time.

County Donegal *Dun na Gall*
The Fort of the Foreigners

According to Ptolemy's map, a tribal group called Vennicnii occupied this north-eastern part of the island in the centuries around the birth of Christ. Its ancient Gaelic name was 'Tír Conaill', the land of Conall, given as it was to the second son of Niall of the Nine Hostages, the other being Eoghan, who received Tír Eoghain [Tyrone] as his fief. As a county it is large and unwieldy, having

several peninsulas, a long and rugged coast and some of the highest mountains in the country. It has a long association with the sea and regularly receives the strongest storms of the Atlantic against its coast. The main part of the Irish fishing fleet is based at Killybegs, on the Glencolmcille road and the vessels there are the equal of any in western Europe. The county also has a large peninsula, Inishowen, which lies between Loughs Swilly and Foyle and tapers toward Malin Head. It is mountainous, rising to Sliabh Sneacht [Snow Mountain] at 616 m [2,019 ft]. Six-and-a-half kilometres [4 miles] south of the chief town Buncrana is Fahan, home to an 8th century Uí Néill prince, Niall *Frossach* of the Cinel nEoghan [d. 773 AD]. He received his name when a 'shower' [frossach] of wheat fell on his rath at Fahan at his birth. Like his predecessor in the high-kingship, Domhnall Midi, he was also a religious man, not just giving nominal lip-service to Christianity but abdicating from the high-kingship of Ireland on two occasions to retire briefly to a monastery.

Cloghaneely

Cloch Chionnaola [Cionnaola's Stone] **Blood Stone**
This area, including 'Bloody Foreland' derives its name from the deeds of antiquity. Balor, a formidable giant, god and general no-good was based on Tory Island, travelling to the mainland every now and then to terrorise the inhabitants. He was killed by his grandson for murdering his son-in-law, Cionnaola, on a stone that lies between the road to Falcarragh and the sea.

Fahan Cross
7th-Century Art
OS 1C.34.26
Approximately 7 km [4½ miles] south of Buncrana is the village of Fahan which holds one of the finest examples of Early Christian art in Ulster. There was a monastery here in the 7th century, founded by St Mura and his 2.5 m [8.2 ft] cross has superb stone carvings and

The 7th-century cross of Fahan, Co. Donegal, perhaps the burial slab of the founder of the monastery, St Mura.

One of the series of Megalithic tombs in Straleela, Glencolmcille, Co. Donegal.

Opposite page: The circular fort of the Grianan, or sun palace, of the northern Uí Néill.

interlacings. The inscription on the north edge of the cross reads [in Latin] 'Glory and Honour to the Father and the Son and the Holy Ghost', part of a prayer first approved by the council of Toledo in 633 AD.

Glencolmcille
Ancient Necropolis
OS 3G.52-54.82-85

This small valley was reputedly the place where St Colmcille of Derry fought the remaining demons of Ireland until he drove them into the sea. Every year, on 15 June, St Colmcille's day, a long 'pattern' or pilgrimage takes place to sites associated with the saint. Most of the sites involved have earlier, pagan connections, subsequently Christianised. The valley has several impressive megalithic tombs, at Farranmacbride and Malin More, where there is a group of 'court' cairns. On the north side of Malin in the townland of Straleela are a further 12 chambered tombs.

Grianan of Aileach
[Sun Palace of Aileach] 5th-Century Palace
OS 1C.37.20

This 23 m [77 ft] diameter stone hillfort was constructed, possibly by the Uí Néill in the centuries preceding the Christian era. It may have been roofed and was certainly a royal residence until the 11th century, when it was systematically destroyed by the O'Briens in retaliation for the destruction of their chief seat at Kincora, Co. Clare. The fort is surrounded by concentric earthen rings and may originally have been a Bronze Age settlement. It sits on a hill overlooking the Swilly estuary and commands a prospect of several counties. It is curiously lacking in atmosphere, as if it was gutted and neutered during the Victorian restoration of the last century. Nevertheless, it commands fantastic views over the surrounding countryside as far as Lough Swilly.

Lough Derg
Dragon Lair

Ulster contains in the county of Donegal, on remote Lough Derg, an ancient Christian pilgrimage site, venerated since the Middle Ages. It was originally sacred to the Caorneach, a beast of huge and devouring appetite that lived in the cave that now lies beneath the Catholic basilica of Station Island. Pilgrims came to the cave to experience the terrors of hell and it was a popular 'tourist attraction' until the overnight experience was banned by Popes Alexander VI and Pius III. The cave entrance was blocked by the puritan Cromwellians in 1649 and never re-opened. The stone seat of the Caorneach's 'keeper', St Dubhtach, remains on the island, and offers quietude to those who rest upon it. Further down the lake is Saints Island, an earlier place of pilgrimage before Station Island was established.

County Tyrone *Tír Eoghain*
Eoghan's Country

The Cinel nEoghan were a subsidiary of the Uí Néill and their territory was the peninsula between the Swilly and the Foyle in what is now Co. Donegal. In 563 AD they crossed the narrow strip of land between Donegal and Derry

Part of the 'Danes Cast', the legendary border of eastern Ulster.

intending to conquer central Ulster. They were met by the Cruithin, a long-settled people who lived east of the River Bann and a battle was fought at a site called Moin Daire Lothair in which the Uí Néill were triumphant. The Uí Néill gradually pushed the indigenous Cruithin across the Bann, forcing other indigenous tribes, especially the Ciannachta of mid-Derry to accept them as overlords. The Tuatha-Eoluirg, another tribute–paying tribe, were possibly from northern Europe and may be a later Celtic arrival, bringing the La Tène art style to Ireland, although it is more likely that La Tène art as it appears in Ireland is local, in both execution and inspiration.

Although the administrative boundaries of this county were only established in the 17th century, it was traditionally 'Eoghan's Territory', Eoghan being one of the sons of Niall of the Nine Hostages, who attempted to rule from Tara in the 5th century. It is important to remember that the Uí Néill were not a tribal grouping with separate

and perhaps different origins, but a dynasty intent on conquest and tightly bound to each other.

Tyrone, in early times, was broadly the territory of the Airgealla, a tribal 'federation' of about nine family *tuath*, whose submission to Niall after his defeat of the Ulaidh gained him the accolade of 'Niall of the Nine Hostages', one from each of the Airgealla tribes. The area comprising most of the county, some of Armagh and bits of Monaghan were their homelands and the Uí Maic Cairthinn, Uí Thuirtí, Uí Mac Uais and other early groups ended up paying a tribute to the Uí Néill of military service [though not in spring or autumn], and giving a third of all 'booty' taken by force of weapons to Niall's descendants.

Beaghmore
4,000-Year-Old Lunar Observatory
This place-name, meaning 'the place of the large birches', contains several large stone circles and alignments over an area of 2–3 acres. This

SECRET SIGHTS — *Unknown Celtic Ireland*

relatively unknown site was buried under peat for almost 4,000 years until the 20th century and could be astronomical in purpose, although fertility may have been the function. A series of standing stones close to the complex was found by Professor Thom to be aligned to observe the rising moon and was dated to around 1640 BC.

The site has several cairns or burial mounds which contained cremated individuals, presumably the founders of the tribe or individuals considered special for some other reason. Isolated individual burials in a large site such as this would lead to speculation as to what meaning could have been given to such elaborate funerary arrangements, unless the singular remains formed a foci for a larger inhumation burial site, perhaps remaining to be discovered under the surrounding peat. A Tievebulliagh axe of a kind popular with Stone Age communities was found buried in a cairn at the end of a series of stone alignments. Although this site is Bronze Age, later Christian custom also surrounded churches with graveyards, while the

bones of a founding saint were often interred under the church itself.

Clogher

Clochoir [Golden Stone or Stony Place] **Site of Oracle**
This ancient assembly place, burial site and medieval enclosure stands on the southern intersection of two ancient trackways travelling across an Oghmagh, the 'sacred plain' that joins Tyrone and Fermanagh. It lies in the well-wooded Clogher valley that stretches from the Armagh border to Fermanagh. There is a Bronze Age burial mound known as *Clochar mac nDaimhine* [the stony place of the sons of Daimhne], possibly the ancient site of an oracle, a stone idol called Kermann Kelstach described by Cathal Maguire [d. 1495] as 'being covered in gold'. St MacCarthinn, reputedly St Patrick's 'minder', was the first bishop here and the remains of his monastery are scattered around the village. In Clogher demesne are the remains of a ringfort, a burial mound and other earthworks, comprising what could be the seat of the Airgealla, the ruling

Sesskilgreen, Co. Tyrone, the remains of a tomb and observatory from 2000 BC.

SECRET SIGHTS — *Unknown Celtic Ireland*

This hillfort of c. 100 BC was reputedly the site of the mystic 'Oracle of Clogher', guarding the routeway between east and west Tyrone.

family of the area. Eight kilometres [5 miles] south-east is *Alt-a' Deamhain* [Spink-ana-gaev] 'The Demon's Cliff' where there is a stone seat with cup-marks and a holy well.

Tullaghoge, Iron-Age residence of the O'Hagans and inauguration site of the O'Neills, rulers of Tyrone for centuries.

Sesskilgreen
4,000-Year-Old Solar Observatory
OSNI SHEET 1 36.26

Near the agricultural town of Ballygawley is the Bronze Age stone of Sess Kilgreen, one of many stones found to have astronomical alignments, in this case for observing the summer solstice. The un-roofed tomb is 3.5 m long and 2.5 m wide and may be related to Cairn U at Sliabh na Cailleach [Meath] in that the main symbol of interconnecting spirals is almost a copy of the Meath example. The former roof slab to this ancient structure stands in a field and has an extraordinary collection of sun-wheels, stars, and other heavenly bodies. The significance of these and similar markings at megalithic sites was ignored by Irish archaeology until research

by Martin Brennan in particular demonstrated their accuracy.

Tullaghoge
Tulach Óg **Royal Inauguration Site**
OS 4H.825.743

This was the inauguration site for the Uí Néill from the 11th to the 16th century and is a secluded and silent place. Its literal translation is 'hillock of the young' but Óg is often used to denote youth and virility, rather than the innocuous sense of children cavorting on a grassy mound. The site was near the Uí Néill fortress of Dungannon and was itself the rath and dwelling of the O'Hagan sept [clan] who were justiciars of Tír Eoghain. It was they who inaugurated the Uí Néill as princes of mid-Ulster by touching the incumbent on the shoulder with a hazel twig and presenting him with a shoe. Usually the king or chieftain would wear special clothes of silk with gold embroidery, or arrive on a special horse, all to become the property of the person who performed the inauguration.

Geraldus Cambrensis in his book about Ireland in the 12th century describes a ceremony in Tyrconnell whereby the king bathes in a broth made from a slaughtered horse and offers the ritual stirabout to his companions so as to share in his kingship. This ceremony, alluded to in Vedic manuscripts of India, is Hindu in origin and seems to have been unique to the Uí Donel and probably the Uí Néill also. Perhaps the Irish ceremony was a tradition, something from antiquity, an ancient Indo-European rite surviving into the historical period within scattered descendants thousands of miles away. Cambrensis, who wrote about the ceremony, was never in Ulster and the same book contains fables about women falling in love with lions and stones being turned into pigs. None of the witnesses to Irish ritual inaugurations report anything like Cambrensis's lurid story and Edmond Spenser, writing in the 16th century, describes a more mundane ceremony when a chieftain, after receiving a symbolic shoe upon the inauguration stone;

'then hath a wand delivered unto him
by some whose proper office it is;
after which, descending from the stone,
he turneth himself around,
thrice forward and thrice backward.'

County Fermanagh *Fir Manach*
The People of Manach

A major portion of this county is taken up with Upper and Lower Lough Erne, 144 sq. km [90 sq. miles] of water containing numerous islands, low hills and narrow tracts of land separating lake and river. Historically, the waterway was a major route through the drumlins, bogs and woodland separating Ulster and the rest of Ireland. The expanse of water was named *Eirne*, after a

daughter of Buirc Buiredeach, a legendary early king. This curious name Buiredeach may derive from *Barrekios* or *Barreci*, a version of the female ancestor Brigantia who was the titular deity of Leinster [where the Uí Bairrche originated]. A 13 m [43 ft] in diameter stone circle at Drumskinny [Kesh–Castlederg road] which dated to around 2000 BC when excavated may be the ritual site for some of these early peoples. Another ritual site nearby at Kiltierney is an 'L'-shaped embanked roadway, of which 1,100 m [3,609 ft] have been excavated and which may have had a function similar to the embanked approachway to the Mound of the Hostages at Tara in Co. Meath and the Mucklaghs at the ritual site at Cruachain in Roscommon [Waddell, 2000].

Another possible source of *Fir Manach* 'People of the Manaigh' may be the Menapii who are recorded in the early historical period as a Belgic people, Celts who came to Ireland perhaps around the 5th century BC. In the archaeological record, however, there is little to suggest massive emigration from northern Gaul and the tentative connections may have been through trade or mercenary activities. The name is more likely to refer to the Fir Monach, the descendants of Monach, who had killed Enna, a relative of the king of Leinster and had to flee for his life to the remote lakelands of Lough Erne. The Fir Manach may therefore be descendants of an early ruling family in Leinster. The Uí Bairrche of Leinster appear in the later records claiming Daire Barriche Mar as their ancestor and one of triplets born to the goddess Maedb who mated with their ancestor Cathair Mair.

Boa Island
Inis Badhbha [Badhbha's Island] **War Goddess Site**
OS 3H.085.620
This long, narrow island is named after the war goddess of the Celts, who sometimes appeared as a carrion crow, notably on the shoulder of the

Left:
One of the enigmatic and possibly pre-Christian stone idols from Boa Island, Co. Fermanagh [The island of the Badhbha, or Banshee].

Right:
The Soisceal Molaise, named after St Molaise, founder of the monastery on Devinish Island. The shrine is mainly 11th century, created to hold a copy of the four gospels.

warrior Cú Chulainn, after his death in battle [see Louth entry]. The island contains a collection of idols, perhaps related to Badhbha and her cult. They stand in a churchyard at the eastern end of the island and are perhaps Byzantine in appearance as if from the Eastern Mediterranean, but strangely familiar in that they resemble somewhat indistinctly the figures that appear in the Christian manuscripts in hair, moustache and clothing.

What is more important about these figures is that the precedents for such stone carvings lie in Gaul, rather than Britannia. No similar carvings, or even decorated stones such as Turoe or Castlestrange, have been found on our nearest neighbour and the conclusion must be that whoever brought the worship of these strange figures came from Europe. Perhaps they were Gauls fleeing the legions of Caesar and following the old trade routes to Ireland. They may well have been the Menapii of Ptolemy, a sub-group of the Belgae, whose particular and recognisable artistic sense appears on various objects of bronze in Gaul, Cornwall and Ireland.

Devinish Island
Monastic Site
OS 8H.224.469

At the southern end of the lake, near Enniskillen, is the island of Devenish, *Daimhinis* the isle of the oxen. This island was on the 'border' between several disputed territories, and was known as 'Devenish of the Assemblies' due to the fact that it was 'neutral' and could be used for parleys and the resolution of contentious disputes. The monastery was established in the 6th century and the various buildings, although of a much later period, are generally associated with St Molaise, its founder. Its greatest treasure is the *Soiscel Molaise*, a book-shrine of bronze plates and silver filigree made to contain a copy of the Gospels. It has an inscription in Irish in the base asking for a prayer for Cenn Faelad, the successor to Molaise and for Gilla Baithin, the artist who made it. It dates from the 11th century and is now in the National Museum Dublin.

Also on the island is a perfect example of a round tower, over 26 m [85 ft] in height and unusual in its having sculpted stonework around the top. On

White Island, north of Devenish, there is a small romanesque church which has a series of curious miniature statues mounted on the outside wall. The six figures may represent pilgrims as they are not obviously ecclesiastics and some of them appear to be holding animals or swords and shields. These short figures probably date from the Early Christian period as one of them has a carved 'brooch' probably of a style popular in the 8th century (de Paor, 1958).

County Derry *Doire*
Place of the Oaks

The area to the east of this historic city was important in Neolithic times, when the rich chalk deposits of the hills were quarried for axes and the earliest farmers began to till the soil. Near the mouth of the River Bann at Coleraine are the oldest habitation sites on the island, where prehistoric hunter-gatherers enjoyed a 'menu' many people would choose today, eating mussels, oysters, fish and occasional seabirds. This site at Mount Sandel produced radiocarbon dates of 7000 BC from the post-holes of several ancient timber houses. Later arrivals, who probably came from a northerly direction, began building the court-tombs and dolmens around 4000 BC and started to change the landscape by clearing the woodland and planting crops. They were more agriculturally advanced than the early hunter-gatherers and may have enslaved or otherwise subjugated them.

Ballybriest
Double Chamber Grave
OS 4H.762.886

Approximately $1\frac{1}{2}$ km [1 mile] north-west of Lough Fea is a double-galleried grave, where two chambers are constructed back-to-back for the remains of [usually] cremated individuals. A point to bear in mind about the construction of these tombs is that they suggest a differentiation in status within the population group and a need

to place a reminder in time and space that 'this area was theirs'. Another tomb was discovered nearby when turf cutting revealed how the spread of bogland around 2000 BC overgrew the early farm systems causing a population shift to more arable land. This climate-related phenomenon is repeated at several sites throughout Ireland, notably at the Céide Fields at Behy in north Mayo.

The area possibly had gold resources during the 2nd millennium BC, resulting in the manufacture of gold 'lunulae', semi-circles of gold, possibly representing the moon. These decorations were probably worn around the neck and may have been a 'badge' or mark of distinction for a special caste, perhaps involved in religious ceremonies.

As we move toward more relatively recent times [*c.* 700 BC], bronze objects including swords, scabbards, brooches and pins appear in the northern archaeological record. The swords, described as 'Gundilingen' type from their close similarity to German examples, have been found in various rivers and lakes throughout Ireland, but especially in the River Bann at the eastern edge of Co. Derry. They may have been placed there as a votive deposit to the gods, or possibly as a symbolic gesture after the decease of a prominent warrior or noble. The swords have an average length of 67 cm, with some as long as 84 cm [Waddell, 2000]. They suggest the arrival of a warrior group, perhaps of small numbers, but certainly heralding the beginning of Ireland as a 'Celtic speaking country'. It appears certain that, during the centuries before the Christian period, the bronze working skills were developed to a high degree in Ireland and while these may have been the result of cultural cross-fertilisation from Britain and elsewhere, the evidence could equally suggest the arrivals from outside of small numbers of mounted warriors, perhaps Halstatt Celts from Europe

Bronze sword, c. 800 BC, Ballyharney, Co. Westmeath.

seeking a new land away from whatever strife or pressure existed on the continent at that time.

Derry City
17th-Century City

St Columcille founded a monastery here in the 6th century, which was destroyed by the Vikings and rebuilt several times during its history. Derry is the last walled city to be built in Europe [*c.* 1613] and Londonderry is the name preferred by its unionist inhabitants. It received this name after London merchant guilds were offered tracts of land following the Ulster plantation of 1608. Many of Ulster's chieftains and landowners were dispossessed at this period and northern Ulster's noble Gaelic families like O'Doherty and O'Cahan and their hereditary brehons, the Magilligans of Magilligan Point, were obliged to take commissions in the service of the Spanish army or navy. Many, however, remained and some prospered, finding other outlets for their talent and intelligence.

Derry city, built on the site of Colmcille's 6th-century monastery, was originally a wooded hill, surrounded by water.

Limavady
Leim an Mhadaidh [the dog's leap] **6th-Century Parliament**

OS SHEET 1 42.27

South of this town in Roepark demesne is a low, grass-covered hill where one of the earliest 'parliaments' in these islands was held. In 573 AD, the high-king Aed, son of Ainmuireach, called the Convention of Druim Ceatt to debate outstanding issues. Attending this gathering were bishops, abbots, kings, bards, warriors and brehons, all assembled to discuss and settle matters relating to law, property and international affairs. By far the most eminent person present was St Colmcille who had travelled from Iona for the event in the company of monks from his community. He, together with King Aedan mac Gabrain of Dal Riata, wanted the community in Iona to be free of Uí Néill jurisdiction, and the high-king, a relative of Colmcille, agreed. This was not without a certain negative partisanship shown by the Irish monks who heckled the saint and jostled and pushed his supporters. There was also a political dimension to the parliament which agreed that only the fleet of Dal Riata would be available to serve the Uí Néill high-king, but all Dal Riata possessions in Antrim and Derry would remain subject to Aed mac Ainmuireach of the northern Uí Néill.

Another important matter was resolved at Druim Ceatt. The kings of Ireland were finding the poets a burden on income and a threat because of their wicked and occasionally lethal satire. They had resolved to put this matter to the convention and have the poets banished forever. Unexpectedly, Colmcille spoke on their behalf and his intervention saved their livelihoods. They did, however, agree to stop recruitment and encourage some 'early retirement'. In thanks, perhaps, a professional poet composed an elegy when the saint died in 597 AD and this, the earliest example of Irish literature, can be taken as an example of the fruitful collaboration between monk and filí, a process repeated in the christianised Anglo-Saxon lands of England [Byrne, 1973].

The 'Long Tower' Church
'Living' Christian Site
This mid-19th century church is believed by its parishioners to be the site of Colmcille's original church. It has a beautiful classical interior, embellished by columns donated by the Protestant Bishop and Earl, Dr Hervey, in 1843.

On an exterior wall, beneath a pieta, are two quern stones dating from the Bronze Age of 200 BC and similar to many found particularly around the province of Ulster.

Romans
In the 4th century AD Roman Britain was in decline and legions were being withdrawn from the Welsh borderlands. There was a concurrent increase in raiding across the Irish Sea and the hoard at Balline [Limerick] and Coleraine could have been plunder, as the Scotii are recorded as penetrating deep into rich areas such as Wroxeter and Gloustershire at that time. Equally, the Scotii were often employed as mercenaries in the Roman army and the Attacotti, possibly a Celtic tribe from Ulster, are recorded as fighting in Gaul for the Romans [Cunliffe, 2001]. A hoard dating from the early 5th century was found at Ballinrees, Co. Derry and contained over 1,500 coins and over 5 kg of silver bars, ingots, fragments of plate and some silver spoons [Waddell, 2000].

Tironey
Grave
This portal dolmen [on B road, 1.6 km (1 mile) north-west of Maghera], supported by three of its original six upright stones, is almost a piece of visual art in the countryside. It has a sculptural quality in the dramatic positioning of the capstone within a simplistic architectural form.

The Hill of Drumcett, where the great convention of 8th-century Ireland was held.

The Province of Leinster

The Iron-Age promontory fort of the 'Baily', reputedly home of Creevan Nionaire, a pirate and raider of eastern England.

This province of 12,560 sq. km [7,850 sq. miles] takes its name from the Norse *stadir* or *place* and *Laighen*, hence 'place of the Laighen'. Much of its northern segment containing the great passage graves of Newgrange, Dowth and Knowth and the other sites of the Boyne valley were historically in *Mide*, the original fifth province, and were not seen as part of Leinster's history. Tara, however, was a symbolic 'capital' until the 5th century while the royal sites of Leinster, upon the hilltops of Dún Aillinne and Dind Righ, were to the south.

Sometime before 2000 BC, a people from northern Europe travelled down the Irish Sea and settled along the east coast of Ireland, from what is now Antrim as far south as the Hook Peninsula. They may have been the *Laighe* of mythology, spearmen from the east who brought a more advanced weaponry with them. They were to prove resilient to expansionist threats

from the Eoghanacht of the south and the Connachta of the west, and although various high-kings attempted to oust the Leinstermen from Tara, their ownership of the hill, in symbolic form at least, was never relinquished.

They also brought with them a form of pottery, with an elaborate rim and incised decoration, perhaps reflecting agricultural practices from their homeland. The burial at Drimnagh near Dublin City centre, an elaborate wigwam shape of alder rods and turf, contained a cist burial of a presumably important individual. There are five known burials of this type in Leinster and also one of a similar type in the Phoenix Park, Dublin. These form a different type of burial rite to the previous Megalithic multiple burials and would suggest new arrivals and new agricultural practices. The Phoenix Park burial is of two individuals 'folded' to fit into the cist shape. They were buried with pieces of a dog; a rite which anthropological studies suggest denotes a sacrilege had been committed, in this case presumably involving both individuals.

Exported from the Rhineland in the 9th century, a Viking sword, engraved with Ulfebehrt, *the maker's name, was found in Ballinderry, Co. Westmeath.*

Early Territorial Boundaries

Leinster was a clearly outlined *fifth*, the *Coiced Laighen* in the early historical period. Its northern boundary was defined by forest and the River Boyne and its western by the great Bog of Allen. It had three partly navigable rivers, the Liffey, Barrow and Slaney, and it was bounded by the Irish Sea itself. Its centre of power was in Kildare, at the great hillfort of Dún Aillinne. Although cattle was the 'currency' in calculating wealth and Leinster has much fertile land, the actual number of ringforts, the 'corralls' of the small farmers who tended the cattle, are relatively low compared to west Limerick and Clare especially. It could be that Leinster was a tillage area from the earliest times, as wealth was still required for the

exercise of political power and the purchase of materials and mercenaries when required.

During the many internal dynastic feuds between the competing rulers of Leinster, it was frequently the losers' 'lot' to retreat over the Wicklow hills to the valleys within or the coast beyond. These rejected dynasts in turn displaced the subject tribes, the *Fortuatha Laighen* whose territory the Wicklow Mountains traditionally were. These peoples were not seen as ethnically 'Laighen' although they apparently enjoyed a status higher than other unfree peoples elsewhere on the island. They may have been the descendants of the miners who worked the ores of Wicklow in the preceding millennia. Like most unfree peoples their role in history was restricted, being subject to tribute and service although one of their number was reputedly St Brigid, and Kildare was an area where they enjoyed some autonomy as a subject people.

Leinster Counties and Sites

Dublin *Dyfflyn* [Norse] *Baile Átha Cliath*
Town at Ford of the Hurdles [County and City]
Viking City

This is Ireland's capital city and has been an area of habitation since before the Bronze Age. It was probably the spot where many early arrivals landed, clearing the forests of Moynalty which stood north and south of the ridge where Christchurch Cathedral and Dublin Castle now stand. Their river crossing point, the *Áth Cliath* of Dublin's Celtic name was probably in the area of Watling Street Bridge. Early manuscripts suggest that the ford of hurdles was a popular crossing spot for sheep stolen in Leinster by north Dublin rustlers. The name of the city is derived from *Dubh Linn* or Dyfflinn, the 'Black Pool' a low-lying area used by the Vikings as an anchorage during the 9th century until it was eventually drained to become the gardens for Dublin Castle.

The northern part of the county was known as *Fingall* 'elder foreigner' from the Norwegian Vikings who first settled there, as later Danish Vikings were known as *Dubh-Gaill* 'new foreigners'. This part of Dublin contains several thousand acres of prime agricultural land and some possibly Bronze Age burial mounds. Two of these, at Coolock and Glasnevin, are un-excavated, as far as I am aware, but the siting corresponds to a familiar pattern of being near the crest of a low hill near a river. These were possibly the resting places of the local ruling tribe, the 'first' to establish a settlement. The tomb probably functioned as a centre of worship for the area, being the hub of the tribe and its ancestral beliefs. The long-established residential area of Glasnevin, lying on the north side of the Tolka, was the tribal area of the *Gaelinga*, a Gaelic grouping whose local saint, Mobhi, established a monastery on the hill above the river sometime in the 6th century. The monastery church was probably on the site of the present Anglican church of St Mobhi at the back of the Bon Secours Hospital and is recorded as having 50 pupils in the *Life of St Colmcille*. The trainee monks had their humble beehive huts, *bothys,* along the opposite bank of the river probably where the Church of Our Lady of Dolours now stands. The Gaelinga were later displaced into Meath by the Vikings, who were being pushed northwards by the Normans in the 12th century. Approximately 1.6 km [1 mile] further north, at the area around the junction of what is now Ballymun Road and Collins Avenue, was the site of a fine house and farm called 'Stormanstown' from a Viking chieftain, *Strum* whose area of control it was.

In 1835 in the southern part of the county a series of graves were uncovered on Bray Head where copper coins of the Emperor Trajan [97–117 AD] and Hadrian [117–138 AD] were found. These coins had been placed in the mouths of the desceased in the Roman manner as payment for Charon, the ferryman of the River Acheron, the other side of which was the land of the dead. It is more than probable that Bray, or near to Bray, was a small Romano-British settlement or trading post [Waddell, 2000].

Baily Promontory Fort
Celtic Coastal Fort
OS DUBLIN DISTRICT 36.30

This multi-vallate fort is home to the Baily lighthouse and sits at the northern entrance to Dublin Bay. According to the annalists it was the fort of Dún Creevan in the Iron Age, home to a king Creevan Nionaire, who was notorious for his predatory raids upon Britain, returning from one raid with 'a golden chariot, a gem-laden chessboard, a cloak embroidered with precious stones and a conquering sword inlaid with serpents of refined gold'. He was rumoured to have been the exiled chief who invited Agricola, the Roman general, to invade Ireland and also to have established the 'market' at Loughshinny. In an earlier period, the Baily was reputedly the 'lair' of a well-known rustler and poet, Atherne, who also acted as an *agent provocateur* against the Leinster Celtic dynasties. In a foray into the lands south of Dublin, Athearne kidnapped wives and daughters of the local nobility as well as stealing hundreds of sheep and 700 cattle. Cú Chulainn and his Ulstermen obligingly came south to help the rustler and poet when warriors from the enraged families attacked his fort at the Baily. This was all part of Ulster's plan, and Atherne retreated behind the walls of his fort at Baily while the clansmen hacked and tore at each other to avenge wrongs and ancient grudges. In this way, Ulster was able to assert its authority as far south as Dublin. Atherne may have been a descendant of the Menapii, a northern European tribe as they are shown in the area on Ptolemy's map. The map, however, was drawn several centuries after the observations were made and few actual correlations have been made between the tribes recorded on the map and insular Celts.

Bohernabreena

The Road of the Hostelry Battle Site

OS DUBLIN DISTRICT Q25.9

Togail Bruidne Da Derga [The Destruction of Da Derga's Hostel]

The *bruden* of the manuscripts was a type of ancient rath-hotel wherein all travellers could stop and be fed and Da Derga, a Leinster lord, had such a hostel beside the River Dodder where the Bohernabreena Bridge now stands. Sometime in the Early Christian centuries King Conaire, whose reign was particularly popular, chose to banish his three foster-brothers who had committed rape and murder and would normally have been executed. As they were his 'family' he forced them into exile and they went unwillingly across the Irish Sea. Tragically for Conaire, the villains met up with a particularly disturbed individual called Ingcel the One-Eyed and a gang of crooks which included some of the worst miscreants of both islands. After a short time of anarchy and murder in Britannia, they decided to return to Ireland and landed near Howth. They sent out spies to see what was

'going on' and found that their hated brother Conaire intended staying the night at an undefended hostel and that he was accompanied by a rich retinue.

The annals record that King Conaire had been enjoying himself that evening. He was surrounded by people he liked and the juggler, a '*clessamnach*', provided by Da Derga was better than his own. Conaire watched the *clessamnach* juggling with nine gold balls and the noise they made was 'like the buzzing-whirl of bees on a beautiful day' [Joyce, 1913]. There was plenty to drink, the roast boar and ale was plentiful and the hostel's musicians had begun to play . . . In the darkness Ingcel's gang had followed the trail to Da Derga's rath and peered through the wattle fencing to see who was with the king. By the light of the great fires they recognised Conaire's three sons and his champion, Conall of the Victories. They would have seen his black-cloaked Pictish bodyguards from Ulster, and watched Conaire's steward fussing over the food and drink. The noisy snoring of mac Cecht, a

The ancient ford over the River Dodder at Bohernabreena in the Dublin Mountains, site of the epic tale, Togail Bruidne Da Dearga [the Destruction of Da Derga's Hostel].

famous warrior accompanying Cormac, son of the king of Ulster, could be heard from the ante-room off the main hall.

Suddenly there was uproar outside in the darkness and the smell of burning thatch. Ingcel's thugs had blocked the river upstream to deprive the hostel of water and their fire-arrows had set the walls and roof blazing. The warriors Dubhtach and Conall led the charge against the marauders and one of Conaire's Pictish bodyguards was killed by an archer. The other, Sencha, fought the attackers with his *matan*, a huge bronze spiked club of blackthorn. The entire hostel was now ablaze and the defenders were surrounded, fighting blindly in the smoke as King Conaire gasped for air and water. The warrior mac Cecht left to get water for the king but did not return. Conall of the Victories eventually escaped the slaughter and made for Tailtu, his father's rath. Mac Cecht returned at dawn to find a smouldering pile of burnt timber and the remaining attackers escaping with Conaire's head. He caught them and killed them, finally giving water to the bodyless head of his king. The hostel was never rebuilt.

In the early Mediaeval period, the territory around Glenasmole and Bohernabreena was part of a territory known as Hy-Maile and ruled by the princely family of O'Kelly. A poem written in the 12th century describes the glen as 'always full of witchcraft' although this may be a reference to the fact that it was heavily wooded and a refuge for the displaced 13th-century Irish of Co. Dublin.

Castleknock
Warriors and Lovers
OS DUBLIN DISTRICT 37.9

Castleknock College, a prestigious boys' school to the west of the city, is the site of a bloody confrontation in pre-Christian times first described in the 12th century *Book of the Dun*

Cow. In the fight, a young warrior, Cumhall, is slain by an experienced and ruthless killer Goll mac Morna in the final episode of a story of elopement, love and revenge. Cumhall had been driven insane with desire for a girl of exceptional beauty called Muireann *of the fair neck* but he was poor, and Tadgh mac Nuadat, her father, rejected him. Muireann, however, fell in love with Cumhall and he responded by abducting her. They married, but mac Nuadat refused to accept his daughter's choice and vowed to avenge the dishonour she had brought to his name. As he was a druid, mac Nuadat could not bear arms and gave the task to Goll mac Morna, who caught up with Cumhall and Muireann at Cnucha. It was a one-sided combat. Goll mac Morna, a member of the Fianna and therefore a professional warrior, killed her young lover after

Castleknock College, site of the bitter 'duel' between Goll mac Morna and Cumhall, father of Fionn, founder of the Fianna.

a brief and fruitless defence. Shortly after the death of Cumhall, Muireann found she was pregnant and this drove her father to decide to burn the girl as punishment. She fled to the great Rath of Conn Cetchathach [of the hundred battles] and not even Goll mac Morna would challenge such a fearsome fighter. After the baby was born, he was brought secretly to the great woods of the Sliabh Blooms to be reared as Fionn, son of Cumhaill [see Offaly entry].

Drumanagh
Roman Trading Post

A Roman galley of a type used for trading along the Atlantic coast of Europe and possibly between Ireland and England, during the Roman occupation of Britain.

This promontory fort beside a small harbour in Loughshinny, north Dublin, is where evidence would suggest Roman and Irish merchants established a trading post in the first centuries AD. As to what was traded? Labour in those days was needed for everything to do with agriculture and war, and a cheap way of acquiring labour was slaves, of which Ireland, like West Africa centuries later, was a plentiful source. Exports from Ireland recorded at the time were wolf-hounds, wool, grain and hides. Britannia at this time had an estimated population of around 3.5 million and Gaul [France] about 8 million. Ireland was probably under 1 million in population but despite its small population may have been exporting some goods to Gaul direct, as the Roman army required 25,000 tons of grain annually and this was sourced from all the 'provinces'. The preponderance of quern stones

in the north midlands would suggest, perhaps, more grain being grown than could be consumed by a relatively small population, but available for sale to merchants at east coast harbours.

Feltrim Hill
Faildruim [Hill of the Wolves] **Wolf's Lair**
This ancient site has produced an interesting harness mount from the 2nd century AD and a Roman coin from *c.* 300 AD. It was the ancient seat of the Fagan family, a branch of the O'Fogartys of Éile and there was a village here in the early Mediaeval period which has now disappeared.

Glenasmole
[The Glen of the Thrushes]
Ancient Hunting Ground
This area, famous in antiquity for its rowan trees, was reputedly a hunting ground for the 3rd century *Fianna* or warrior band, especially its leader Finn Mac Cool and his son, Ossian. There is a spirited account of a chase involving Finn and his hound Bran wherein a beautiful female deer is chased and eventually changes into a beautiful woman who changes into a witch. In a poem entitled 'The Hunt of Sliabh Truim' Finn fights and kills serpents, monsters and an arroch or dragon in the valley of Glenasmole.

Glencree Valley
Remote Valley
OS DUBLIN DISTRICT Q16.15
This was once a great forest designated a deer park during the 13th century and bounded by a double ditch to contain the wild animals for the chase. These woods, containing thousands of acres of oak, were cut for the palace of Queen Mary and further reduced by the establishment of iron works during the 18th century. Described as 'a fit hall for a thief and a rebel' the woods of this and other Wicklow valleys provided local inhabitants with materials for houses, game as a food supply, and importantly, cover against the English military in their campaigns against [primarily] the

O'Tooles and O'Byrnes of the Dublin and Wicklow mountains.

Hellfire Club

A Bronze Age cairn from *c.* 2000 BC stood on this spot commemorating a local tribe until it was demolished by Thomas Conolly of Castletown House to build a shooting lodge for himself and his friends. Legends about this eerie site include black cats, horned demons, orgies, black masses and all the usual paraphernalia of folk imagination. The reality is more prosaic, in that Conolly built this lodge against local wishes and superstition, and apparently held meetings of the hell-fire club on the premises, wherein large quantities of champagne, pretty girls and gambling combined to produce extravagant local tales of debauchery and rumours of demonic appearances.

The Hill of Howth *Benn Etair*

Hooth [Viking] headland

This hill overlooks the city from the north and is named after the legendary hero, *Etar* who died from grief after the loss of Áine his lover. His grave is reputedly on the hill, and may be the portal tomb in the Howth Castle demesne. The tomb is on a rocky platform, at the foot of a steep cliff on the north side of Howth Head. It faces south-east, inclined toward the rising sun.

Lambay Island

Island of the Celtic 'Brigantes'

After their defeat by the Roman army in 74 AD, small numbers of the *Brigantes*, a northern British tribe, made their way across the Irish Sea to this small island off the Dublin coast. The items found on the island include many bracelets, a sword and shield and several other decorated

Glencree Valley, originally a vast forest, famous for its deer and its oakwoods.

St Audoen's. Within the vestibule of this 12th-century church is the 'lucky stone', an early Christian slab which pilgrims were obliged to touch in veneration before setting out on their pilgrimage to Clonmacnoise.

brooches, all of which indicate strong Roman influences on their artistry and manufacture. The choice of the island of Lambay has precedents in ancient Greece and the Atlantic coasts of Europe. A trading group would often choose an off-shore island to establish themselves, as it formed no threat to the existing communities and was an easy place to access for outgoing and incoming trade. The island therefore formed a separate community and a distinct territory with its own recognisable borders, and as such was ideally placed to conduct business with both natives and those from abroad.

St Patrick's Well, part of the Priory of the Holy Trinity, and visible below the Douglas Hyde entrance to Trinity College.

Monastic Road [Carrickmines]
Ancient Roadway
Hidden up a small by-road in Carrickmines is a stretch of a penitent's way where pilgrims would walk barefoot to a small church a short distance away. The Early Christian cross at the beginning of the 'way' probably signals the boundary of the

monastic site and has been in this situation since around the 7th century. Unfortunately, horse-trekking and local motorbikes are damaging the stony floor of the penitent's way and changing it from a dry, stony path to a muddy boreen.

St Audoen's Church
1,300-Year-Old 'Lucky Stone'
OS 16O.15.34
In the porch of this recently restored Anglican Church, there is an incised Christian stone, perhaps an early grave-slab. It has been there since the 8th century, when St Brendan built a timber church on the site, marking the beginning of the *Slighe Mhor*, the 'great road' to the monastery of Clonmacnoise and points further west. Pilgrims leaving on the long trek to Clonmacnoise would touch the stone and pray for a safe journey. As they murmured their prayers, they may have repeated the ancient saying, *'Tonga na dia thungus mo thuath'* 'I swear by the god my people swear by', for the older pagan beliefs continued into the Christian era and the general word for a god, *dia* was used for pagan and Christian deity alike.

St Patrick's Well
5th-Century Well

Hidden behind the wall of Trinity College as it runs along Nassau Street, the ancient well of St Patrick dates to the 5th century and was part of the Priory of the Holy Trinity that stood on the site now covered by the college. It can be reached by going through the gates at Leinster Street, turning left and walking about 200 m [656 ft] as far as an iron gate set in the wall. You are now at a well where reputedly St Patrick blessed converts to his new faith in the 5th century AD.

'St Patrick's breastplate', a hymn attributed to the saint, was reputed to be a *Fe-Fiada*, an incantation for invisibility or shape-changing, apparently allowing the saint and his followers to appear [in one instance] as a herd of deer to evade assailants who waited in ambush during his 5th-century missionary travels.

Thingmote
Site of Viking Throne and Burial Ground

At the junction of Suffolk Street and Church Lane, where St Andrew's Church [now Dublin Tourism] stands, was the Viking 'Thingmote'. This conical hill, levelled in 1632 for Nassau Street road material, was the Viking ritual centre of Dublin. On its summit, generations of Dublin's leading Vikings were inaugurated and the paved area surrounding the church covers the graves of many of Dublin's Viking kings.

County Kildare *Coill Dara*
Church of the Oak Wood

This county was bounded by geography, having the rivers Barrow, Liffey, Slaney and Boyne forming natural declinations to its frontiers. It had a high density of woodland, as well as the extensive peat 'sea' of the Bog of Allen, covering almost 200,000 acres of its southern terrain. The Curragh of Kildare is a famous grassland plain that lies to the east of Kildare town. For centuries

it has been a home to horse racing, stud farms and the bloodstock industry in general. It covers around 5,000 acres and has several ringforts and other prehistoric earthworks within its 9.6 km x 6.4 km [6 mile by 4 mile] shape. It has many small burial mounds [barrows] and was probably on the periphery of the tribal area dominated by the ritual site of Dún Aillinne. It is usual to find burial grounds on the border of tribal sites of importance and Cnoc Áine, for example, in Limerick has an extensive burial ground to the south. It was an ideal location for hunting deer, and the early tales frequently refer to a headlong rush southwards across the plain of Kildare and on to what has been the Great Heath of Maryborough since the 17th century.

During the early Middle Ages, Kildare contained the territory of the tribal group called Uí

The site of the 'Thingmote', burial mound of Dublin's Viking kings from the 8th to the 10th centuries.

Muirchedagh, of which the O'Tooles were the most prominent. This patrimony was forcibly taken by the Anglo-Normans and the O'Tooles became outlaws in their own country, retiring to harass the newcomers from the Wicklow glens. The lands of the Uí Muirchedagh became the county palatine of the Fitzgerald family who became reasonably hibernicised through intermarriage with the leading Gaelic families. They also succeeded in making political alliances with the competing power structures of the English establishment and offered a considerable degree of artistic patronage to poets and bards in a similar way to their Gaelic cousins.

Opposite page: Dún Aillinne, the massive hill-top site where a great 'stadium' for gladiators or bull-fights was built, c. 100 BC.

Ballyshannon

Áth Senaigh [Battle Site]

[Crossroads on N78 — 7 km (4.4 miles) south of Kilcullen] On Tuesday 19 August in the year 738 AD, a pitched battle was fought at this bridge between rival dynasties fighting for control of the rich grasslands of Kildare. The Leinstermen, led by their king, Aed MacColgan and accompanied by nine princes of the *Laighen* and two kings, were defeated by the Uí Néill and their king, Aed Allan of Tara. All the Leinster nobility fell on that battlefield, with MacColgan being beheaded by a blow from the battle-sword of Aed Allan himself, thereby ending his reign and breaking the power of the Uí Cheinnselaig for several hundred years [O'Cronin, 1995]. A monk from the monastery of Clonard described the slaughter as *'an overwhelming victory, trampling under foot,*

Group of warriors with swords and shields, from Monasterboice high cross [Joyce, 1913].

prostrating, over-throwing, consuming their rivals to the point of annihilation with few left to tell the tale'. Fergus and Dub-da-Chrich [the kings of the Fothairt], nine other princes of the Uí Cheinnselaig and Sil Maeliudir and countless unnamed fighting men died, perhaps buried under the mound near the ford.

Clane

Kings and Warriors

Almost 2,000 years ago, the chariot road *Slighe Mhor* forded the Liffey where Clane Bridge is now situated. South of the village was a *Nineadh* or sacred place of refuge and sometime in the 2nd century AD, Mesgedra, a bleeding and mutilated king of Leinster, sought desperate and final shelter within its ancient yew trees. He had fled a disastrous battle against Conall Cearnach, a ruthless warrior, and was running from the victorious Ulstermen and their ferocious leader. Despite the king being wounded, Conall Cearnach refused him sanctuary within the *Nineadh* and called him 'coward' baiting him to fight. Cearnach bound one of his arms behind his back to make the contest even but still he slew the weakened king and took his head as a trophy. When Buan, Mesgedra's wife, came with her ladies-in-waiting to seek her husband, she was confronted on the road [where the hamlet of Mainham now stands] by his murderer, who taunted her as 'widow of Mesgedra' and attempted to seduce her. She and her retinue raised a great lament or *caoineadh* for Mesgedra, so piteous and so heartbreaking that she died as it finished. She lies buried within the mound at Mainham and legend suggests that a hazel tree grew upon that spot. Hazel was still abundant along the banks of the Liffey until the 17th century and is remembered in the name 'Hazelhatch', a corruption of hazel hurst, meaning a wood of hazel trees.

In a much later year [704 AD] ambitious warlords from the Sil nAedo Slaine [the seed of Aodh of

Slane, a branch of the Uí Néill] were met and defeated by Cellach Cualainn, the overking of Leinster, at a pitched battle beside the village.

Dún Aillinne
Gladiator Arena [Site]
OS 16N.82.08

The well of St Brigid, who was probably the goddess Brigantia, near to Kildare town.

This hilltop fort of 40 hectares was an important site for the kings of Leinster from the earliest times. It has a circular embankment surrounding the top of the hill which is 5 m [16 ft] high in places. Although the bank is not defensive, in that the ditch is on the *inside*, the scale of the bank is very impressive from the bottom of the ditch. When excavated by Bernard Wailes, the remains of a series of extraordinary structures dating to the early Iron Age were discovered. In or around 390 BC, highly organised activity took place on the summit of the hill and a ritual structure of 40 m [131 ft] in diameter was built. This stadium, involving two circles of tiered seating [perhaps for participants and spectators] was designed possibly for contests of some sort as an iron sword was found near the site. It would not seem impossible to imagine some form of gladiatorial contest taking place within these walls over 2,300 years ago.

The Hill of Allen
Site of 3rd-Century Druid's Hall

This hill, once the home of the Fianna and famous in legend and song, is gradually being destroyed by quarrying and gravel extraction. Perhaps the needless and wilful despoliation of this ancient and romantic site was foretold in the tale *The Death of Oisín*, for when he returns from Tír na nÓg [the land of the ever-young] he

finds an Ireland of few forests and no leaders. He travels to the Hill of Allen where the Fianna, a band of travelling warriors, had their headquarters and from where they hunted and coursed the county. He finds that everything he loved — his friends, his hounds, his house, the noble and free life he lived — has vanished.

'He called out loudly for Fionn,
For Caoilte and for Faolan,
But there was no reply,
No great fortress was visible,
Only scrub, briar and moss covered ruins'

Long before, Allen had been the residence of Tadgh mac Nuadat, who had arranged the murder of Cumhall, Oisín's grandfather, out of fear of losing Allen. Fionn took the hill from his father's murderer and left it to Caoilte.

Kildare Town
Powerful Goddess
OS 16N.72.12

The town came to prominence through the endeavours of its native saint and possible pre-Christian seer, Brigid, [perhaps] of 'the Fiery Arrow', the most popular saint in Ireland after Saint Patrick. In Professor MacCana's words, 'It is clear beyond question that the Saint has usurped the role of the Goddess Brigantia and much of her mythological tradition' [MacCana, 1983]. Brigantia was the tribal deity of Celts living in Gaul, Northern and Eastern England, and possibly what is now Wexford. They may have arrived in Ireland fleeing Caesar's legions in either Gaul or England, but they were a numerous and powerful tribe, and may have originated from several sources. And yet the nature of their goddess would suggest a tender edge to their activities and a respect for tradition and continuity.

It is difficult to say precisely who Brigid was, in that it appears likely she was a living human

being, the daughter of an unfree woman from the *Fortuatha*, the subject and tribute-paying tribes of Celtic Ireland — but reputedly fathered by a king. She was also a pastoralist — in that she 'tended her own cattle'. This seemingly benign phrase [Haverty, 1860] suggests that the land she received from the local Gaelic lord was grazing land and not arable. This would add to the probability that Brigid was pre-Christian, in that almost all Early Christian monks were given land in the river valleys, generally too low-lying for cattle. A nun with pastoral land would be unthinkable in Early Christian Ireland.

In many ways Brigid was the most well-known of the individuals who were both pagan holy and Christian holy and who managed to be venerated by both traditions. Perhaps she was a pagan priestess with a retinue of virgins who became a convert to Christianity. Her legendary goodness and enduring spiritual vitality enabled her shrine and sacred flame to survive the closure of the monasteries under Henry VIII and it only succumbed to destruction under Cromwell in 1649.

The remains of the fire-house where the eternal flame was kept is visible beside the Romanesque cathedral that stands on the site of her oak-grove. It is more than possible that the remains of her pre-Christian temple lies beneath the floor of the present building. Today, the round tower of the monastery and her holy well endure and are visited and prayed at all year round. Special attention is paid to her feast day of 1 February, the start of spring and the Celtic festival of *Imbolc*, when ewes begin to lactate. In many parts of the country, straw babies were left outside cottages on Brigid's eve until they were 'invited' in by the families, thereby making 'Brigid' welcome. She is recorded as having died in 525 AD and her remains lie at the side of the altar in the cathedral in Kildare town.

SECRET SIGHTS — *Unknown Celtic Ireland*

Punchestown

Ritual Phallic Stone

OS 16N.92.17

This standing stone is one of a series of three in the area. It is quite a tall and slender example, tapering to a point some 3.5 m [11 ft] from the ground. The function of these monoliths is unknown, but they were probably related to events or individuals of significance to their tribal grouping. They may have been boundary markers or indicators of where valiant warriors fell in battle, as a cist grave of the Bronze Age was found beneath this example when it collapsed in the 1920s. The stone, box-like grave contained the cremated remains of one male individual. If their shape and phallic appearance is relevant to their function, they may have been a focal point for orgiastic activities around certain times of the year, as the European Celts tended to procreate *en masse* according to Tacitus when the omens were deemed appropriate. The May celebrations of late Mediaeval rural life, involving dancing around decorated and festooned maypoles, were probably a symbolic continuation of the celebratory nature of these activities.

County Wicklow *Cill Mhantain*

St Mhantain's Church

Although the name itself is Viking, from 'Vickluuw' meaning a thorny woman, it was, according to Ptolemy's map, the territory of the Cauci, a sub-group of the Belgae. The geography of the county is dominated by the granite peaks of the Wicklow Mountains, rising to 1,000 m [3,280 ft] on Lugnaquilla, the 'god of the forest', a dark and mysterious mountain that has claimed many lives, even those of experienced climbers. The county was also the reputed source for much of the gold that was used in the manufacture of the exquisite gorgets and collars of the late Bronze Age, although for a county with alluvial gold in the Avoca River, few gold artefacts have been found within its borders.

Near to the village of Avoca is the townland of Tigroney [*Teach-na-Romhan*, the house of the Romans], perhaps Romano-British merchants who may have been attracted to the copper ore from the nearby mines.

Baltinglass

Bealach Conglais [Cugla's Road] **Royal Stronghold**
This ancient habitation site on the River Slaney has a history stretching back to Early Christian times and before. As mentioned previously, it lies to the west of the great hillforts of Spinans Hill and Brusselstown, but has its own unique antiquities and history. To the north of the town are two forts, Rathnagree, with a double rampart containing an area of 14 ha and Rathcoran on the summit, some 383 m [1,256 ft] above sea-level. The remains of this fort are still impressive and the ramparts have a circumference of almost a quarter of a mile, enclosing an area in excess of almost 50 ha.

During the 6th century Baltinglass was known as *Bealach Dubthaire* and was the power 'hub' of Brandubh mac Echach of the Uí Cheinnselaig of Leinster. He achieved a great victory in the Battle of Dunbolg in 598 AD when he slew Aed mac Ainmerech, the Uí Néill high-king and thereby ended northern plans for expansion in Leinster. Brandubh hoped to use the ensuing weakness of the southern Uí Néill to further his plans for dominance over the fertile Liffey plain of south Kildare and established the forts at Baltinglass as an 'outpost' from his Rathvilly base. The Uí Cheinnselaig hoped to move northwards along the foothills of the Wicklow Mountains toward their goal of *Magh Life* [the Liffey plain] but were thwarted by the Uí Dunlainge, a powerful grouping based around the royal hillfort of Dún Aillinne. Ultimately, the more enterprising of the Uí Cheinnselaig moved across the Blackstairs mountains and established themselves around Ferns and the monastery of St Maedoc [Byrne, 1973].

Opposite page: Punchestown standing stone, erected to commemorate the body placed underneath it during the Bronze Age.

The massive stones of the 4,000-year-old Castleruddery circle, Co. Wicklow.

The ancient monastic site of Glendalough, founded in the 6th century by St Kevin.

Castleruddery Stone Circle
Solar Observatory

OS 16S.91.94

This is a more substantial circle than Athgreany and has several massive recumbent stones, some over 3 m by 4 m [10 ft by 13 ft] in scale. Like the great circle at Grange, Co. Limerick, Castleruddery has an enclosing earth bank, an eastern facing entrance and portal stones. It probably dates to the same period, about 1800 BC and in common with other circles was not used for habitation [Ó Ríordáin, 1966]. This last point, however, is open to some dispute, as Dutch examples suggest that these circles were

constructed to resemble houses and were originally roofed. Other evidence from Britain suggests that many stone circles were roofed 'temples', the timber and thatch materials having deteriorated over time. This would seem a reasonable proposition, in that the circles may well be a descent in a built form of the Megalithic tombs of 3500 BC, and if constructed with more simple and available materials could be built in reasonable time and without the huge outlay of energy and materials that the great tombs of preceding generations required.

Glendalough
6th-Century Celtic Churches

OS 16T.10.95

This popular site is subject to mass invasion by coaches and cameras during the tourist season but is worth visiting on misty or otherwise inclement days. There is a comprehensive 'visitors centre' with a detailed model of how the monastery looked in its heyday. The monastery was founded by St Kevin in the 6th century and has several interesting buildings and remains, among which are St Kevin's bed, a man-made cave about 10 m [33 ft] above the upper lake and St Kevin's kitchen, a 12th-century church. The original monastery was situated around the shore of the upper lake and moved down the valley, perhaps in the 10th century when numbers increased and more buildings were needed. It is a wonderful location for a monastery and St Kevin lived there in a small, stone, beehive hut near the shore of the upper lake.

The treasure of Glendalough, comprising books, altar silverware and a shrine, was moved when the Vikings first attacked and has never been found. Folklore suggests it was hidden somewhere on the hill between the churches and Glenmalure, and as those responsible for its concealment were killed by the marauders, it presumably lies buried still.

Hollywood

Dun bolg [Fort of the Bags] **Battle Site**

OS 16N.93.03

[Dunboyke Townland] The quaint village of Hollywood sits near the scene of a violent confrontation in the year 598 AD between Brandubh mac Echach of Uí Cheinnselaig, king of Leinster, and high-king Aed mac Ainmerech. The high-king was intent of avenging the murder of his son, Cummusach, by the Leinstermen earlier that year and brought a contingent from Ulster to fight on his behalf. Brandubh, having only a small force, went to meet the Ulaidh warriors at their camp on Sliabh Nechtain [possibly the hill to the left of Hollywood village] the evening before the battle to see if he could persuade them to abandon Aed and join his army instead. The Ulstermen remembered the harsh threats made by Aed against their poets some years previously and agreed to join Brandubh's army, making a *cro-cotaig* [a blood-covenant] with Brandubh 'that should never be broken'.

That night, the guards at Aed's camp were diverted by a leper who arrived at their fireside, saying he had heard the Leinstermen were preparing to submit. Shortly afterwards several score of cattle were driven toward them carrying large woven sacks. They examined the leading containers and found them carrying bread, ale and other provisions, 'for the high-king, from his benefactors in Leinster' was the message. The cattle were brought into the centre of the camp and corralled. Within a few minutes, each bag was torn from the inside to reveal an armed warrior. The Leinstermen drove the cattle onto the sleeping army of Aed while the Ulstermen attacked from the outside. It was a total success. Brandubh had destroyed the king's army through a combination of tactics and daring, and still dressed as the leper, personally hunted down and slew Aed, although the king was surrounded by a *cro-bodba* [a shield of spears]. Becc mac Cuanach, prince of the Airgealla, also fell in the battle, representing the Uí Macc Uais sept of mid-Ulster, allies of the northern Uí Néill.

Dunbolg townland, near Hollywood, Co. Wicklow, scene of a violent battle between Brandubh, king of Leinster, and the high-king, Aed mac Ainmerech, in the year 598 AD.

The battle was known as *Dunbolg* [the fort of the bags] after Brandubh's plan.

Lough Nahanagan

Loch na hOnchion [Lake Monster]

This lake of some 45 sq. km [28 sq. miles] is reputedly one of several homes of the *Onchu*, a ferocious water-dog. The *Onchu*, illustrated in mediaeval heraldry as a dragon/dog type of beast, may have been some form of large otter. Access to the lake is difficult, as it forms the lower reservoir for the ESB power station within the adjacent Turlogh Hill. Between the lake and the public highway is St Kevin's Road, the Mediaeval route taken by pilgrims descending toward Glendalough. It is marked by timber stakes and is a popular route for the wild goats of the valley to wander.

The Piper's Stones

Athgreany Solar Observatory

OS 16N.93.03

This stone circle lies on a heath at the north-west end of the Wicklow mountains on the Baltinglass road. This was an important routeway toward the ford across the River Slaney at Tullow and the stone circle may have had some relevance to the community that used this thoroughfare. There are several circles in this locality and one, Ballyfolan, had a cairn [burial mound] at the centre. When excavated, it was found to be empty, probably due to earlier disturbance.

These circles themselves are exercises in space and time. They are usually constructed in relation to solar position and frequently relate to other geographic features in the surrounding countryside. They are a restraining space, with a circumference, entrance and focal point, yet allow access to the ritual temenos within. They are secretive yet open, sometimes with a hidden single burial at the centre, and, I would suggest, are completely different in concept to the chambered burial mounds of earlier times. Ritual now appears to be outdoor, communal and personal, no longer hidden and collective. Likewise their circular shape, while perhaps being natural and even ovoid, do not have the gloomy and suffocating sense that the earlier tombs appear to have. They are less claustrophobic, and

The Piper's Stones, a ritual circle of 13 standing stones, dating to c. 2000 BC.

even if roofed, would have been spacious structures, large enough for a group. Perhaps the rituals performed within the 'court' tombs had dried up, become fossilised and the community needed a new and fecund source of transcendence within a reformed architectural space.

Poulaphuca

Poll an Phúca *The pool of the Pooka Water-Spirit*
This wild and deep gorge is now almost dry, the river having been diverted for a hydro-electric scheme in the 1940s. Before the bridge was built across the top of the waterfall, it was the dwelling place of the *puca* [pooka], an apparently lonely spirit of malign intention and black humour. Pookas are usually found in these wild and desolate places, suitable perhaps for their solitary and mischievous nature. This crossing of the Dartry River was always a dangerous place at night, especially when the river was in spate, and there are several stories from the 18th and 19th century of unwary travellers being swept off their horses and lost, due to the malice of this notorious goblin.

Rathgall

Hilltop Fortress

This hillfort is one of a series of tri-vallate and bi-vallate hillforts on the western slopes of the Wicklow Mountains. It has three stone walls with exterior ditches and was used for the manufacture of weapons in the Later Bronze Age. There was a climatic deterioration in *c.* 1500 BC and this may have caused considerable pressure on the population groups in the area. It is also in this period that votive deposits began to be made, primarily around wet or marshy areas, and these may also have been related to the disturbed nature of that time. Spinans Hill and Brusselstown Ring are further examples of the hillforts in this area. Most are unexcavated and were probably for use in emergencies, as a refuge, rather than habitation sites. The interesting

point about these hilltop sites is that they suggest a separate 'culture' to the La Tène 'Celtic' material more common in the midlands and east Ulster.

Shillelagh

Siol Ealigh [*The Descendants of Elach*] **Ancient Forest**
This was once a mighty wood, stretching from Baltinglass almost to the coast at Arklow. When the Gaelic order was defeated at Kinsale [1601], the Boyne [1690] and finally at Aughrim [1691], voracious entrepreneurs who had financed the English army were granted thousands of acres of what was primaeval woodland. Formerly providing shelter for the king's Irish enemies, these woods and their sister Leinster forests at Coillaughtim were also a symbol of the old order. When the woods were gone, a way of life was also gone forever. The 'new men' of the late 17th century were ruthless in their exploitation, nervously afraid of the Irish returning and therefore cut everything above ground for a quick profit. Possibly several million acres of prime oak were clear-felled in this way as well as holly, larch, elm and spruce. Gallery forests along the river valleys were cleared for barrel staves and exported to the Azores, while the best timber, felled over successive centuries, provided the roof for Westminster Hall [*c.* 1200], the palace at Whitehall and the Dutch Stadthaus at Amsterdam [*c.* 1700] [Stopford-Green, 1908].

Spinans Hill

Hilltop Fortress

In the vicinity of this hill is the largest collection of hillforts in Ireland. There are eight in total, some with one bank, other multi-vallate. Most are unexcavated, but Rathgall, a tri-vallate hillfort, showed evidence of the manufacture of bronze weaponry during the 6th and 7th centuries BC. Hillforts pre-date the arrival of 'Celtic' groups in the country and may have been the centre of a rudimentary administration for the Bronze Age people of the locality. Another

SECRET SIGHTS — *Unknown Celtic Ireland*

possibility is that they existed to prevent any significant Celtic incursion into Munster, perhaps forming a strong series of prominent defensive positions to deter invaders and settlers alike. They may have had a similar significance to the Black Pigs Dyke, forming a barrier across Ireland except that the hillforts 'defend' a substantially larger tract of territory, possibly that of a conglomeration of tribal domains. Perhaps at this time population pressure, the rise of an elite, the beginnings of status related to possessions was changing the hitherto egalitarian Bronze Age people into a 'society'. At Baltinglass, the overlooking hill is certainly a defensive and domineering feature and would have reminded residents and intruders alike as to who was in charge and to whom obedience or fealty was due.

In cultural terms, the people who built the hillforts were European but pre-Celtic, and the erection of these defended sites may be related to a marauding Celtic threat from the north, in that the forts continued in use during the period when La Tène objects began to appear in the northern half of the country [*Atlas of the Irish Rural Landscape*].

Sugarloaf
Warrior Hunting Ground
OS DUBLIN DISTRICT Q25.13

[N74 Enniskerry–Roundwood road] In a townland near the base of this mountain are several *fulacht fiadh*, the Bronze Age cooking sites associated with the *Fianna*, a band of male warriors reputedly comprising valiant and brave individuals ready to defend the honour of women and the territory of a chief, sometimes demanding a price. Their origin is in groups of males surplus to the needs of the tribe and capable of being a nuisance. They were encouraged to travel around and remain unsettled and formed recognised outlaw bands similar to the American West and were also the subject of romantic embellishment. They had a

useful function, however, in that they removed potentially dangerous individuals from the tribe while giving them a certain status and function, i.e. hunting wild animals and being heroes. The narratives they appear in form one of the richest series of tales from early Europe and are poignant, witty, sad and violent. If the use of landscape around the Sugarloaf and Dublin mountains is similar to other areas in the country, a high number of *fulachta fiadh* ['deer roast'] suggests a considerable barrow cemetery in the vicinity — these 'cooking sites' may also have been sweat houses and part of a wider settlement pattern [Mitchell, 1976].

County Wexford *Wiess Fjiord*
A Viking Term for a Wide Anchorage
This county of over 236,552 ha enjoys a generally benign climate situated in the south-east corner of Ireland. It has several fine rivers, the Slaney, Barrow and Suir which drain the interior, and a hilly western border rising to 796 m [2,612 ft] at Mount Leinster. It has suffered more than other counties from the destruction [through farming and other developments] of Iron Age ringforts, with some 70% destroyed by 1981, compared to 31% on the Dingle peninsula and only 11% in parts of Roscommon. Wexford contains some of the best soil in Ireland and over 48% of the county has this fertile brown earth. Unsurprisingly, the early farmers were good judges of soil and over 300 of their ringforts were located on land suitable for cultivation and grazing. The lack of ringforts in the west and north-west of the county may suggest forest cover was still extant into the Early Christian period [JRSAI 119, 1980].

O'Rahilly and others suggest that a Celtic tribe from Gaul, the Laighen, landed in the vicinity of Carnsore Point around 300 BC. Presumably they could also be the Menapii who established a settlement of sorts at the mouth of the Slaney

Opposite page: Sugar Loaf mountain, Co. Wicklow, where many fulacht fiadh, *the cooking and domestic sites from the Bronze Age, have been found.*

where Wexford town now stands. The National Museum of Ireland has an interesting collection of spears from the late Bronze Age which may be related to the mysterious 'spearmen' from Gaul. These spears are more accurately 'javelins' — throwing spears for cavalry or infantry — and are found at sites in Scotland and northern England also. Wexford is not a county that is associated with 'Celtic' Ireland in the popular mind, yet it was part of the pre-Christian, pre-literate society from which Ireland developed.

'Duck' freshwater pearl mussel.

The Slaney was a rich source of mussels and examples were recorded in the 17th century as '*taken out of itt about fowre, five and six inches long in which are found pearles for lustre, magnitude and rotundity, not inferior to any oriental*' [Solomon Richards, 1656]. The Irish word for pearl was *sed* or *set* and it seems reasonable to assume that pearl mussel fishing was popular in the Celtic period although there is no record of their use as ornament earlier than the 14th century.

Ard Ladrann
Burial Mound
OS SHEET 19 54.20

[On sea-cliff, 2 km (1.3 miles) south of Courtown, on Kilmuckridge road] The mound at Ardamine is by tradition the burial site of Ladru, one of the primal gods of pagan Ireland. He was a brother of Cesair, another founding goddess and they were the children of Bith, a cosmic deity. Ladru featured in Leinster dynastic mythology and his name as a 'great steersman' was invoked as a protecting ancestor. This ancient site became a seat of the Uí

Cheinnselaig, one of a group of ruling families that claimed descent from Cathair Mair, a primal father-figure of Leinster. Ard Ladrann was part of the *Timna Cathair Mair* [The Testament of Cathair Mar] an 8th-century manuscript that described how the different branches of the Leinstermen were given their lands by their primal ancestor [Byrne, 1973]. St Maedoc, whose cross is at the mound, is said to have landed at this spot in the 6th century before establishing his church at Ferns.

Carnsore Point
Sacred Site

This remote headland has been a sacred site since before Early Christian times. It was the spot where unknown sailors were buried when washed ashore and the place where many of the first arrivals on this island touched land. They were possibly Brigantes, whose Irish tribal and territorial name Ua Barriche, became the barony of 'Bargy' in the Mediaeval period. An early church was founded here by St Veoc [Beoc] who died in Brittany in 585 AD and a holy well and cross inscribed stone remain. It is especially evocative of the sea, as part of the short peninsula has a inclined shingle beach and the tidal swell creates a rhythmic crashing noise reminiscent of surf on a great ocean.

Forth Mountain

This mountain was the border between two ancient baronies known as 'Forth and Bargy'. Forth was the tribal area of the *Forthairt*, a tribute-paying people of the Uí Cheinnselaig, but of an independent nature. They had a favourable status, in that they were not required to be obsequious, being 'reliable vassals' and not mere subjects, and Uí Cheinnselaig kings demanding payment had to call *in person*, in order that honour be satisfied. They had their own kings, two of whom fell at the Battle of Ballyshannon [Co. Kildare] in 738 AD. They had a further Kildare connection in that the famous St Brigid was of their family line. The Forthairt were often to be found in close relation to the Uí Bairrche [Bargy], another tribute-paying tribal group who claimed descent

from Cathair Mair, a shadowy ancestral figure whose ancestors were probably Brigantes who settled on the south Wexford coast, perhaps in the Early Christian centuries.

Lady's Island

Cluain na Mban [The Meadow of the Women]
Sacred Site

OS SHEET 23 6.12

This popular pilgrimage site is an island in a large saltwater lagoon, reached by a small causeway across the mudflats. There are several raths visible beneath the grassy meadow behind the church and a statue of the Blessed Virgin faces the sea at the far end of the island. It was probably a pagan site in antiquity, in that the area was renowned for sun-worship and the

Ard Ladrann, the burial mound of Ladru, legendary 'steersman' and founder of the Uí Cheinnselaig, one of Leinster's ruling families.

Gold head-band, possibly of the Brigantes of northern Britain, many of whom retreated to Ireland after their defeat by the Romans during the 1st century AD.

*Above:
Lady's Island, Co.
Wexford, pagan
and later
Christian
pilgrimage site.*

*Fishing during the
8th century
[Knights
Engravings of
Old England,
1845].*

'women' in the name of the island were probably druids. It seems likely that the coming of St Abban christianised these women and their dedication was switched to the Virgin Mary. On the western side of the island is a tiny holy well which may have been the original used by the female druids before Christianity [Healy, 2001].

Wexford Town

9th-Century Viking Town

The town itself has had Viking connections since the early 9th century when the Norse first raided the island hermitage of Beggerin in Wexford Harbour. The hermitage was originally founded by a curious 5th century 'bishop' called Ibar, or Ailbhe, whose name has connections to the yew tree, a symbol of the Eoghanacht tribal grouping of Munster and possibly the Eubores [People of the Yew], a Celtic people who were defeated by

Caesar in 55 AD. As Ailbhe had been in Ireland 'first', he was particularly incensed at Patrick becoming 'Bishop' of the Irish, remaining a vociferous rival to the saint until he died. In 835 the Vikings arrived, having sailed down the Irish Sea attacking settlements along the coast and they used the area where the town now is as a base for raiding and slave-taking from the surrounding countryside. Ultimately they became traders and set up a permanent settlement on the riverbank. It grew into a town and retains some interesting remnants of its 14th-century town walls and bastions. It has a network of narrow streets and alleyways, many dating from those Mediaeval times.

The Banshee

There is one tradition which is unusual for towns and cities and that is the *banshee* or fairy woman.

She is an ancient Irish tradition, dating back to at least the 8th century, and in Munster, particularly the Decies or Waterford area, she was known as The Bow [bough]. In Wexford town, this wailing banshee was known to be particularly prevalent in the Bride Street parish in the town between Cromwell's Fort and Bernadette Place [Rosslare road east of 'The Faythe']. She is described as 'wearing a grey cloak over a green dress' and having 'red eyes from continually weeping'. She is the fairy death messenger, sent to warn ancient families of an impending death, though not causing it. It is unusual to find the banshee in a town, as sightings or 'hearings' are usually in the countryside.

County Louth *An Lú*
The Plain

The name of this county is uncertain but may mean 'a plain'. This appears reasonable as Louth was probably cleared of trees early in the Bronze Age and has certainly been in pasture since then. It is a county of surprising vistas of husbandry and care, frequently bisected by the main Dublin–Belfast motorway endlessly carrying containers, tourists and trade to and from the other Ireland across the border. The fertile countryside of north Louth attracted the earliest farmers and their associated art form is to be found on over ten decorated stones in the triangular plain between Dundalk and the towns of Louth and Inishkeen. Many rectangular stone cist graves of the Bronze Age [*c.* 2000 BC] are to found in this area also. The county features in the 8th-century *Táin Bó Cuailigne* with the action travelling across *Ath Lethan* [Dundalk Harbour], around the Cooley Peninsula to *Finnabair Cuailigne*, the rath on the R173 above the village of The Bush and back across the county to the ford across the River Fane *Ath da Ferta*, below Knockbridge on the R171 to Louth village [Kinsella, 1988].

The county has a scenic coastline with many pretty villages and the ancient Viking harbour of Annaghgassan. This was a base for the Danish fleet, in that Dublin, while a trading port and ship repair 'depot', was not where the fleet was kept. This harbour and its inland embanked settlement was attacked by the Norwegians in 851 AD, on their way north after attacking Dublin.

Ardee
Warrior vs Warrior

The river crossing near this pretty town was the scene for the epic four-day struggle between Cú Chulainn and Ferdia during the *Táin Bó Cuailigne*. Among the prizes offered to Ferdia by Queen Maeve for defeating Cú Chulainn was a 'great reward in rings' [*buinne*] which may refer to the gold ring-clasps used to close a cloak or mantle. It was also the place where Murtagh of the Leathern Cloaks, Prince of Aileach, was killed by Vikings in 943 in revenge for sinking their fleet 14 years earlier.

To the west of the town lies the reduced area of Ardee Bog, formerly covering over 20 sq. km [12.5 miles] until its exploitation by state bodies from the 1840s onward. To the south of the town, where the N52 meets the R165, is approximately the southern shore of the huge lake that existed in about 8000 BC, and it is in this area that several finds of Irish Giant Deer skeletons have been made. The lake ultimately became a bog, providing fuel, grazing and fresh water for the inhabitants of the area. By 1000 BC bands of hunters camped around the shore of this great lake and constructed *fulacht fiadh* perhaps as part of a habitation or to cook what they caught. The cooking was done by digging a shallow trench, lining it with timber to make a trough, heating stones and dropping them into the water until it boiled. This was tested by archaeologists in the 1940s and found to be a succulent way of cooking a piece of venison.

Carlingford Lough
Viking Battlefield

Beautifully situated between the Mourne Mountains to the north and the Cooley Peninsula to the south, this bay was the site of several bloody contests between Norse and Danish 'Vikings', vying for the plunder of Ireland's monasteries. The ferocious rivalry came to a head in 852 AD in a three-day battle on sea and on land, involving a fleet of 150 Norwegian Viking ships sent to destroy the Danes. The fighting was brutal and merciless on both sides, and the annals record warlords being hacked to pieces and beheaded during the melee. The fighting moved onto the shoreline and the Norwegians, through force of numbers, were winning the contest when the Danes prayed loudly and swore fealty to St Patrick. They won,

The standing stone of Clochafarmore, Co. Louth, reputedly the site where Cú Chulainn, the champion of Ulster, died in battle.

and days later, when Patrician emissaries arrived to collect the 'tariff', they had to step over thousands of unburied putrid bodies of the slain to collect the amount. Buried in the mud of Dundalk Bay are the remains of ships of a later Viking fleet captured and sunk in 926 AD by Murtagh, Prince of Aileach, who beheaded 200 of the captured Vikings. Later in the same century another Viking fleet was defeated by a Munster prince who was unluckily kidnapped by his defeated foes, but was rescued after a fierce battle in which three Viking leaders, Tor, Magnus and Sitric, were killed.

Clochafarmore
Ancient Battle Site
OS 9J.01.04

This fine example of a standing stone is reputed

to be the spot where the greatest of the mythological heroes, Cú Chulainn, died. He was the greatest of the Ulster heroes and his death, after tying himself to the pillar stone, was in true mythological fashion. Just as he died, the Morrigan, the goddess of death, landed on his shoulder in the form of a raven and his enemies knew he was no more. The stone is on a slight prominence in a field and appears to be roughly carved into a phallic shape. It competes with Garrihy in Westmeath for the site of Cú Chulainn's final battle and has a more romantic setting. It faces over rolling countryside and is certainly sited for maximum visibility. Like many similar stones, it is probably Bronze Age in origin, perhaps around 2000 BC — and is one of at least seven examples in the hinterland of Dundalk.

Dún Dealgan
Warriors Fort

OS DISCOVERY SERIES 36J.08.03

This wooded site is reputedly the ancient birthplace of Cú Chulainn, hero of the Red Branch Knights and a fierce warrior and lover of women. In his boyhood, he was known as Setanta, a name identical with the Setantii, a tribe known to have been in Lancashire in the 2nd century AD. This imposing mound stands at Castletown outside Dundalk and is comprised of a Norman motte and surrounding rampart. The motte was built on top of the Dún in *c.* 1187 by Bertram de Verdun, before he departed for the crusades. There are a further seven ringforts and some 24 souterrains in the vicinity of Dundalk. These underground chambers, also found in great numbers in Brittany, may have been for personal retreat from attackers or storage — the saved seed being placed underground for later planting and perhaps the space offering a final refuge for a family. This would perhaps account for souterrains being more common in areas that in the Iron Age may have been in tillage, rather than pasture. Over 3,500 are known in the

country as a whole, with concentrations in Louth, east Ulster and Connacht.

County Longford *Longphort*
A Fortress

In many ways Longford was the quintessential Irish county, in that it was recorded as having, at the close of the 12th century, extensive woodland, bogs and lakes. It is an inland county, bounded to the west by the River Shannon and adjoining the counties of Westmeath, Cavan and Roscommon. It shares with those counties a combination of bog and farmland, with pleasant views of lake and river along its western border. Judging by the place-names beginning with *doire*, oak certainly was in abundance in ancient times along Lough Ree, and Paul McMurry, prior of Saints Island near Ballymahon, was renowned as the man who cleared the woods of *Doire na gCailleach* [the wood of the enchantress] in *c.* 1360. Longford, in common with its sister county, Westmeath, was hidden behind the lakes and bogs of the midlands and probably enjoyed a degree of independence due to its inaccessibility. In earlier times, an ancient highway, possibly for use with chariots, passed through the bogs near Lough Ree on its way from Tara in Meath to Cruachain in what is now Roscommon. Part of it has been excavated at Corlea near Keenagh. Areas possibly connected with this routeway have produced spear-butts and horse harness of La Tène style. The county also produced several beehive querns, a hollowed-out stone used for grinding corn and common in northern England, in the territory of the Celtic Brigantes. Lough Ree is one of the lakes on the Shannon waterway and contains several islands with Early Christian and pre-Christian connections. Iniscleraun, reached from Coosan Point near Athlone or from Lanesborough, contains six churches which were part of an early monastery founded by St Diarmuid in the 6th century. It also has a church

SECRET SIGHTS — *Unknown Celtic Ireland*

*Dún Dealgan, Co.
Louth, birthplace
of the Ulster hero,
Cú Chulainn. In
his boyhood he was
known as Setanta,
a name
synonymous with
the Setantii of
Northern Britain.*

dedicated to the Blessed Virgin called the Woman's Church. St Sionach [d. 719] is buried here as are some of the O'Farrells, princes of Annally, the ancient name for the area. The legendary Queen Maeve died on this island after she was struck by a sling stone fired from the shore as she was bathing.

Corlea Trackway
Chariot Road of 150 BC
OS SHEET 12.63.09

[L121, Ballymahon–Lanesborough road] Possibly as early as 150 BC a causeway was required across a stretch of bog running toward a ford across the Shannon at what is now Lanesborough. This small Longford town is at a narrow part of the Shannon, at the top of Lough Ree and lies midway between two important cult and ritual sites, Cruachain in Roscommon and Uisneach in Westmeath. There was an existing small causeway across the bog, a *togher*, suitable for pedestrians, but for whatever reason a larger routeway was required. The timber trackway was constructed of 10 m [33 ft] birch planks laid lengthways with lateral oak planks laid across and pinned into place with dowels and wedges. This roadway is wider than what would be required for foot travellers and may have been intended for chariots, although these elusive, rumoured vehicles have never been found in Ireland. The nine townland names surrounding Corlea are suggestive of oakwoods; Derrygeel, Derryaghan, Derryad, Derryglogher, Derryoghill, Derrygowna, Derrymacar, Derry Lake and Derrynagalliagh [the Wood of the Witch], near Saints Island on Lough Ree. These woods and other woods of birch were probably in existence at the time of the roadway construction and at least 300 oak trees, centuries old, were used by the carpenters in a skilful and creative way [Raftery, 1994].

The Corlea visitors' centre must be one of the most elaborate and expensive in the country. It sits above and in front of what was a wonderful and inspiring late Bronze Age roadway like a cinema on top of a holy well. Inside, there are beautiful miniature models of 'Celts' chopping trees, 'Celts' carrying timber, and more 'Celts' transporting and fixing the roadway. There are books, postcards, assistants, coffee, audio-visuals and all surrounded by a vast tarmac car park. Of the original 2 km [1.3 miles] oak roadway, only some 10 sad metres [33 ft] is available for indoor observation, the rest being obscured behind concrete, stainless steel and fussy officialdom.

The Duncladh
The Great Wall of Ireland
OS SHEET 12 83.34

As wealth and status in the Early Iron Age were closely related to cattle, control of illegal livestock movement was certainly a priority. Cattle rustling was one way in which landless young men and those of substance could become rich and gain status as warriors. Sometime in the last centuries BC, the rulers of Eamhain Mhaca in what is now Co. Armagh decided to fortify the extremities of their territory against marauders. Their claimed jurisdiction, containing *Tuath* of their Ulidian people and also of the Airgealla, a separate and subservient population group, ran from the Drowes River in Donegal to the Boyne at Drogheda. Although this was a slightly optimistic claim, they endeavoured to fortify this borderland through the construction of various embankments and ditches, utilising natural features where possible. This largely unknown 'Great Wall of Ireland' is recognised by many names in its perambulations across the island and has probably been ignored due to its unfortunate affinity with the more contentious border of Northern Ireland.

In north Co. Longford a portion of this early frontier exists in various states of denudation and accidental preservation. The portion known as the 'Duncladh' or the 'Black Pigs Race'

Opposite page: The Duncladh of Co. Longford, ancient boundary between Ulster and the rest of the island, constructed c. 100 BC.

stretches for 9.6 km [6 miles] from a point 1.6 km [1 mile] north-east of the town of Granard and forms a barrier between the Lakes of Kinale and Gowna. It is described as having a large bank with an internal and external ditch. Attempting to find stretches of this embankment can be difficult, however, as sections have been ploughed out and other parts are surrounded by boggy, waterlogged soil. There are several sections reachable from the public road, although pursuing the route of the Duncladh in general involves wading through marshland, possibly the result of woodland being clear-felled centuries ago, thereby raising the water table. It finishes as a rounded slope like a buried finger pointing toward Lough Kinale with sedge and waterlogged gorse on either side. Other sections as pointed out by locals appear little more than gentle undulations beside a tall hedged ditch. Directly north of Granard the otherwise archaeologically empty north Longford landscape is positively crowded with standing stones, stone circles and raths, all directly north-east of the Duncladh in the townland of Tullygullin, *the hill of the holly*. There are over 15 raths perhaps of the Early Christian period within 1 km [0.6 miles] of the indicated line of the Duncladh and if the related stone circles are included, it would suggest an area of continuous social, cultural and commercial activity, not dissimilar to most 'border' areas today, where trade, both legal and illegal, is an enduring feature.

Of the raths in the area, most appear to be single ditch and bank enclosures, the homes and enclosures of low-status family groups. It was, however, quite usual in a *tuath* to have one or more raths that functioned as defensive 'barracks', near to the borderland of the [Lord] Tighearna's demesne. These were sometimes multi-vallate and within sight of the Tighearna's high-status residence. The large

oval rath of Carrickduff may be such a billet and comes into view as a miniature citadel at the top of a short hill. It appears as a 'bulwark' for the Duncladh earthwork, in that its function would appear to be that of a barbican, or fortified gateway. A hawthorn-topped, steep-sided ditch circumnavigates its massive central dike on three sides and has a soggy leaf till of at least 1 metre [3.2 ft]. The banks of the surrounding ditch are over 5 m [16.4 ft] high in parts, and with the corresponding high central platform, form a broad 'D' shape. It is of a type that the writer has never encountered before and requires further investigation. Without conclusive excavation data, it could possibly be a high-status habitation site, or an example of a reputed 'ringwork castle' — it sits right on the OS 'Black Pigs Race' indication and is simply too colossal to be a farmer's banked enclosure.

From personal observation, it would appear that the Duncladh in Co. Longford may have been a series of fortified positions between the lakes, with some portions being continuous like a rampart and others like watchtowers, wherein the necessary garrison and sentries could rest and camp in relative safety. The conclusion being that the Duncladh is in appearance a series of 'links', some large, others small, between natural defensive features.

Granard
Ancient Royal Residence
OS SHEET 12 80.33

[N55 Edgeworthstown to Cavan] This busy market town has an Anglo-Norman motte at its south-east corner which was originally the royal residence of Cairbre, eldest son of Niall Mór [died *c.* 452]. The area around Granard was always contentious, lying between rival kingdoms and battles were fought here in 485 and 501 AD against the 'Leinstermen'. Granard was the power centre for a branch of the southern Uí Néill who at one time held sway over a considerable portion of Longford and Westmeath. Cairbre or Coirpre was resolutely opposed to St Patrick's missionary work in Ireland and attempted an assassination at Tailtu during a royal assembly. His descendants were cursed by Patrick and his name deleted from later king lists, but they continued to use his name as a patronymic, creating a kingdom which at times stretched southwards through Westmeath toward Offaly along the eastern shore of Lough Ree [Byrne, 1973].

Sliabh Golry
Entrance to Otherworld

[Ardagh Hill near Ardagh village] This 200 m [656 ft] high hill was once the site of Bri Leth, a *sidh* or otherworld residence, of the god, Midhir. Beneath this hill is reputed to be the land of Tír na nÓg, where Midhir seduced the beautiful Etain and kept her trapped within, until her restoration to the land of mortals. Midhir was the foster-brother of Aengus Óg, the god of love, but had a wife, Fuaimneach who disapproved of his affair with Etain and pursued them both ruthlessly. This tale has murder, incest, infanticide and a seductive quality; in that the narrative drives along, always seeking its object of desire which changes into water, a butterfly, a swan and ultimately, a union with the goddess of sovereignty. Midhir as a prince was always in splendid costume — *'and the tunic he wore was purple in colour, his hair was yellow and his eyes were grey'.*

In a translation from the *Book of the Dun Cow*, the description of Bri Leth gives a foretaste of paradise:

'There shall be neither grief nor care;
White are the teeth, black the eyebrows,
Pleasant to the eye the number of our host;
On every cheek is the hue of foxglove.'
[Hyde, 1923]

County Westmeath *An Iarmhí*
West of Meath

This county was the western half of *Mide*, the ancient 5th province of Ireland, originally a patrimony of the Mac Lochlainn [a branch of the northern Uí Néill]. Access to the 'county' was difficult, lying as it did broadly to the west of a series of large lakes, among them Loughs Owel, Iron and Ennell. The enigmatic and swan-shaped Lake Derravaragh, 10 km [6.3 miles] long, was home to the Children of Lir, whose father was also the father of Manannan, the sea god. These mortals, changed to swans by a step-mother, lived for three hundred years on the lake until a 'woman of the south mated with a man of the north'. From a later period, the remains of a Roman boat over 8 m [26 ft] in length, together with oar fragments were found in Lough Lene and this would suggest that Roman

The Motte of Granard, Co. Longford, residence of Cairbre, eldest son of Niall of the Nine Hostages, founder of the O'Neill dynasty of Ulster.

merchants were trading in the midlands and especially with the wealthy crannóg dwellers in or around the 1st century AD. This and other evidence from several counties would suggest that Ireland was not as removed from Roman Britain as had been thought and small groups of either Romanised Britons or Romanised Gauls traded and settled in the country in the Early Christian centuries.

Until the Mediaeval period, trackways across the bogs and along the eskers were the only ways to the west through what must have been difficult territory. The county was inhabited, however, during the Bronze Age of *c.* 2000 BC, and the high ground, rising to 200 m [656 ft] in some areas, provided these 'Beaker Folk' with arable land and security from enemies. They had pottery among their skills and created a corded-impressed ware, crude perhaps, but useful and in funerary rites, effective. Their stone box-like graves, 'cists', turn up from time to time along the glacial Kame ridges that run from Rathconrath to their sacred place, Knockastia. The western part of *Mide* was the centre of southern Uí Néill power and the Clann Cholman Mair [Colman the Great] claimed the title of *rig Uisnig*, 'king of Uisneach'. Their 10th-century descendants resided at Dún na Sciath beside Lough Ennell or at Cro-inis, a crannóg on the lake itself [Byrne, 2001].

Created by an Act of Parliament in 1543, Co. Westmeath was a conglomeration of tribal regions and principalities and, by 1573, most of the land had been shired and families like the McGeoghegans were now Senechals of their sovereign territories. Prior to the largely ignored piece of 1543 legislature,

The 9th-century cross of Bealin, Co. Westmeath, erected c. 800 AD by Tuathgal, abbot of Clonmacnoise.

Westmeath was known by its separate and independent family principalities as Dalton's country, Dillon's country, O'Molloy's country and O'Kelly's country.

Westmeath is also the county in which part of the ancient sage of the *Táin Bó Cuailigne* takes place. The language of the tale is 8th century, but may refer to events taking place several centuries earlier. It is a tale of war, incest, slaughter, humour and magical happenings, somewhere between a mythological narrative and a protracted dynastic feud. During the epic, the armies gather at the hill of Sleamhian [Slanemore, 4.8 km [3 miles] from Mullingar on the L18, Ballynacarrigy–Longford road], which features in several ancient narratives and was the site where the king of Meath celebrated *Samhain*. The armies involved in the Táin gathered at the hill from several territories and marched southward for a huge battle against the Connacht army of Queen Maeve that took place near the gates of 18th-century Jamestown Court, in the townland called Garrihy [Mullingar – Moate road], from *gaireach*, a great cry. In 1962, the Garrihy cist grave, known from local folklore as 'The Grave of the Warrior' was opened, but had been despoiled at some time in the past.

Bealin
Art of 1,200 Years Ago
OS 12N.10.43

[Twyford] This 9th-century cross has an interesting collection of carvings showing animals with birdlike heads, similar to the *fantastic* animals on the base of the high cross at Moone in Kildare. Bealin has a scroll of coiled animals and hunting scenes showing mounted riders and a hound and is probably part of a series of crosses related to

Tuathgal, abbot of Clonmacnoise, who died in 811.

Cloghstucca Borderland

[Up Private Avenue to Jamestown Court] In a field close to an 18th-century house stands Cloghstucca. This 1.75 m [5.7 ft] standing stone, probably of the Bronze Age [*c.* 2000 BC] is contemporary with the many cist graves that lie along the intermittent escarpment that skews across Longford and Westmeath. This high ground rises above the wetlands to a height of 153 m [500 ft] at Mount Dalton, an estate beside the village of Rathconrath where several of these early grave sites have been unearthed. Beaker people of 2000 BC lived along the midland escarpments, above the morass to the south and east, and safe from the wolves of the Slieve Bloom Mountains. The Jamestown monolith is possibly an intertribal boundary, a discarded glacial erratic that assumed a significance for the peoples in the vicinity. These stones were re-used by the 'Celts' as focal points for the tribe, representing continuity over time. It stands in an ancient landscape of over 12 ringforts of varying sizes, evidence of occupation back to the Iron Age and beyond. These ringforts formed part of a settlement area for the southern Uí Néill dynasty of Clann Cholman Mair, with the largest fort, on high ground to the west of the house, probably the residence of the local *flaith* or prince. His immediate family would have lived in the smaller units, and other 'free' people would have occupied smaller but similar residences. The slaves would have lived in mud huts on the perimeter of these thatched dwellings.

The Hill of Uisneach
Druidic Heart of Ireland

OS SHEET 12 29.49

[Mullingar–Ballymore road] For anyone attempting to travel across the midlands today, there is an efficient road system that has motorway, dual carriageway, fly-overs and so on.

Modern rest-stops and service stations have replaced the 'hostels' or *brudens* of Gaelic legend where 'twice three hundred boar were slain for a guest'. Small villages, once important staging posts to the west have been bypassed, and the River Shannon is no longer any barrier to travel. In the Bronze Age of *c.* 1000 BC the lakes of the midlands [Loughs Iron, Owel, Ennell and Lene] formed, with the great Bogs of Allen, a morass covering hundreds of square kilometres. In the winter, the 'low road' through the current villages of Rochfortbridge and Tyrrellspass was impassable, and all travellers, on foot, horseback or in chariot, took the 'high road', from Mullingar to Athlone. That road, beginning at Tara, and travelling via Killucan, Mullingar and Rathconrath, stopped on its way west at what is probably the least known and most enigmatic of the Celtic hillforts, Uisneach.

The Hill of Uisneach, ancient centre of Celtic Ireland.

'Nuadh of the Silver Hand, the king
In those days held a fair at Uisneach on the hill
A great fair meeting and the people came,
And filled the plain in their thousands, and the chiefs
Were all assembled there, and not a man,
Of the Dé Danann race of any mark,
But showed himself among his fellow men
In that great throng that pressed around the king.'
[*The Fate of the Children of Tuireann, c.* 8th century]

Ireland's five ancient provinces met on this 205 m [673 ft] hill and twenty of Ireland's counties can be seen from its summit today. On the west side of the hill is a tall craggy limestone boulder, *Ail na Mireann*, the stone of the divisions, mentioned by Geraldus Cambrensis [Gerald of Wales] in the 12th century as *'the navel of Ireland'*. It sits within a small banked enclosure, as if awaiting attention. The area surrounding the stone appears barren and without noticeable features, until one notices a small grove of hawthorn. When visiting the hill in 1997, rain began pouring from the sky in a summer deluge, and this writer ducked into the hawthorn grove near the stone. Inside the copse, the remains of red and green ribbons, faded and mildewed, hung from the hoary branches. The ground was flattened by the hooves of cattle, but the hidden nature of the interior, the remains of those votive offerings and many curious, worn-stone formations suggested a venerated site, perhaps in use up to recently. The casual observer might easily pass by this small intimate liminal space, with its eerie sense of forgotten importance.

Druids

The *Yellow Book of Lecan* describes how the god Fintan, son of Oisín, returned to the hill: 'It is long since I drank a drink of the deluge over the navel of Uisneach'. It is recorded as being the seat of King Tuathal Techtmar 'the *acceptable*' around the end of the 1st century AD, but was in use as a ritual site before that. The hill received its name according to the *Annals of the Four Masters* when Midhe, the son of Brath, son of Detha, lit the first fire on the hill. The druids of Ireland complained that it was a slight to them to have such a fire, whereon he had their tongues cut out and buried in the earth. He sat over them and his mother commented; 'It is Uisneach [proudly] you sit there tonight' [*Yellow Book of Lecan*]. Uisneach was reputed to be the centre of the territory of the *Fir Bolg*, who may have been Belgae, a tribe of Celtic Gaul. The Belgae are also recorded in northern England around this time, and trade and ultimately settlement may have occurred during the 3rd century BC, when the embankments were erected and ritual activity began on the hill. Caesar commented on the druids of Gaul travelling to a sacred hill in the territory of the Carnutes, whose lands were believed to be the centre of the world.

Uisneach was certainly the site for the 1 May festival of Bealtaine, an important part of which involved a purgative rite with cattle being driven through two potent and magical great fires, dedicated to the god Baal. The hill, therefore, would seem to be a ritual/assembly site, used perhaps for annual festivals and law-giving, in conjunction with a royal tour by a important king. During excavation in 1931 a large bed of ashes was discovered within one of the circular enclosures on the hill containing the charred skeletons of animals. Ritual slaughter of animals and sometimes humans is recorded in Gaul and insular sites of the Celts around the same period, so we may assume that the druids of Uisneach *'having made preparation for a sacrifice and a banquet beneath the trees, bring hither two white bulls whose horns are bound together for the first time . . . then they kill the victims'* [Green, 1996].

An embanked circular enclosure of some 76 m [250 ft] in diameter remains on the summit, possibly the remains of the fortress-palace of

King Tuathal Techtmar who ruled *c.* 200 AD. On the apex of the hill several underground chambers [souterrains] were discovered in 1929 by the Scottish archaelogist, R. A. Macalister. They lie beneath a possible site of Techmar's 'palace' and illustrations of their layout resemble, in a primitive way, a symbolic stallion and mare.

Knockastha

Cnoc Aiste **Burial Ground for Ancient Royalty**
OS SHEET 12 25.43

This 190 m [623 ft] hill is steep but rewarding to the climber. It appears out of the gentle undulations of Westmeath like a slice from another, more exotic county. Kestrels nest annually near the burial ground and will screech at the visitor if there are fledglings nearby. In early summer, its slopes reflect the pale green and

gold of hay awaiting its first cut and in winter its sharp prow juts into the cold easterlies that bring sub-zero temperatures to the high midlands pasture.

It was a sacred place from the earliest of times, and the Urnfield peoples of *c.* 2000 BC chose this wild and beautiful place to bury their princes and leaders. When excavated in 1932 [Hencken and Movius], the remains of over 40 high-status individuals were discovered within the low burial mound on the apex of the hill, some buried with tusks of wild boar as a mark of distinction. In the 14th-century *Annals of Clonmacnoise, Cnoc Aiste* is mentioned as being 'the home of schools', perhaps referring to the large ringfort on the southern slope [Walsh, 1957]. The 360-degree summit view is striking, showing well-cultivated pasture and industrious-looking farms. Tall trees

Ribbons tied to hawthorn beside the 'Catstone' on Uisneach.

SECRET SIGHTS — *Unknown Celtic Ireland*

The mound at the top of Knockastha Hill, Co. Westmeath, burial site for the midland Urnfield peoples of 2000 BC.

grace many of the fields and the northern skyline is bounded by Uisneach and the distant wooded citadel of Mount Dalton, itself a model demesne.

Lough Ennell
Lake Fort of Important Dynasty
OS SHEET 12 40.45

This lake held the royal crannóg of the southern Uí Néill dynasty of Clann Cholman Mair and their second residence, Dún na Sciath, a large ringfort, was on the adjacent lakeshore beside where Kilcooley House now stands. Cro-inis, the name of their crannóg on the western side of the lake, was exempt from providing the ample food and cheer required for accompanying warriors when kings visited, but was obliged to supply 'a lad to tend his [the king's] horses'. Uisneach was their ritual site, and the lands between Uisneach and Lough Ennell are populated with numerous ringforts of varying sizes and importance.

Lough Ennell, part of the territory of Clann Cholman Mair, a sept of the southern Uí Néill, whose king drowned the Viking Turgeis in the lake in 845 — to general acclaim.

Maelsechnaill, high-king of Ireland from 846–862, won the acclaim and thanks of many in the year 845, when he captured Tugeis, a particularly vicious Norseman, brought him to Lough Ennell, tied stones to his body and dropped him in the lake. He also defeated the Norse at the Battle of Skreen [near Tara] in 848, a year that saw the Norse Vikings defeated in four battles by Irish kings and their allies. To celebrate and give thanks, a small deputation led by an important scholar, Sedulius Scottus and including Olchobar mac Cineada, abbot of Emly and king of Cashel, went to the king of the Franks, Charles the Bald, with gifts and a request for free passage to Rome to give thanks and to make pilgrimage. Maelsechnaill celebrated by pillaging the Viking city of Dublin the following year. His descendent, Maelsechlainn, son of Domhnall, king of Ireland, died on Cro-inis in 1022 AD and a poem of Flann Mainstrech

[d. 1056] about the kings of Mide mentions:

'Five and forty years exactly
Was the reign of Maelsechnaill
Great king with sweetness
He died in Cro-inis.'
[Walsh, 1957]

County Meath *An Mhí*
The Middle [Province]

Established according to legend by Tuathal Techmair in the 1st century AD, Mide [meaning 'Middle Piece'] was to be a principality for him and his heirs for all time. He appears to have been a shrewd and capable man, holding fairs and celebrations at the various sacred and ceremonial sites of preceding dynasties and peoples, with the aim of giving each tribal grouping an equal 'visitation', thereby avoiding charges of favouritism or corruption. As agricultural land, Meath probably has some of the best in Ireland, being cleared of forest before the Early Christian period. It is also worth noting the ongoing commercial and social intercourse between Brega [Meath] and Anglo-Saxon England during the 7th to 9th centuries when Irish kings fought alongside Anglo-Saxons, and Fin, daughter of the Uí Néill High-King, Colman Rimid, was the mother of Aldfrith, king of Northumbria from 685–704 AD.

As well as the important tombs and ritual centres on the Boyne, Newgrange, Nowth and Dowth, Meath also contains the Iron Age royal site of Tara, hence its sobriquet 'The Royal County'. Kings of Tara also had significance for other parts of Ireland and in several instances, early

The 4000-year-old tomb of Fourknocks, containing the earliest representation of a [female] deity in Ireland.

and perhaps Bronze Age peoples attributed their descent to semi-divine individuals such as Conaire Mor mac Eterscelae, a 'primordial just king' whose tragic demise is told in the *Destruction of Da Derga's Hostel*, a tale set in the centuries around the birth of Christ [Byrne, 1976].

Castlekeeran

Diseart Chiarain [The Hermitage of Ciaran]
Celtic Christian Site

This small monastic site was founded by a monk from nearby Kells and contains three high crosses of middling quality. It has a small, ruined church and beside a well-marked Ogham stone there is an ancient stoup for penitents to bless themselves which fills with refreshing rainwater for the troubled brow. The monastery was destroyed by Vikings in 949 AD, and it was probably they who flung one of the high crosses into the nearby River Blackwater, where, according to tradition, it remains.

Fourknocks

Tomb with Goddess Image
OS 13O.11.62

This passage grave is probably one of the series of tombs which lie along the wide strip of fertile land between Garristown on the Dublin–Meath border and the sea. It is a circular structure with a large central chamber and many internal lozenge rock carvings. These carvings, similar to other sepulchre art of the Neolithic age, may have been of a religious nature, or may, as has been suggested [Brennan, 1978], replicate certain motions of the moon or other celestial bodies. Most remarkable, however, is the figure carved in stone inside the chamber. This figure has a certain benign and perhaps maternal appearance, a cheerful welcome for the spirits of the dead whose cremated ashes were laid within the tomb. It is a very early representation of a humanised deity, as the tomb has been dated to 2300 BC. The remains of over 28 individuals were found in the tomb and it was possibly the family vault for a dominant tribal grouping. The importance of the carved figure lies in its being the first recorded instance of a reasonably human representation in such an early structure.

Kells

Monastic Site

This historic town has existed in one form or another since the 6th century. It lies in the partly wooded valley of the Blackwater and was the monastery where portions of the world-famous *Book of Kells* were so beautifully illuminated. This book, arguably the finest piece of illuminated art ever produced, is now on display in Trinity College Dublin. The monastery was founded in 804 AD, probably by monks fleeing from the Viking attack on Iona in western Scotland where the composition of the book may have begun. Its most famous page is the 'Chi-Rho' which contains the Greek initials 'XP', the first two letters of *Christos*. Taking perhaps years to complete, and involving the hands of several monks of prodigious skill, this stunning page of calligraphy and design has the Christian symbolism of an otter swallowing a fish, playful Celtic interlacings, all combining into a tumult of lustrous detail celebrating the glory of God. It also has two tiny cats playing with four mice, one of whom is nibbling on a communion wafer.

Near the remaining tower of the monastery is St Colmcille's house, a high-roofed early church of impressive solidity. There are several high crosses at Kells and the largest has a wealth of detail showing scenes from the bible showing interesting carvings including a deer, a chariot and elaborate interlacings.

Lagore

Loch Gabhair [Horse Lake] **Warlord Fortress**
[1.6 km (1 mile) east-northwest of Dunshaughlin] This crannóg, 159 m [520 ft] in circumference and some 6.4 km [4 miles] south-

west of the Hill of Tara, was a royal residence, possibly of the Sil nAedo dynasty who were the dominant warlord grouping in the Blackwater Valley in the 7th and 8th centuries. It was built on an enormous foundation of animal bones [150 cartloads were removed for fertiliser in 1839] and occupied from *c.* 600 AD to the year 934 when it was destroyed. It was constructed in the autumn, as many hazel nuts were found in its multi-layered flooring. In a later period, Tigernach, prince [*flaith*] of Lagore, fought and defeated the Norse in a ferocious battle fought in 848 AD near Skreen in Co. Meath [Laing, 1975].

During excavation, skulls, presumably of the workmen, were found with the back of their heads sliced off, but whether this was due to disobedience or ritual sacrifice followed by deposition is open to speculation [Laing, 1975].

Newgrange
5,500-Year-Old Observatory
OS SHEET 13 00.72

This circular tomb and observatory is part of a series of three giant tombs and other ritual enclosures within the bend of the River Boyne at Oldbridge. The farming communities who constructed the great mounds probably came from somewhere along the Atlantic coast of Spain or Portugal around 3500 BC and their art form of spirals and lozenges are found on many tombs in Ireland and several in Wales. Newgrange is also unique in its alignment to the summer solstice, wherein the sun shines through a 'roof box' illuminating the inner chamber, some 19 m [62 ft] inside the tomb.

It also functions, I would suggest, as a 'philosophical device' for estimating time and space, by establishing a relation between the physical world and the motions of the sun and stars. Although the recognition of the equinox determined the seasonal and agricultural objectives of that community, the use of the roof box also established a 'space' between Newgrange and the sun itself. It showed that there was a distance between objects, and that that distance and its relation to movement could be measured and foreseen from year to year. It would have established the notions of *past*, *present* and *future*, which are all related to the concept of time and motion. In the observation of daylight entering the chamber on the summer solstice, the elite of the tribe would have witnessed the creation of time itself and perhaps a glimpse of the fleeting and unseizable nature of infinity.

Opinion is divided as to whether the Megalithic tomb builders brought an advanced system of agriculture with them to Ireland or whether it was developed before their arrival, but we may be certain that they were advanced enough to have an ample supply of food, and thereby the surplus of labour required for tomb construction. This would suggest some relationship with the developments in farming that began in the Near and Middle East, spreading westwards into Europe as a gradual movement. As agriculture became more productive, greater material wealth was available to provide the labour and materials necessary for elaborate cultural organisation and concurrent funerary structures. Whatever the means available, the construction of the monuments in the Boyne valley in particular may well have been the total culture, with the utilisation of such enormous amounts of time and labour depleting the tribe's resources beyond recovery.

In a more general sense, Neolithic burial structures are the bedrock of what popular Celtic archaeology is built on, and form the template for speculation on astronomy, mysticism and a popular conception of ancestral descent. Archaeologists have suggested that similarities in shape and configuration to the Boyne structures and the possible aperture alignment being south-

south-east would suggest Brittany and its *Allees Couvertes* as a potential original homeland.

Skreen
Battle Site
In the 3rd century, Cairbre, son of Cormac the High-King, was involved in a bloody conflict with the Fianna, a militant, but subject race at Gowra [Garristown, near Skreen], that left him mortally wounded. He was brought to Skreen where his camp was and his wife keened over his dead body for so long that it became known as *Cnoc Ghuil*, 'The Hill of Weeping'.

According to the later Annals, this 55 m [180 ft] hill was the site of a battle between the Ulaidh of Ulster under their leader Ellim MacConrach and a young Tuathal Techtmar, reputedly king of Tara in pre-Christian Ireland. Ellim and three brothers [known as 'The Collas'] had killed Fiachu, Tuathal's father and king of Tara, 20 years before in what was described as an 'uprising' of the tribute paying tribes [MacNeill, 1920].

Tuathal claimed descent from the legendary queen Maeve and was the grandfather of the famous 'Conn of the Hundred Battles', the ancestor of the Connachta, the dominant grouping west of the Shannon. It is worth remembering, however, that because of the complex series of kings, dynasties and rivalries that surround the kingship of Tara, some of the names given in the genealogies may refer to founding deities, rehumanised into ancestors by later chroniclers.

Sliabh na Caillighe
The Hill of the Witch
OS 13O.00.72
This is a site with significant 'mana', that quality of presence. The view across several thousand acres of fertile and cultivated land is rewarding after the brisk grassy climb. The 25+ tombs are

Sliabh na Caillighe, 'The Hill of the Witch', a series of Megalithic tombs re-used over centuries by the rulers of Brega, a warrior dynasty based in the Blackwater valley.

scattered and several show [perhaps] evidence of early 'tomb raiders'. They follow what could be described as a cruciform internal shape, with sun [?] and moon [?] inscribed radial engravings on the stones. There is no doubt it was an important site, and chosen for its proximity to the sky, and its visibility above the early farming community for which it represented a burial site, observatory and ritual temenos. It is primarily a neolithic burial ground, with over 30 tombs spread across three hills — Cairnbane East, Cairnbane West and Brennans Hill. The Hill of the Enchantress was first used as a burial site before 2500 BC but re-used by the Sil nAedo Slaine, kings of Brega, to bury their nobility in the Early Christian centuries. The sun enters the chamber of cairn T on the spring and autumn equinox and progresses from left to right across representations etched on the interior monoliths which may represent the sun's position at seasonal intervals. The connection between art and astronomy seems rational and perhaps conclusive as the traversing sun follows a 'pre-engraved' path across these massive stones [Brennan, 1983]. The society that produced these massive tombs and their counterparts, notably in counties Sligo and Clare, disappeared or went into such serious and rapid decline so as to vanish from the record. Although this societal phenomena is rare, it is not unknown and the history of Europe and the Near East has many instances of notable tribes, with recorded civilisation, cities, commerce and a language who simply cease to exist. Perhaps like the individual situation, circumstances sometimes create a solvent of sufficient proportion to efface what had been a prominent and thriving society. Current theory suggests that the *proto-Celtic* tomb builders did not progress to further developments in their society but rather became subservient to later and more vigorous intruders. The individual tombs did not lose

their numinosity, however, and some became sites of homage for Celtic La Tène craft workers who deposited votive offerings of carved bone, concept items for future pieces of art, presumably in recognition of the resident goddess's bounty in bestowing talent and ability on her followers.

Tailteann
Goddess Site
OS 13N.80.74

This was the site of the reputed great annual meeting of kings, with concurrent country fair and athletic games, called *oeneach tailteann*, which survived up to the Viking raids into Meath in the 9th century. The games were also a 'wedding fair', in the sense that alliances relating to relationships, marriage and dowries were arranged at that occasion. Part of the site was carelessly damaged in 1999 by a local builder and there are plans to excavate and restore what remains.

The *oeneach tailteann* were held on Lugnasa, 1 August, the feast of the god Lugh, a multi-talented god known across early Europe by similar names. Manuscripts suggest that the *oeneach tailteann* had a national status as an annual 'conference' of kings and subkings, with different documentary sources naming Ua Conchobhair kings from Connacht, Cerball mac Dunlainge [king of Osraighe] and others in attendance. The local dynasty, the Sil nAedo Slaine [kings of Tara] were the hosts for this annual gathering and the failure to hold it every year was seen as a blow to their prestige, as well as foreboding poor harvests and sickness for the people of the *Tuath*.

It is the resting place of the benevolent corn-goddess Tailtiu and the legendary site of a great battle between the Tuatha Dé Danann and the incoming Milesians which may refer to a conflict between gods of pastoralism and those of agriculture. When Tailtu died, her prophesy was that should every prince accept her, Erin would

not be without perfect song.

Tara
Ritual and Royalty
OS 13N.92.60

This hill is probably the best known and most famous of all royal sites. Its summit has several ringforts and a Bronze Age burial mound, the *mound of the hostages*. Lining up with the entrance to this mound is a partially hidden well, one of the 'mouths of Tara', an ancient and venerated site reputedly a cure for eye ailments and headaches. Tara was the site for the triennial *feis* which was a great national assembly wherein laws were enacted and disputes settled. There is a standing stone, the *Lia Fáil*, a phallic pillar reputed to cry out when a king touched it, although some tales suggest that the potential king had to ride his chariot around the stone in such a way as to cause the iron hub to screech against the stone, thereby demonstrating his ability to control a war chariot.

A king of Tara in the 3rd century AD, Cormac Ulfhada, wrote a tract called *Teagusc-na-Rí* [Institutions of a Prince], a sort of early Machiavelli with instructions as to manners, morals and government. He was rumoured to hire assassins when needed, and to impose tributes on friends and relations alike. As a result of losing an eye in a battle, he expelled the opposing tribe in the disagreement, the 'Deisi',

The Hill of Tara, Co. Meath, ceremonial, ritual and symbolic site of importance for over 3,000 years.

from their adjacent lands, forcing them to emigrate to what is now Waterford. Some two centuries later the Deisi established settlements in south Wales at Dyfed, after raiding and plundering western Wales for several years.

Tlachtga

[The Hill of Ward] **Ritual Site for Human Sacrifice**

This was one of the four fortresses of the high-king of Tara, Tuathal Techtmar, who ruled perhaps as early as the 1st century AD. Uisneach in Westmeath and Tailteann [Meath] were his other residences. According to the *Annals*, Eochu, the king of Leinster, married Fithir, Tuathal's daughter, but changed his mind shortly after. He told Tuathal that Fithir had died and married her sister Dairine instead. As one might expect, the two sisters eventually met and the story relates how they died of shame. Tuathal and Techtmar, their foster-fathers, the kings of Connacht and Ulster, flew into a rage, and hunted and slew Eochu for his bigamy and the dishonour he brought to Techtmar's family. As further punishment, they levied an *eraic* or blood-fine of thousands of cattle, pigs, cows and calves and silver, bronze and other valuables to be paid in perpetuity. This blood-fine was levied for centuries, with the Leinstermen fighting 35 successful battles against its imposition.

There are also parallel linear embankments on the site, similar to those on Tara and Rath Cruachain, the royal site in Connacht. These curious parallelograms may have to do with the ritual enthronement of kings and a ceremony involving progress toward a sacred stone or site. The sorceress, *Tlachtga*, daughter of the wizard Mug Roith, after whom the hill is named, is reputedly buried on the site, having died during childbirth. Geoffrey Keatinge, writing in the 17th century, described this as the site for the night ceremony of Samhain, when burnt human sacrifice was made to the gods and all men were forbidden to kindle fires except from that fire. The hill, some 116 m [381 ft] above sea-level, is surmounted by the damaged concentric rings of a massive 149 m [478 ft] diameter ringfort, encircling a raised but disturbed mound, presumably the dais for the ritual immolation of the victims.

County Kilkenny *Cill Chainnigh*
Canice's Church

The origins of this county lie in the contested area of the ancient kingdom of Osraighe based on the valleys of the Barrow and the Nore. Traditionally, any Ulster or north Leinster army marching south to collect tribute or inflict damage, crossed the Barrow at Leighlinbridge and then continued south across the plain of Mag Mail and the pass [*bealach*] of Gowran. Although the county is 'Norman' in appearance and cultivation, its origins are earlier and like the rest of the island, marked by boundary, ritual and conflict. The core of what was probably the dominant tribal grouping of the Dal Maic Cuirb and Uí Gentig territory was to the west of the present city of Kilkenny, in the fertile plain between the rivers. In general terms, what makes the area centred on Gowran unique is the suggestion and evidence that it was an area of settlement favoured by returning or fleeing subjects of Roman Britain, who inscribed their names on several of the numerous Ogham stones in the area. The ancestor 'myth' of the Osraighe peoples centres on Buan mac Loegairi Birnd and his sons Ailill, Oengus and Fiacc, who were possibly related to early Munster Eoganacht dynasties, who may also have originated in Roman Britain. The northern border of Ossory is marked by a linear earthwork, Rathduff Dyke [T51 Paulstown Junction, in Shankill Castle demesne] which runs for 11 km [6.9 miles] from the River Barrow to the foot of Sliabh Margy [Castlecomer Plateau]. This earthwork is probably of the early historic period and has an

Ogham stone within its embankments at Shankill. A further linear embankment exists at Grevine West [N10 Kilkenny–Stonyford, 5 km (3 miles) then turn for Grange], perhaps the western boundary of the same territory. Hillforts at strategic points are Cottrellrath [between R697 and N10, 8 km (5 miles) from Kilkenny] and Ballinkillin in Co. Carlow, at the western extremity of the terrain. The area around Dunbel [N10 to Carlow, junction to Maddockstown], where a ringfort was ploughed out in the 19th century, produced Roman-type pins as did Bramblestown [5 km (3 miles) to the south-east] where an enamelled bronze ring, based on a Roman prototype, was found.

A king of Osraighe in the 9th century, Cerball mac Dunlainge, found that by dominating the river valleys of the Barrow and the Nore, he could control the Viking forays into Leinster. By a combination of tactics, bribery and manipulation he succeeded from 870 to his death in 888 in controlling the Norse of south Leinster. He married his daughter into the Dublin Vikings and acted as 'protector' of the Dubliners for an annual fee.

Cerball, like many Irish nobles of that time and later, found that it was far more profitable to exact tribute from the Norse of the towns than levy sub-kings with all the possibilities of treachery and non-payment involved.

Dunmore
Giant Cat

Up to the 19th century, wild cats, about twice the size of the domestic variety and reputedly highly dangerous, existed in mountainous parts of Ireland. In Early Christian times several were famous for being giants and man-eaters and one in particular, *Luchthrigern* [Lord of the Mice] lived in *Derc-Ferna*, the cave of Dunmore. He was eventually slain by the *bean-gaisgidheach* or female champion of Leinster. His epitaph was written by a monk called Broccan the Pious who included this demon among the many ejected from the newly Christianised kingdom.

In 928, the Vikings of Dublin and their leader Godfrey raided the kingdom of Ossory and the inhabitants hid in the chambers of the cave. Numerous human bones found in the cave testify to the vicious and brutal fate they suffered.

Freestone Hill
Roman Site
OS SHEET 19 50.56

[T51 Kilkenny–Paulstown, north of junction with L30 to Gowran] This 142 m [464 ft] hill was the ritual centre of a population area bounded by Ogham stones, embankments and territorial markers. The hill itself is surmounted by an oval enclosure over 155 m [508 ft] in diameter with an Early Bronze Age cairn in the centre. Originally occupied around 800 BC when the burial mound was constructed, later use began before 400 AD when a coin of the Roman emperor Constantine the Great, minted between *c.* 337–340 was [accidentally] deposited. Other Roman items included ear-scoops, nail cleaners, bronze bracelet fragments and finger rings similar to items recovered from excavated villas in England of the late 4th century [O'Floinn, 2001]. It would appear that Freestone Hill was a sacred *temenos* and, although glassblowing and iron smelting took place in its vicinity, it was also a domestic habitation site.

Other items recovered suggest ritual deposition on the hill, as a particular type of bracelet found has been identified as Romano-British and of a type deposited at the ceremonial site at Lydney, Gloustershire, dedicated to the god Nodens. The same Nodens is the Irish 'Nuada' *of the silver arm*, a forceful warrior figure from mythological tales and kingship origin fables. If the peoples who came to Ossory were Romano-British they were

Freestone Hill, site of a Romano-British settlement and possibly a centre for glassblowing and iron smelting in the ancient kingdom of Ossory.

possibly connected to the Silures or Dobinii, tribal groups living along the River Severn who at different times opposed or supported the Roman conquest. They certainly had relations with the Deisi of Munster who had established themselves in south Wales during the later years of Roman Britain and erected Ogham stones to commemorate their worthy fallen and delineate boundaries in their tribal territory.

Freshford
Sacred Settlement
OS SHEET 18 40.65

Freshford, Co. Kilkenny, founded as a Christian settlement in the 7th century.

[T49 Kilkenny–Urlingford road] St Lachtain, who was of the Muscraighe *Bealach Febrat* people of west Limerick, founded a church at this ancient crossroads in 622 AD. The settlement that grew up around the church eventually received a royal charter, a sort of

'duty free' status for all fairs and markets held there. The original 7th-century church was probably of timber, with a crossed gable rafter, a stone representation of which [including a depiction of the Saint] is beside the holy well in the village. St Lachtain's simple building was replaced by a Romanesque church in the 12th century, and a doorway from that church is built into the gable of the present 18th-century building. He was a notable member of a people that included the Corca Baiscind of west Clare, the Corca Duibne of Kerry and the Dal Riata of Antrim. They, the Muscraighe and their related tribes, were a vassal or rent-paying people of pre-Celtic origin, but had their own kings and 'sub' vassal tribes beneath them. They contributed many clerics and monks to the Early Christian church including the notable St Ciaran of Saighir, the patron saint of Ossory.

The 12th century reliquary of St Lachtain's arm is a striking example of rhythmic scrollwork and confident design. It was created to hold a relic of the saint and is 38.5 cm tall, made of bronze on wood and inlaid with silver and silver gilt. It has the distinctive Scandinavian-Celtic-*Urnes* motifs of interlacing foliage and spiralling tendrils, banded and contained within panelled rectangles. The interior of the base is conical, with a large inset rock-crystal, to allow the relic of the saint to be viewed, probably on his feast day. It is a splendid example of Hiberno-Scandinavian ornamentation, a hybrid art-form that re-introduced earlier Celtic styles with more three-dimensional animal modelling.

Eight km [5 miles] south-west of Freshford is the townland of Tubbrid [T19, 5 km (3 miles) to junction, 3 km (1.9 miles) to crossroads] which has a well, *Tobar-na-nDruad* [the well of the druids], which taken with another townland on the opposite side of the town, *Clontubbrid* [water-meadow of the druids] would suggest a certain amount of occult activity around Freshford prior to Christianity.

Knockroe
Ruined 4,500-Year-Old Observatory

[3 km (1.9 miles) north-west from Tullahought village] This is a relatively unknown semi-ruined Megalithic tomb close to Sliabh na mBan, a mountain with two burial cairns at its summit and sacred to the ancient Celts. The tomb lies close to the River Lingaun on the 300 m [984 ft] contour and is visible from another tomb at Kilmacoliver Hill. Although the tomb itself is unimpressive in terms of site or size, it contains the largest collection of megalithic art outside the great tombs of the Boyne Valley. In all, there are 16 decorated stones, and the possibility of several more beneath the surrounding farmland. The art itself is broadly similar to what can be seen at Newgrange and, while of the same period, is of a restricted range of symbols. In general the tomb appears to have been an oval mound, 30+ m [98+ ft] in diameter and bounded by kerbstones. At some stage in the past it was re-used as a boundary and it

continues in this function today. The original tomb had two burial chambers concealed within the cairn but there is no record of any archaeological finds at the site [JRSAI, Vol. 117, 1989].

Stonyford
Roman Site

[N10 Kilkenny–Knocktopher road] This small picturesque village may have been a Roman trading post in the first or second century AD. It lies close to a crossing of the River Nore and could have been reached from Waterford harbour with ease. In the 19th century, a burial was discovered in a rath close to the village, possibly to the north of the Kells road, containing a delicate glass funerary urn covered with a bronze disc mirror. This Roman ritual burial is presumably that of a woman, containing as it did a small glass bottle, perhaps for perfume [Raftery, 1994]. Other items from the rath included a nail-cleaner and a ring with millefiori glass inlays. Opinion is divided as to whether these items are 'Roman' or native copies of Romano-British originals. The site is also within the general area dominated by Freestone Hill, a ritual and manufacturing site associated with early Romano-British coins, rings and bracelets.

Proximity to Roman Britain would have been beneficial to Irish traders and the possible market site at Drumanagh in north Dublin would be another example of a location where buyers and sellers alike could meet. Roman Britain had many market towns where craftsmen worked to customer's specification in bronze and glass, often selling a pottery ware called *samian*. This particular type of pottery was

The 12th-century shrine of St Lachtain's arm, decorated in Urnes, *a Hiberno-Scandinavian art style, combining riotous foliage within panelled rectangles.*

manufactured in the Colchester region of the west of England and shards have been found in ploughed land near the Drumanagh site in Co. Dublin.

By 300 AD Rome was experiencing 'inflation' and the emporor Diocletian issued an edict specifying the prices that could be charged for goods from the 'provinces'. Imported premium beer, Cervisa, was to be no more than 4 denarii a pint, Celtic cloaks were 8,000 denarii and pairs of men's shoes, double soled for farm work . . . 80 denarii.

Ballymoon, the site of the battle where Cormac mac Cuilennan, king-bishop of Cashel and one of early Ireland's most learned men, was killed.

County Carlow *Ceatharlach*
Four Lakes

The two tribes associated with the area now called Carlow, the Brigantes and the Coriundi, are names associated with regions in *Britannia* around 100 BC. These British tribes were of a similar 'stock' to the Scotii, as the Irish were then referred to. Trading and marital links across the Irish Sea for generations before Caesar would have led to a degree of familiarity with the east coast of Ireland and an inland settlement,

especially using the Barrow as a route, would have been relatively easy to accomplish. They may have travelled to *Hibernia* to escape the Roman legions or in the hope of a better life, as many tribes often did due to famine, plague or war. The meaning of the name Ceatharlach, perhaps 'four lakes', may refer to a seasonal flooding of the River Barrow which forms its western boundary.

Aghade
Clochaphoill [Healing Stone]

This holed stone now leaning close to the ground, though originally upright, was used for the healing of sick infants up to the 18th century. It has legendary origins, reputedly being the stone used to restrain Eochaid, son of Eanna Cinnselach in the 5th century. Eochaid broke the chain and killed the assassins sent to kill him.

Ballymoon
Ancient Battle Site
OS 19S.74.61

[On the L33 from about 3.5 km (2.2 miles) from Bagenalstown] Toward the end of the 9th century, Cormac mac Cuilennan was both

bishop of Cashel and king of Munster. He was a learned and cultured man and had compiled a psalter which contained a fine collection of the psalms of David and early origin tales of his tribe. He was king of the great Eoghanacht dynasty, who controlled of most of the south of Ireland from the coast of Kerry to the Sliabh Bloom Mountains on the Leinster border. They had been in this position of power for almost 500 years and Munster had been more prosperous than other provinces under their astute control.

Unfortunately, due to the goading of Flahertagh, abbot of Iniscathy and some Eoghanacht chiefs who were greedy for Leinster's riches, king-bishop Cormac decided to invade the easterly province on the pretext of an ancient tribute unpaid. He marched from Cashel and crossed the Barrow to await the army of the Leinstermen at *Bealach Mugna*, the Pass of Moon. He had a foreboding of his own death and wanted to parley with the Leinstermen, but Flahertagh, apparently a violent and hot-headed man, would have none of it and insisted on the battle.

On the morning of the encounter, Cormac was crestfallen to see that the king of Connacht and his army had joined his adversaries as had the king of Tara with a large contingent of warriors. He was hopelessly outnumbered and his men lost confidence in their leader and the cause. The fight quickly became a rout and Cormac's horse threw him in the confusion and slaughter. He was beheaded by a common soldier and his head was brought with excitement to the victorious king Flann Sinna as was the custom. Flann Sinna, however, was upset at the death of such a learned man and having kissed the head three times, and turned around three times, ordered that it be interred with the body at Disirt Diarmada [Castledermot]. Three thousand of Munster's fighting men were buried in great pits at Ballaghmoon [Ballymoon] and the Eoghanacht

were never to recover their power and position [Keating (Ed. Cunningham), 2000].

Browne's Hill
Dolmen
OS 19S.75.77

This impressive late Neolithic dolmen is one of over 1,200 megaliths in Ireland. In common with similar structures in Atlantic Europe, it probably served as communal burial mound for the dynastic family of the area and perhaps as a ritual site also. 'Portal tomb' is the correct term for this type of burial structure and they are mainly found in the east and north of the island. The builders and farmers may have come from northern Europe, as wheat types introduced around this time and pottery shards within the cairns indicate a Scandinavian origin for the arrivals.

When we look at these remarkable and sturdy monuments, strength and durability come to mind. Perhaps it was also the intention of the builders to embody the 'character' of their race and descent in the structures they created. This huge dolmen was the residence of an evicted

Browne's Hill dolmen, erected c. 2000 BC by a farming community that placed great importance on the veneration of the dead, perhaps seeing the dolmen as the centre of their territory, or a visual marker of their ownership.

The ditch between the immense mound of Dind Righ in Co. Carlow and the exterior earthen 'wall'. The fortress is hidden behind a jungle of beech and alder in a private demesne beside the village of Leighlinbridge. It is a massive dún, partly surrounded by an earth bank 6–8 m high. The dún itself is partly protected by the River Madelin on its western side and rises to at least 15 m high within its protective embankment. The undergrowth makes it difficult to assess the structure, and the flat-topped centre is a mass of nettles and thorn. It is the largest dún this writer has seen in all 32 counties. Permission to visit can be difficult to obtain and care should be taken, as horses and sheep frequently graze the adjacent fields.

family in the 19th century who presumably found it homely. The capstone weighs over 100 tons and is embedded in the earth at one end.

Dind Righ

[The Fort of the Kings]

Murder, Revenge and a Kingdom

High above the Barrow on a narrow ridge sits the ruined fortress of Dind Righ, a seat of power since before written history. Its ancient name was *Duma-Slainge*, the *Duma* or burial mound of a Belgic king, Slainge, and early kings of Leinster raised a fort over his tumulus. The remaining mound is steep and flat-topped, some 72 m [237 ft] in diameter at the base narrowing to 41 m [135 ft] at the top.

Sometime in the distant past, centuries before the Christian era, a prince of Dind Righ, Coffagh Caelbra was bypassed in inheritance by his father in favour of his brother, Laoghaire. Coffagh fell into a deep jealous depression and consulted a druid as to how this sickness could be lifted. The druid suggested *'feigning death to get death'* as his brother would never visit without bodyguards. Coffagh sent word he was dying and when Laoghaire arrived with his son Ailill and without bodyguards, Coffagh murdered them both.

In sadistic triumph, he forced Ailill's only son, Maen, to eat part of his father's and grandfather's heart and a mouse and her young. From shock and disgust, the child was struck dumb and Coffagh therefore thought him inoffensive and spared his life. The child spent several years in the kingdom of Munster, safe from Coffagh's spies until he was old enough to travel to Gaul, the country of his grandmother's birth. There he entered military service probably as one of thousands of Celtic mercenaries in the wars around the Mediterranean and was long forgotten by Coffagh. Some years later, a small, well-armed group landed at the mouth of the River Slaney in Wexford, led by a seasoned soldier and sailor, with a new name, Labra Loingsech, *The Mariner*. He was joined within hours by followers of his murdered father and grandfather and sailed up the Barrow to Dind Righ for revenge.

When Loingsech arrived at the high mound at nightfall, Coffagh was hosting an assembly with his followers inside the great timber hall, protected by guards along the perimeter and within the compound. The guards were surprised and Loingsech and his mercenaries set fire to the halls and all the buildings. Anyone who tried to escape was hacked to pieces and King Coffagh perished with his nobles and warriors in the inferno. Loingsech, son of Ailill, was declared king by the foreign auxiliaries brought by him to Ireland. Their name was *Gáileóin* and in Irish they were known as *Laighne* or spearmen, possibly of the same 'family' as the Gestatii, Gauls who invaded Italy in the 3rd century BC.

Haroldstown
Dolmen
OS 19S.90.78

This is another portal tomb similar to Browne's Hill and both were an offshoot of the court-

The fortress of Dind Righ as illustrated in Joyce's Social History of Ancient Ireland *(1913).*

Haroldstown dolmen, perhaps a creation of the peoples who arrived on the island 5,000 years ago, beginning agriculture and cultivation.

cairns that were possibly constructed as early as 3000 BC. The creators of that 'tomb culture' were the first farmers to arrive on the island and it was they who created the complex field systems in Co. Mayo, at that time heavily forested along its northern coast. Haroldstown was probably covered by a long-vanished mound, and would have been an impressive monument to the ancestors of the local tribe.

As Herity and Eogan have pointed out [Routledge, 1997], the route southwards into the Irish Sea from Jutland and points north and west is now being accepted as a route for commercial and cultural contacts and is a new 'direction' in Irish prehistory. It explains to a degree the derived similarities between Irish gold ornamentation of the early Bronze Age and precursors in central Europe. Irish goldsmiths, like their bronze-using colleagues, were probably itinerant craftsmen, travelling from place to place and offering their skills to anyone who had the required goods for barter.

St Mullins

Ancient Monastery

St Moling, who died in 696 AD, was an active politician and mediator in Early Christian Ireland. As well as establishing the monastery that bears his name, he successfully persuaded the Leinstermen in 694 to no longer levy the *Boromha*, the heavy tribute annually levied on Munster in retribution for an insult to the daughter of a king centuries before. The king to whom St Moling appealed was the generous Finsneachta Fledach who granted the remission of the tribute until 'Monday'. Unfortunately for the king, the Monday St Moling had in mind was the biblical judgment day, traditionally believed to be a Monday. The irate king of the Sil nAedo Slaine [related to the Uí Néill] berated the saint in such a fashion that Moling cursed him roundly and with great venom. Fledach was assassinated by cousins from the Fir Chul Breg in 695.

Although the monastery was burned by the Vikings in 951, it retained its importance and many kings, including the McMurrogh-Kavanaghs, kings of south Leinster in the Mediaeval period, are buried in the churchyard.

Things were not always amicable between the Early Christians and their druidical opponents and on one occasion St Moling was being pursued by hostile 'religious' when an apostle Motharen, waiting at the monastery, became aware through divination that his friend was in trouble. The apostle called up a *ceo druidechta*, a 'sacred fog' to surround and envelop the saint so that he might escape. It came and he did.

County Laois *Laoighseach*
Laoighseach[s] Territory

This county began as a loose confederation of related families who are believed to have overcome the indigenous tribes in the 3rd century AD. The manuscript tales relate how a group of warriors led by Laoighseach Conn More, son of Conall Cearnach of the Red Branch Knights of Ulster, came south to help defend Leinster against attack from the Munster Eoghanacht. In return, they were granted what is now Laois. The legendary queen Maedb [Maeve] who was probably a goddess of sovereignty of Tara was reputed to have poisoned Laoighseach's descendant Lugaid Laigse, a king of the Laoigis, thus dividing and separating the tuath into seven different groups throughout Leinster.

In a later period, the O'Mores and their seven related families [the seven septs of Leix] created a principality that survived into Elizabethan times, with the O'Mores holding the title of kings and princes of Leix. They survived until New Year's Day 1577, when they and the O'Kellys, O'Lalors, Devoys, MacAvoys, O'Dorans and O'Dowlings were summoned to

Mullaghamast rath in Kildare under the queen's protection and were ambushed and murdered. Over 400 were killed within the rath and more would have been killed but for the bravery of Harry O'Lalor, who fought his way out and warned his arriving companions. Another dispossessed Leix family, the O'Connors, became hereditary physicians to notable families across Ireland and frequently appear in other countries during the Middle Ages studying to advance in their profession.

Female Druids
The county contains the Sliabh Bloom Mountains, originally heavily wooded and the home of the pre-Christian female seers, Lia

Luachra and Bobhmall. These extrasensory women were given the task of raising Fionn, son of a murdered chieftain, and they hid him in the deep woods to protect him from the sons of Morna, his family's sworn enemies. Fionn's father, Cumhall, was a leader of the Fianna, possibly an early Celtic group in Ireland related to the Gaulish Gaesatae of the Upper Rhone, described by the 2nd century BC Greek writer Polybius as high-status 'spearmen' or 'mercenaries'.

The Fianna probably became tribute-paying tribes by the Early Christian period but always had serious internal rivalries between themselves and Fionn's tribe, the Corcu [clan] Baiscne, were mortal

The view south-west from Dunamase, looking across the fertile lands of Laois, a tribal territory of seven septs, established perhaps as early as the 3rd century AD.

100 BC stone from Autun, France, showing druids in costume.

Pair of 2nd-century AD horse-bits, decorated with stylised bird heads and a palmette design. Probably a votive deposit to appease or placate the gods, they were found in a bog in Attymon, Co. Galway.

enemies of the Clan Morna, led by Goll Mac Morna. Fionn spent many happy days exploring the woods that covered the Sliabh Blooms and the tale *The Boyhood of Fionn* gives a sense of an immense forest with great trees where a boy could climb;

'and gaze across
an impenetrable roof of leaves,
above and below,
sway and motion,
the whisper of leaf on leaf
and the eternal silence
to which one listened
and at which one tried to look'
[Stephens, 1923, Trans]

Dunamase

Dun-Masg [the Fort of Masg]

Ancient Fortress

OS DISCOVERY SERIES 55 S53.98

[N80 from Portlaoise to Stradbally] This dramatic hilltop site stands in the strategic gap between the present counties of Laois and

Dunamase fortress, perhaps established by the Dumnonii, a Celtic tribal grouping from Britannia.

Kildare and has been a defended site since Early Christian times. It may have been the original fortress of the pre-Christian king Mes Delmonn of the Domhnainn, or Dumnonii, a P-Celtic-speaking people [similar to the Welsh language] found in Devon and Cornwall. He is described as an ancestor of the Leinster peoples and a prince who fought the Formorians, possibly seaborne pirates from the west coast of Scotland [Byrne, 2001].

Although the original ramparts are submerged beneath fern and somewhat collapsed, the later mediaeval stonework gives a sense of the defended nature of the site. Dunamase affords spectacular views across the lush green countryside that surrounds the ruined fortress from the Slieve Bloom mountains in the west, to the River Barrow in the east. By the 12th century Dunamase was part of the MacMurrogh Kavanagh territory and was acquired by the Norman adventurer Strongbow as part of the

wedding dowry of Aoife, Art's daughter, whom he married in 1167.

The tranquil scenes that surround the hill give little indication of the contested nature of the area, especially the later violent confrontations between the incoming Elizabethans and the O'Mores, princes of Leix, who fought the usurpers several times in the 16th century in the area around Stradbally.

Killeshin
Ancient Art and Architecture
OS 19S.67.78

This old monastic site was established in the 5th century by St Comghan and it produced several notable saints of the Early Christian church, including St Aodhan [d. 843] and St Diarmait, abbot until 847. Dubhlitir Ua hUathgaile, a monk of this monastery, translated the Latin manuscript *De Sex Aetatibus Mundi* into Irish. The door of the later church is one of the finest pieces of Romanesque stonework in Ireland, having foliage, scrollwork, animal motifs and heads with intertwined hair [Harbison, 1970].

County Offaly *Ui Fhailghe*
The Descendants of Failghe

According to the *Book of Rights* as translated and published by the antiquarian John O'Donovan, Cahirmore, monarch of Ireland in the 2nd century AD, made a will for his thirty sons. Cahirmore was slain by the famous Conn of the Hundred Battles in 123 AD and in his will he bequeathed to 'my fierce Ros, my vehement Failghe' [Ros of the rings] a territory which then formed a considerable portion of Kildare and Laoighse. His descendants became Hy Failghe, the descendants of Failghe and from their patrimony, the present Offaly came into existence. Tullamore, its chief town, was the site of a ferocious battle between the Connachtmen under Goll mac Morna and Frejus, an Iberian

Celt who had come to Ireland to assist a chieftain called Mug Nuadat. The battle took place at a crossroads called Meelaghan [L108 Portarlington] and Goll mac Morna was victorious. Low mounds near the crossroads are reputed to contain the remains of Mug Nuadat and his Iberian friend. The same Mug Nuadat appears in several early pedigrees as an 'ancestor' and may be a divine personage inserted into early genealogies to give a more noble descent. Near to the town of Tullamore is the site of Durrow Abbey, a 5th century foundation on land given to St Columba by Aedh, son of Brendan, a local prince. A fine high cross sits in the woodland amid the graves of Donal, king of Tara [d. 758], Murchadh, grandson of Brian Boru [d. 1068], and other kings whose tombstones were probably destroyed by Hugh de Lacy in 1186. *The Book of Durrow* is one of the earliest Christian manuscripts, probably created around the year 680 but of uncertain origin. It may have been

The grave slab of Aigide, whose ancestors claimed to have granted the site of Durrow Abbey to Colmcille.

created at Iona, or Northumberland, but it did, however, arrive at Durrow in the 10th century and a shrine was made for it there. Stylistically, it represents the four evangelists in a strikingly different way to later, more 'religious' iconography. St Matthew is shown wearing a very smart cloak with embroidered millefiori enamel, similar to Irish metalwork examples and represents a 'borrowing' of styles — in this case a Pictish-Mediterranean hybrid example. As the demand for sumptuously illustrated books increased, purely Celtic sources were no longer strong enough nor available in a three-dimensional form for the illustrators. Hence the sources for the illustrations were varied and eclectic, and Irish calligraphers and artists used Anglo-Saxon, Byzantine and Celtic motifs and symbolism to produce a unique art form, drawing on many sources yet totally Irish.

The county forms part of an ancient region that also included portions of Kildare, Meath and Westmeath. Its centre was the imposing ruined citadel of Dunamase [now in Co. Laois], where the chieftains of this territory had their seat of power. As in most present Irish counties, its boundaries and extent changed as early dynasties came and went and the current territory is approximately that which existed at the time of the shiring of Ireland around 1650 when its principal families were dispossessed.

Crannóg in Lough Gara. These lake dwellings were often the residence of high-status individual families and functioned like a ringfort, only with more security. They date from the last centuries BC well into the Christian period.

Ballinderry
Ancient Homestead
This lakeside site, a crannóg from the Bronze Age of *c.* 800 BC had three human skulls placed under the floor before it was inhabited. This sacrificial or ritual placement occurs at other crannóg sites and suggests either propriation of the spirits of the water or the place or perhaps the transgression by workmen of some taboo. The people who lived here were not of high status but kept cattle, sheep, pigs and goats and hunted red deer. The site continued in use until the Christian period and accumulated layers of artefacts and debris from each succeeding generation. According to Harbison the *'inhabitants were a self-contained group that kept domestic animals, grew grain and spun thread'* [Thames & Hudson, 1988].

Ballykilleen
Dynastic Fortress
[South of Edenderry, on the T41 from Enfield to Daingean] On a low 110 m [360 ft] hill is a multi-vallate ringfort, probably one of the 'lost' sites of the Uí Failge, 5th-century kings of Leinster. This ruling dynasty occupied Ballykilleen over several periods and it would have been a suitable fortress to oversee their territories in Offaly and Westmeath. It also lies on the route of the Slighe Mhor, the ancient chariot road from Tara to Clarinbridge, but as the Uí Failge had their major fort at Rathangan, 12 km [7.5 miles] south on the other side of the great Bog of Allen, there may have been a trackway across the great bog where the road through Clonbulloge joins the two sites.

Birr
Ancient Border Town
Between the town of Birr and Banagher on the Shannon is the townland of Ballaghanoher [*Bealach-an-fhothair* the pass of the forest], which was the location of the 'Great Forest of Delvin' felled in the 16th century, possibly for the needs

of the iron foundries which were starting in Ireland at that time. The town was important in the Early Christian centuries, being a 'border' town between the southern Uí Néill and the Eoghanachta of Munster and, perhaps like any frontier town, it was a place where rivals could find refreshment in a neutral venue. In 697 AD the *Cain Adomnain* ['Law of Adomnain'], a type of early human rights charter, was proclaimed in Birr for all of Ireland, attempting to guarantee the lives of women, children and clerics in wartime. It also forbade women to participate in military operations. Birr also lay at the intersection of several routeways and the small town of Clareen, 5 km [3 miles] to the west lies at the junction of the routeway from Birr to a series of large ringforts between the Little Brosna River and the Sliabh Bloom Mountains. The trackway connecting these settlement areas lies to the west of the T9 from Kinnity and runs south from Seirkieran behind Leap Castle toward Roscrea, to meet the chariot-road Slighe Dala which ran from Tara to Munster.

In the early 9th century the abbot of Birr, MacRiagail Ua Magleni, completed and signed a magnificent illuminated manuscript known as *Macregol's Gospels*, which suggest that a scriptorium existed in Birr at that time. The 350 mm x 270 mm manuscript subsequently ended up in the monastery of Harewood, England, where two scribes wrote a commentary in Anglo-Saxon explaining and underlining the confident, freehand Irish majuscule script of MacRiagail [O'Neill, 1984].

Clonfinlough
Healing Stone
Not far from Clonmacnoise is the decorated stone of Clonfinlough. It lies in the middle of a field and has many curious decorations, perhaps resembling the human form. Respected sources would suggest these markings are similar to those in Galacia in northern Spain which date from around 2000 BC. This is not unreasonable as it is more than probable that the first 'settlers' on the island of Ireland travelled via

Clonmacnoise, founded in the 6th century by St Cíarán, on lands donated by the O'Conors, kings of Connacht.

the Atlantic seaways along the coast from Iberia to a landing point perhaps on the south-west coast.

Clonmacnoise
Sacred Land for 1,500 Years
OS 15N.01.31

This great monastery, founded by St Cíarán, was endowed with land by the O'Conor kings of Connacht from its inception in the 6th century. It quickly became a market as well as a monastery, and school and merchants from Gaul and the Mediterranean are recorded as visiting and trading with the Irish and the monks. Wine in particular was popular and Irish wool and hides were a commodity much in demand in Europe.

It was robbed by a farm-worker about 100 years after its foundation and the *Annals of the Four Masters* recorded '*the theft of a silver model of Solomon's Temple, a silver cup, a silver drinking horn, a silver chalice, a paten and other objects*' — presumably all expensive gifts from the O'Conors whose kings were buried at the monastery by tradition. St Cíarán's foundation grew into the greatest of all the Irish monasteries including a school, teaching the works of Virgil, Horace, Ovid, Juvencus and the Scriptures. It drew students from Britannia and Gaul but unfortunately it attracted the greed of the Vikings and they plundered the monastery in 834, 835 and 842.

Gallen
Celtic Christian Site

Gallen, founded in 492, was on an important routeway through the bogs of Co. Offaly. This significant vein of communication followed the well-drained Brosna valley and the trackway runs along the north side of the river for a considerable distance from Gallen to

The Nun's Church, Clonmacnoise, endowed by Dervorgilla, wife of Dermot MacMurrogh, king of Leinster; she retired here towards the end of her life.

Lemanaghan, or St Managhan's Church. Gallen itself has a fine collection of Early Christian cross slabs, many attached to the church on the site. Just north of the monastery between The Doon and Ballycumber, another trackway runs along the south side of the existing road and between the two trails are several high-status ringforts, the residences of the local *Tighearna* or Lord and his 'palace guard'. He and his immediate family would have granted land to the monastery, making sure that the monks remained on the lower ground, suitable for tillage but not for cattle, the *Tighearna's* prerogative.

The Nuns' Church, Clonmacnoise
A Queen's Church
OS 15N.01.31

This entrance arch, part of the ruined monastic settlement of Clonmacnoise, is the entrance to a Romanesque church built towards the end of the 12th century by a repentant queen of reputedly great beauty. Her affair with a neighbouring prince brought the Anglo-Normans to Ireland, beginning a different and challenging era in Irish history. Queen Dervorgilla retired here after taking holy orders and the arch to her church has a motif of animals gnarling a vine with terrifying heads on the capitals. The church stands just beside the main buildings of Clonmacnoise, *the water meadow of Naoise*, founded by St Cíarán in 548 AD. Like Iona in Scotland it is the burial place of many Irish kings and princes such as O'Meolaghlin of Meath, O'Conor Don of Connaught, O'Kelly, MacCarthy Mor, McDermott and others.

Seirkieran
Centre of Ancient Kingdom

This monastic site of over 10 acres still retains traces of the surrounding earthen wall and defensive ditch. The wall, rising in places to 6 m [19.6 ft] in height, runs for approximately 300 m [984 ft] alongside the road and gives a sense of the defended nature of the settlement. St Cíarán

the Elder, 'firstborn of the Saints of Ireland' founded the monastery sometime in the 5th century on heavily forested lands granted by the local dynasty [probably O'Carroll ancestors]. Cíarán was an interesting saint in that he wore the skins of animals and had, as his first monks, a badger, a fox, a wolf and a deer. St Cíarán went on to use his abilities in a more profitable manner and became the owner of 'large herds of cattle' according to the *Feilire Oengusso*, a Mediaeval Irish commentary on the lives of saints [Edel, 2001]. A trackway, allowing communication between the 20+ ringforts in the area and the high-status bi-vallate and tri-vallate forts, runs to the east of the monastic enclosure. Adjacent to the site is a now obliterated tri-vallate ringfort, probably the main residence of the local chieftain, which formed part of a series of visually connected ringforts of differing functions — defence, farming and habitation — which formed the nuclei of the tuath.

County Leitrim *Liatroim*
The Grey Ridge

Leitrim was the western part of a territory called Breffni, a patrimony of the powerful early Mediaeval O'Rourke family group. These

St Maedoc's Shrine has an interesting collection of ecclesiastics in robes, perhaps depicting members of the Ua Ruairc family, whose patron St Maedoc was.

peoples were Connachta in origin, originating in the plain around Cruachain in Roscommon and only moving into the hitherto desolate lands of Cavan and Leitrim in the 8th century. The lands of the Uí Briuin Breifne were then known as Garbthrian Connacht, 'the rough third of Connacht'. The northern part of this territory was dominated by the ancient wood of *Fasach Coille* which lay between Lough Allen in the centre of the county and Lough Melvin at its northern end. Leitrim has a low density of ringforts, suggesting that the woodland cover was not seriously depleted in the Early Christian period, when small numbers of these 'farmsteads' were occupied in the district around Lough Arrow.

In the year 1084, the king of the Ulaidh, Donn Sleibhe mac Eochada came to Breffni and gave *tuarastal*, special royal gifts indicating dominion to Donnchad Ua Ruairc, king of Breffni. This was an attempt to create an alliance against the northern Uí Néill and the Ua Brien kings of Munster. Breffni, although originally a Connachta settlement, was seen as a possible ally of the Ulaidh against Uí Néill attempts at hegemony over Ulster [Byrne, 1973].

The patron of the family of Ua Ruairc was St Maedoc of Ferns and in later years his shrine [now in the National Museum, Dublin] was carried around the king as part of his inauguration ceremony.

Until the shiring of Ireland in the 16th century, Leitrim and Roscommon formed an ill-defined terrain, although the lands of O'Conor and McDermott to the west were clearly circumscribed and defended. As Leitrim and to an extent Cavan were 'barren' territories, expelled and subject [fortuatha] tribes from other areas found refuge in these unwanted areas. The Gailenga and Luigni formed a tribal

area south of the Ox Mountains and the Corca Ochlainn and Cenel Maic Ercae claimed the Breffni lands along the Shannon and the western shore of Lough Allen.

Black Pigs Race or The Worm Ditch
Great Wall of Ireland
OS 7G.97.46

In the pre-Christian centuries, Ulster was a distinct and separate part of the island and its rulers, the Ulaidh, built a series of embankments to protect their lands, cattle and people from attack. The *Black Pigs Dyke* runs across many of the counties that form a border with today's Republic of Ireland and parallels the existing, if imaginary, frontier. The original claim of the Ulaidh of Eamhain Mhaca [Navan Fort] to a territory from the Drowes River in Donegal to the Boyne at Drogheda is perhaps a little ambitious, but the *Black Pigs Dyke* at least supports that claim in a tangible and solid form.

Identity at that time was closely related to territory and the clear delineation of boundaries was seen as a mark of power, perhaps emphasising where a border lay and that different people lay inside and outside that line. Often, this need for a physical boundary was also a linguistic matter and the Ulaidh may have been P-Celtic speakers [Irish is Q-Celtic], their language similar to Welsh rather than Gaelic. The threat, however, to the Ulaidh of the north came from Connacht, from a warlike and ambitious dynasty whose centre of power was at Cruachain in Roscommon, a complex and extensive series of mounds, raths, linear embankments and Bronze Age tumuli. The Connachta were different to other tribal groups in that they seem to be of one family and their ambitions were for land, *other peoples*, and as much as they could take. Around the time that the *Black Pigs Race* was constructed, there appears to be a general rise in activity on the

Opposite page: The great 'Doon' of Drumsna, Co. Leitrim, which runs for approx. 9 km from Runnafarna, below Carrick-on-Shannon, to the bend in the river below Drumsna village. It may have been part of the series of defensive ramparts collectively known as the Black Pigs Dyke, *dated to around the 1st century* BC.

island, in that trackways are replaced with roadways to facilitate perhaps commerce or intercommunication, and the erection of linear earthworks between tribal groups suggesting 'a rise in the need for territorial visibility' [Barry, 2000].

Therefore, sometime after 200 BC, the Ulaidh constructed a barrier against the dynasty from Cruachain and a 9 km [5.6 miles] stretch of this ancient border runs between Lough Melvin and Upper Lough Macnean on the Leitrim side of the border with Fermanagh. The earthwork is 2.5 m [8.2 ft] wide in places and would have been perhaps 3 m [9.8 ft] high when it was built. The part between Kiltyclogher and Rossinver is worth visiting and can be walked from the junction 3 km [1.9 miles] from Kiltyclogher in a north-west direction. Another 4 km [2.5 miles] stretch runs from the northern end of Lough Allen toward the village of Dowra.

Corracloona
Shamanic Site

This rectangular tomb was originally beneath a cairn of stone some 20 m [65.6 ft] long. It has a small forecourt, where ritual relating to internment could take place, and it also has a curious small entrance hole at the bottom of the entrance stone. This feature may be to allow subsequent burials to take place, although these sites were also re-used by later peoples whose burial rites were different. Later, possibly Celtic peoples used these burial sites for divination, where the tribal shaman would spend the night inside and re-emerge with a vision of the future. The shaman was a forerunner of the 'druid' and if Irish shamans were similar to their Tibetan and Siberian cousins, they went through a considerable period of training, so that their gifts of intuition and 'ESP' could be used to the benefit of king and tribe.

The Province of Connacht

*Dún Aengus,
Co. Galway, a
spectacular Bronze-
Age citadel facing
the Atlantic,
surrounded on its
landward side by a
dense 'forest' of
stone uprights: a*
chevaux-de-frise,
*intended to repel
attack on horseback
but perhaps
symbolic in this
context.*

The western province of Ireland has always been
remote, and to Dublin city dwellers, the most
romantic. It was historically the least known,
having almost no roads into Connemara until the
19th century and almost no clear access to parts
of north Mayo until much later. The Shannon
provided a physical border to the east, and the
restless Atlantic was perhaps a reminder to its
early inhabitants that there was nowhere left to
run. It is the smallest of the provinces at 10,560
sq. km [6,600 sq. miles] and contains vast
stretches of mountain and moorland with tree-
fringed lakes and ancient stone-lined fields. It has
a long jagged coastline, scattered islands within
its bays and ancient Christian sites atop
mountains sacred since people first walked upon
the land. Its mountains are wild and steep and its
sea-cliffs among the highest in Europe. The
landscape bounded by the modern towns of

Tuam, Ballymoe, Mount Bellew and Attymon has a low concentration of ringforts and may have been the great forest of Feadha. Forest was a factor in Connacht's remoteness and Erris, the northern coast of Mayo, was conspicuous for its yew and birch woodland.

Population Groups

In the Early Christian period, the mid-Connacht area was the homeland of the Sogain and Corco Moga, subject tribes of the dominant dynasty of Uí Maine, although their function and geographic position may have been to separate the contesting parts of Connacht and their competing dynasties. Forest also lay along the Atlantic seaboard and, the subject tribes of Conmaicne, Delbna and Partraigh occupied the thin soil between the sea and Lough Corrib. Roderick O'Flaherty, writing in the 17th century, identifies the Partraigh [and other subject tribes] as Damnonii, although a pre-Celtic origin seems more likely for the Partraigh. The 2nd-century map by Ptolemy suggests several tribal groupings within Connacht's geography. The most important were the Fir Domnainn, possibly a sub-group of the Belgae from northern Gaul [France] who were shown as Dumnonni on Ptolemy's map. They came to power in Connacht after a particularly ferocious and bloody battle, in which the king of the Dé Danann, Nuadu, had his arm chopped off. He was henceforth known as *Nuadu Artgatlamh* [of the silver hand]. Following this victory, the Fir Domnainn were left to the western part of Ireland. This grouping remained as rulers of this area until at least the 3rd century AD. The ancestor of the Connachta, Cormac Mac Airt, fulfils many of the requirements for a hero and mythical progenitor, being orphaned before birth, suckled by wolves and a late Christian convert before he died.

In Nuadu Artgatlamh we also find aspects of divinity. He may be the Gaulish deity *Nodens* and as such had a shrine at an elaborate temple at Lydney in Gloustershire [see Armagh and Kilkenny entries]. He is also the Welsh *Nudd* or *Lludd* and his grandson, Fionn mac Cumhail is known as *Gwynn ap Nudd* in Wales [Byrne, 1973].

The Connachta [a tribal group based in Cruachain, Co. Roscommon] were the genesis of the Uí Néill, who dominated Tara during the 5th and 6th centuries and who were the hereditary enemies of the Ulaidh, forever attempting to subdue and conquer their lands north of the *Black Pigs Dyke*. In the Early Christian centuries, Connacht also had 'free states' or territories that were free of tribute belonging to the descendants of Brion and Fiachra, brothers of Niall of the Nine Hostages. The majority of the province was divided, however, into tribute-paying areas corresponding to different tribal groupings, in various degrees of vassalage and power. Umhall, around Clew Bay and Uí Maine in south Galway would be examples [MacNeill, 1921]. This latter area was ruled by Maine, a prince of Oriel, who received the territory after the previous inhabitants, perhaps of Pictish origin, were defeated in battle in the 4th century AD. The Picts appear again in the place name Partry [Partraighe] around Lough Mask and indications are that these peoples occupied a large area of territory before Gaelic-speaking peoples came to the west of Ireland.

Connacht Counties and Sites

County Galway *Gaillimh*
[Town of the] Foreigners
The name probably came into existence as the Gaelic for 'foreigners' — a reference to the Anglo-Normans who established a settlement here in the 13th century. It is a large county and is almost bisected by Lough Corrib, an immense

lake famous for salmon as far back as recorded history. To the east of this expanse of water is the fertile plain of east Galway, extending to the Roscommon border and the River Shannon. It is the west of the county, however, that receives most attention due to its majestic Twelve Bens mountain range with their scattered lakes hidden in deep valleys. The wild Connemara moorland extends to the coast, covering hundreds of square kilometres of what was forest centuries before Christian times.

There was probably a settlement of sorts around the mouth of the Corrib at that time, as its rich salmon fishery would have been much prized even then. When the Normans arrived, the lands west of the Corrib were owned by the O'Flaherty family, with septs such as the O'Hallorans as sub-chiefs. Within a century Norman families such as Joyce, Morris, De Burgo [Burke] and others had become Hibernicised to the degree that they saw themselves independent of England, although not of Gaelic blood. Clarinbridge [N18 to Kilcolgan], a pretty village south of the city, was the 'terminus' for the *Slighe Mhor* [the great road that ran across the country from the Hill of Tara] and was possibly a 'port' in the Iron Age.

Castleblakney Ritual Murder Site

At Gallagh in 1821 the submerged body of a man, placed in the bog, perhaps two thousand years previously, was found with sally rods twisted around his neck and pointed wooden stakes on either side of his body. He was found wearing only a short leather cloak, similar in description to the Roman general Tacitus's description of Germanic peoples of the 1st century BC. Other, similar bodies wearing only a cape have been found, principally in Denmark. In Jutland a female body, thought to be Queen Gunhilda, was found to have been pinioned into the peat by wooden crooks, driven tight across elbows and knees, with her head pointing east and her face toward the setting sun. Old Danish

belief was that '*so long as the stakes stood, the ghost remained pinned in the ground*'. This method of ritual death, the drowning in a bog, was particularly used for witches and sorcerers, who were usually interred alive [Glob, 1965].

A second category of 'bog people' were those found [in Denmark] to have delicate features and neat hands and feet, not worn by the heavy work and toil that would have been the lot of the majority at that time. These people appear to have been chosen for a specific reason, in that the expressions on their faces suggest that their death, while ritualised and caused by either strangulation or drowning, was not violent or resisted. They may have been part of the cult of

Clonfert Cathedral, begun during the 12th century and decorated with a 'bizarrie' of heads, grotesque animals and foliage.

Ishtar or *Astarte*, the fertility goddess of the east, who in turn for granting the increase in cattle, crops and humankind, required a sacrifice from her followers, specifically the sacred priesthood who watched over her shrine. It is perhaps interesting to consider that many Irish pottery finds from the 2–3rd centuries BC often have as decoration around the rim, the impression of a type of wheat popular in Jutland at the same period.

Clonfert Cathedral
Celtic Art and Architecture
OS 15M.96.21

The extraordinary façade of this church is decorated with what appears to be decapitated stone heads in the massive door-case above the entrance. It was founded by St Brendan, a descendant of the Ciarraigh [a Pictish pre-Celtic people whose name derives from *Ciar* meaning black, and *raige* people of]. Ancient law texts describe the Ciarraigh as 'a subject, tribute-paying people'. Many of them were expelled from Munster to Roscommon sometime in the 6th century and one of them, St Brendan, founded the church. The Romanesque decoration consists of animals gnawing tendrils, while strange pagan faces glare at the worshippers as they enter the church. The Celtic habit of decorating their houses with the heads of their slain enemies is carried on here in stone, the closed oval eyes and swirling moustaches of some of the decapitated individuals showing them to be of Celtic derivation, perhaps representing symbolic trophies of the benefactor to the church.

In 838, Feidlimid mac Crimthainn was abbot of this church and was also a prince of the Eoghanacht Caiseal of Munster. He was distinguished by his inability or unwillingness to retaliate against the Vikings who were burning and pillaging monasteries across the south of the country, and instead robbed Clonmacnoise and Durrow himself. He was finally struck down by a curse from St Cíarán himself, dying in 847.

Dún Aengus, Aran Islands
Ritual Solar Site
OS 14L.76.99

Situated on Inishmore, the largest of the Aran Islands, 15 km [9.4 miles] from the Galway coast, this immense Bronze Age cliff-top citadel is surrounded on its landward side by a dense *chevaux-de-friese*, a configuration of stone uprights, apparently a derivation of a sharpened timber anti-cavalry device first used by the Freisians against the Romans in 40 BC. Legend suggests that it is a fortress, built by the Celtic Belgae tribe fleeing westward, perhaps from Caesar's legions. The word 'fortress' suggests habitation, however, and no evidence for occupation has been found although excavations revealed artefacts associated with bronze-working, and the scraps of metal and fragments of crucibles reveal the widespread use of bronze and the prevalence of artisans skilled in its use.

There appears to be a platform of some sort on the edge of the cliff and Bernard Wailes has suggested that the site may have had a ritual significance. This would be a reasonable observation as the ramparts have a stadium aspect to their terracing and appear to focus on the 'stage' adjacent to the cliff. As a semi-circular amphitheatre, it resembles early Roman examples in Tuscany and Provence, albeit in a 'provincial' architectural form. Perhaps Celtic soldiers who had fought against or within Caesar's legions had become familiar with aspects of Roman building techniques and use.

This site suggests most powerfully a ritual enclosure, suitable for contests or dramatic ceremonial events.

Knocknadala

[The Hill of the Assemblies]

Possible Ancient Assembly Site

This is possibly the Teamhar cited by Ptolomy and may be the centre of what is a complex and extensive site. Many of the mounds and oval earthworks may be Bronze Age and some are certainly of the Iron Age and later. Perhaps due to the propaganda of 9th-century Tara polemicists, Knocknadala was ignored by official historians and has suffered from subsequent neglect and official indifference. Local knowledge, inherited from people whose forebears have lived in the area for generations, suggests many earthworks have been obliterated by 'improving' farmers and land reclamation. The very existence of this important and unexplored site is now threatened by a dual-carriageway, a supreme irony given that possible traces of the chariot road from Tara, the Slighe Mhor, run nearby. It was a mini 'kingdom' for some of Niall of the Nine Hostages descendants, specifically Indrechtach mac Muirdaig who reigned from 707–723 and consolidated the Uí Briuin hold in the south of Connacht around Galway Bay. Knocknadala suggests a function as a place of meeting and discussion, possibly for the Uí Fiachrach Muade whose leader, Ailill Medgraige [a son of Indrechtach] reigned in the area during the 8th century [Byrne, 1973]. It was also a possible ritual and residential site for the *aithech-thuath* peoples of the 1st century BC, tribute-paying tribes who may originally have been Belgae, or *Fir Bolg*. The Ordnance Survey 25" map for the area shows extensive earthworks spread over several townlands and the area cries out for systematic appraisal and preservation.

Lough Rea

Battle Site and Lake Monster

This town has a history stretching back to Early Christian times at least. It was the centre of power for the Uí Maine tribal grouping that had as tribute payers, the *Cuircne*, *Calriagh* and *Delbna Bethra* subject groups. The Uí Maine were frequently caught between the contesting

The Turoe Stone, Co. Galway, a ritual stone of the last centuries BC, similar in artistic concept and, perhaps, function to Killycluggin, Co. Cavan and Castlestrange, Co. Roscommon. All of these stones were probably 'markers' of territory and indicators of belief.

dynasties of northern Connacht and the southern Uí Néill and it was the scene of a ferocious battle in 802 AD when Muirgius mac Tommaltaig, a ruthless warlord of the Sil Muirdaig tribe, was imposing his rule on tributary tribes across Connacht. He is one of the earliest rulers to start a policy of territorial acquisition and this could suggest that the Connachta were later arrivals to the island and of different 'blood'. It was unusual for any Irish king to attempt to usurp the lands of the tribute-paying tribes, as 'tribute' in the form of cattle, grain or gold was the usual requirement.

The *Ongamhas*, a large monster of the eel family, was believed to reside in this lake and was credited with pursuing unwary lovers who loitered near its banks. The lake lies in the

Part of the recently excavated stone farm-walls of the Ceide Fields, an agricultural community of 5,000 years ago.

ancient territory of the O'Kelly family, who took the beast as their heraldic symbol, incorporating this Onchu into their coat of arms.

Turoe Stone
Celtic Ritual Stone
OS 14M.62.23

This stone originally stood in or near the rath of Feerwore in the vicinity of Knocknadala, some 6.4 km [4 miles] north of Loughrea. The stone is decorated in a curvilinear style using chisels to cut away the material leaving the design to stand proud. Detailed studies of the stone show it to be 'insular La Tène' with suggestions that its art is derived from British or Breton prototypes. Raftery and others would contend, however, that the stone and its contemporaries at Castlestrange and Killycluggin are of a native art-form and fit well with bronze and La Tène ironwork examples of similar design. The stone is undoubtedly for ritual use and, considering that the design covers all the surface, it would suggest that whatever audience was expected would sit on all sides surrounding the stone. It may well be that stones such as Turoe formed the basis in style and form for the Irish high cross of later Christian Ireland, and Raftery has suggested that some of the Irish high crosses may have been pagan stones re-used in a Christian context [Raftery, 1984]. Excavation of the rath at Feerwore has produced artefacts suggesting a skilled population group arriving around the 2nd century BC, possibly from continental Europe.

County Mayo *Maigh Eo*
The Plain of the Yews

Mayo is a county of muscular, brooding landscapes, dark mountains and prehistoric remains from the earliest periods of ancient history. It contains the wildlife habitats of peatland, bog and estuary, while its mountains and rugged sea-cliffs are breathtaking and fresh to the eye. Often embedded in a human

landscape of immense antiquity, its scenery is the match of anything in Ireland, and yet the county remains one of the most sparsely populated areas of western Europe.

Over 4,500 years ago, farmers arriving in Ireland found tracts of forest along the headlands of the north Mayo coast, regenerated woodland of birch and pine that had re-grown over the earlier forest clearances of 2,000 years before. For the success of their farming enterprise, they needed the best land and cleared the north Mayo woodland with axes made from porcellanite, a sharp and resilient flint found in Co. Antrim and 'popular' with Neolithic farmers across the northern part of Ireland and northern England. They also began building prominent tombs for certain of their deceased, so as to lay claim to the land and its surroundings. Ultimately, climatic change at the beginning of the second millennium BC with increased rainfall and lower temperatures caused an expansion of the peatland, making farming impossible. The peat eventually covered and ultimately preserved the elaborate and extensive field systems near both Ballycastle and Belderg.

In the 1930s at Behy [*birch-land*] near Ballycastle, turf-cutting unearthed part of an extensive field system which would have been capable of sustaining large numbers of domesticated animals including cattle. The range and structure of the wall-systems suggested a large and thriving community, capable of maintaining a stock management system of apparent complexity and efficiency. There is now an 'interpretative centre', *The Ceide Fields*, which offers guided tours and information on this ancient site.

Originally sacred to the pagan god *Crom*, the great conical peak of Croagh Patrick dominates the coast of western Mayo. St Patrick fought the old gods of paganism on this mountain in 450 AD, and his bell, blackened and tarnished from the heat of the encounter, now rests within an exquisite gold filigree shrine in Dublin's National Museum. The tradition of climbing this holy mountain has been maintained for over 1,500 years and every July thousands of pilgrims, many barefoot, climb the Reek before dawn, receiving communion on its misty peak in recognition of its sanctity. Beneath the Reek is the ancient

One of a series of standing stones between the sea and Croagh Patrick, Ireland's 'holy' mountain.

territory of Umhall, where a group of marauding Vikings were surrounded and killed in the 9th century by Uí Máille warriors.

At the southern shore of Lough Mask, beside the quaint village of Cong, is the limestone Kelly's Cave, of importance as a burial chamber in the Bronze Age and still eerie and tomb-like in the 21st century. The Partry Mountains which overshadow Lough Carra and Lough Mask commemorate in name the *Partraigh*, a pre-Celtic tribe that inhabited this area perhaps as early as the 2nd–3rd century BC, before any dynasty existed in Connacht. They may be related to the Garmisch-Partenkirchen of Bavaria, a group with origins in ancient Illyria on the western coast of the Adriatic [Byrne, 1973]. Another ancient tribal grouping, the Domhnainn, settled across north Mayo and they were probably Dumnonnii of pre-Roman Britain whose antecedents may have been originally Belgae of northern Gaul. The Dumnonnii of Britain [Devon and Cornwall] returned to Gaul at the time of Caesar and settled in Britanny, renaming the area they settled in Dumnonnia.

The Battle of Moytura
Battle Site
Between the village of Cross and the village of Kilmaine is the ancient plain of Moytura, centred on the megalithic tomb of Cregnanagh, 4 km [2.5 miles] north-east of Cross village.

The plain was the site of a famous battle on the pagan sacred day of Bealtaine, 1 May, in which an incoming Celtic group, the Dé Danann [people of the goddess Danu] fought and defeated the resident population of the area, the *Fir Bolg* and their leader *Nuada*. The Dé Danann had burnt their ships on arrival, to forbid retreat or return and were determined to stay and become the dominant people of the island. The *Fir Bolg* were probably an early Celtic group, *Belgae* speaking a P-Celtic language [similar to Welsh] and were related linguistically to another Gaulish tribe, the Dumnonnii, also in Ireland around this time. The *Fir Bolg* had a champion called Sreng for their leader and during the fierce fighting, he hacked the arm off the Dé Danann's leader Nuada. This leader is probably the god, Nodens, a deity associated with a population group living along the River Severn in the west of England around the time of the Roman occupation. After the defeat and total rout of the *Fir Bolg*, Nuada's arm was replaced by a silver replica made by the Danann's druid, Dian Cecht with the help of a master blacksmith Credne.

Following their thrashing at a subsequent battle, the *Fir Bolg* only appear in the *Annals* as a scattered population group mainly across Connacht, with a reputation for being 'black-haired, tale-telling, noisy, contemptible, unsteady and churlish'. The N84 from Kilmaine–Ballinrobe forms a northern boundary along what might have been the edge of the battlefield and there are perhaps related burial mounds at Loughanboy, Ballyjennings and Cahercroobeen.

Ballymacgibbon Cairn
OS DISCOVERY SERIES 38.55.18
This 8 m [26 ft] high burial mound was reputedly built to commemorate the first Battle of Moytura, where the incoming Dé

Lough Mask, Co. Mayo, home of the feared 'Onchu' or giant otter.

Danann population, representing perhaps an advance in science and agriculture, fought and defeated the more backward and indigenous *Fir Bolg*. It is over 30 m [98 ft] in diameter, constructed of loose stones in a roughly oval shape, and has several low-standing stones forming an irregular perimeter.

Eochy's Cairn

This curious 50 m [164 ft] in diameter cairn has a later 'chimney' on the summit and legend suggests it is the burial site of a *Fir Bolg* king. It is surrounded by a ditch and bank and has a large *rath* to the east.

Lough Mask

Lake Monster

OS 11M.60.12

The deep and extensive waters of this lake were the home in tradition of the *Onchu*, a fearsome giant water-dog who may have been a form of large otter. The *Onchu*, however, was believed to be a man-eater and its dangerous reputation persisted into the 18th century. The creature was reported on several occasions to have pursued its prey on land and there are several descriptions of a hybrid, dog-like, giant eel that had to be fought off with stones and sticks.

Rosdoagh

[The Wood of the Sand-Bank] **Ritual Circle**

OS 6F.83.39

At Broadhaven, along a remote peninsula of narrow roads lined with fuchsia and yellow butterwort are the low and partially overgrown stone circles of Rosdoagh. These monuments, two circles of 33 and 16 stones respectively, date from the Bronze Age and were probably of religious or symbolic importance. Unlike many other 'henge' monuments, these stones are too low to have been of much astronomical significance but their situation on high ground overlooking the sand bars and estuary of the Glenamoy River is stunning.

Looking toward Broadhaven, Co. Mayo, from the 2,000-year-old stone circle of Rosdoagh.

Ballymacgibbon Cairn, perhaps a passage grave from 2500 BC.

County Sligo *Sligeach*
The Shelly River

Although a small county, Sligo has fine coastal scenery, dramatic mountains and beautiful lakes. Except for its seaward side, the town is encircled by mountains, and lies on the edge of a wooded plain between Lough Gara and the sea. To the north lies the dramatic escarpment of Ben Bulben where Fionn mac Cumhail, a member of the Fianna, hunted. The great woods of Dubhros lay between Ben Bulben and the coast, and provided wild boar and deer for the chase. The Fianna were a war-band, perhaps of Halstatt warriors, who may have been mercenaries to the Irish kings. They were organised into separate 'families' who were often blood enemies, yet sometimes combined to fight others. Fionn, one of their leaders, had a mistress, Sadbh, a goddess and also a daughter of a king of Munster. Sadbh could also shape-change, and as a result of a liaison with Fionn, gave birth to a boy but

Carrowmore, Co. Sligo: a necropolis of over 65 tombs lies east of Knocknarea, the great hill-top cairn of Queen Maeve, who may have been the 'goddess' of the area, watching both the living and the dead.

suckled him as a doe. The boy was Oisín [small deer] and he became a great hunter like his father. The woods around Ben Bulben were reputed to be of *rowan*, the mountain ash, a tree brought to Ireland by the Tuatha Dé Danann and favoured by the druids for divination and also used as a symbolic wand in the inauguration of kings.

Sligo town, first mentioned in 807 when attacked by Vikings, was the main fording point across the broad Garavogue River and lay on the route northwards from Roscommon to Donegal. It was the site of an important battle in 543 AD when a valiant Connacht warrior and prince, Eogan Bel, was killed defending the crossing against the northern Uí Néill. His body was interred upright and armed with his spear in Rath Ua Fiachrach on Knocknarea, facing northwards toward his enemies, thereby preventing them defeating Connacht. After

considering the matter for some time, the Uí Néill disinterred his body, buried it at Lough Gill, and invaded Connacht.

Carrowmore
Ancient City of Dolmens
OS 7G.66.33

This extraordinary site is the largest megalithic cemetery in Ireland with over 65 tombs scattered across a number of fields and alongside modern roads. Many of the tombs have been damaged through re-use for field boundaries but a sufficient number remain to give a sense of the immense importance the site had for the people of 5,000 years ago. These were the first farmers in Ireland and probably cleared the elm forests that existed around Carrowmore at that time. They may have brought the first domesticated cattle to the island and have 'moved on' as resources or land became exhausted or overpopulated.

Creevykeel
Earth Mother
OS 7G.72.54

Situated 8 km [5 miles] from Sligo town, this 70 m [229 ft] structure, when excavated, was found to contain pottery, axes, arrowheads and several cremated burials when excavated in 1937.

Burial chambers and ritual enclosures were of immense importance to their communities, establishing ownership, not only of the bones of their important ancestors, but certainly of the lands surrounding the bones. It is worth noting the shape of these burial chambers, usually called by Irish archaeologists 'court-cairns' or 'lobster-cairns', because if they are viewed from the back, opposite the entrance, upside down, then yes, they do resemble a 'court' or 'lobster' in rough appearance. But if one was to approach many of these structures from the front, as the original users would have done, we see a different shape altogether, that of a reclining female, receptive and awaiting. It would seem perfectly natural that these early agriculturists would see the earth as essentially feminine, and respect this in symbol, thereby combining necropolis and sacred precinct. As the earth was the matriarch who brought forth all living things, so earth mother as sacred structure would seem appropriate for receiving the spirits of her children after death.

Inishmurray
[Muirioch's Island] **Remote Sacred Island**
OS 7G.57.54

This beautiful island lies out in the Atlantic, 6.4 km [4 miles] north-west off Streedagh Point in Co. Sligo. The monastery was founded by St Molaise of Killala in the 6th century and the island had a viable community until 1947. The fierce Atlantic storms did not deter the Vikings who burnt the monastery in 802, but a group of cursing stones placed there subsequently to render a hurt to the northernmen remains.

This unique monastery has a massive surrounding stone wall, 4 m [13 ft] high in places and from 2 m [6.5 ft] to 5 m [16 ft] wide at the base. It contains beehive huts, a primitive church with a Greek cross on its lintel and several other buildings relating to its founding saint. One of these, *Teampuill-na-teinead* ['Church of the Fire'] had a perpetual fire burning in a central hearth,

Creevykeel, built 4,500 years ago as a burial site, perhaps resembling the figure of a reclining woman, a symbol of the religious belief system common to early farming communities.

night and day, with a monk detailed to make sure it was never extinguished. There are over 50 early cross slabs, some with inscriptions in early Irish, probably commemorating local kings rather than monks [Leask, 1955].

Keshcorrigan
Entrance to Otherworld
OS DISCOVERY SERIES 25 72.12

[Near Kesh Village, 6.4 km (4 miles) south of Ballymote] Keshcorrigan caves are hidden on the back of Keshcorran Hill, where in a legend similar to Romulus, a great and early king of Ireland, Cormac Mac Airt was nurtured by a she-wolf. They are accessible via a steep [220 m (722 ft)] climb from the road and will test the endurance of the unfit. They form a series of limestone hollows created many thousands of years ago by water seeping through the porous rock from the hill above and small finds have been made in the caves, especially the largest, which contained wolf, bear, reindeer and human bones. The caves were possibly a ritual site,

representing an entrance to the underworld and feature in the Fianna story where Fionn, the poet Fergus Truelips and the rest of the warrior troop are lured to the cave by three hags, daughters of Conaran, son of Imidel. This putrid trio of magicians, Caevog, Cuillen and Iaran, with *'mouths black and twisted, and a hedge of yellow teeth'* were twisting yarn when the hunters arrived. They ensnared the Fianna in the strands and dragged them inside, the warriors being overcome by a loss of valour and strength. The hunting dogs bayed and howled outside, as the witches produced butchers' knives to gut the warriors . . . and then Goll mac Morna, *'the raging lion, the torch of sunrise, the great of soul'* arrived. For a moment there was a stand-off as the witches circled mac Morna, ready to cut him open. But he was a 'Rambo' of the Bronze Age, a one-man army adept with any weapon and any opponent. The witches rushed at mac Morna but he sidestepped them and cleaved Caevog in two. She fell dead, sliced apart like a piece of red fruit. Her sisters rushed again at mac Morna but he

Inishmurray, an early walled monastery on an island off the Sligo coast, was founded in the 6th century by St Molaise of Killala and had a small separate church for women, outside the walls.

spun and cleaved Cuillen's head from her shoulders. The remaining sister, Iaran, begged for mercy, promising to release the Fianna from the spell if she could live. Mac Morna let her live, but she returned to attack them again and this time he made no mistake.

Knocknarea
Sacred Hill

Three thousand years before the Vikings arrived, the area between Sligo Bay and Lough Gara was heavily populated by a prehistoric farming community. They buried their dead in an elaborate series of tombs covering several townlands and hilltops, culminating in the magnificent Maeve's Cairn at the summit of Knocknarea, 328 m [1,053 ft] above Sligo town. This 55 m [180 ft] diameter cairn is the reputed burial place of Queen Maeve [Maedb] of Connacht, thought to have ruled the west of Ireland in the 1st century AD. She was in the words of W. B. Yeats *'queen of the invisible host, who sleeps high up on Knocknarea, in an old cairn of stones'*. Maeve is often described as having a bird on her shoulder, a Celtic mark of divinity and called 'queen wolf' in respect of her rampant and

devouring nature. Her sexual appetite required a supply of thirty men a day if Fergus, her consort, was away. He had a nickname Ro-ech [great horse] and his member was reputedly so enormous and virile that seven women were required to satisfy him.

Mullaroe

Cnoc na druaid [Red Hill] **Hill of the Druid**
[Overlooking Skreen on the T40] This 17g m [575 ft] hill overlooking the village of Skreen was visited by Daithí, a 5th century king of Ireland on the eve of Samhain [1 November] to ask a seer's advice. He wanted to know what lay ahead during his reign and demanded the druid foretell the future. The druid remained on the summit of the hill all night and returned to inform the king at dawn that he would be 'King of Erin and of Alba' and that he would soon after mount a conquering expedition to Alba [Scotland] and be successful. The *Annals* record that he was [Joyce, 1913].

Rathtinaun Crannóg
Lake Town

In 1952, drainage lowered the level of Lough

Keshcorrigan caves, home to a trio of hags who enticed and attempted to murder a band of the Fianna, the 'freelance' warriors of pre-Christian Ireland.

Gara by as much as 2.5 m [8.2 ft]. This drop in water level revealed almost 400 crannógs [lake dwellings] within the confines of this small lake. Rathtinaun was excavated between 1952 and 1955 by Joseph Raftery and produced material suggesting occupation dating from *c.* 600 BC into the Early Christian period. Included in the finds were hair-rings or ring money, boar tusks and pieces of amber, possibly from the Baltic region. There were suggestions by antiquarians that the crannógs were perhaps interconnected by causeways, thereby forming a 'village' with a water-bound street system.

County Roscommon *Ros Comáin*
Coman's Wood

Maps of early Irish woodland show much of the east of this county to have been a large forested area perhaps some hundreds of square kilometres in extent. The wood, called *Feadha*, stretched along the western shore of Lough Ree taking in where Roscommon town is now and continued north as far as Drumsna in Leitrim. A settlement grew from a small, forest-encircled monastery on the road between the ford at Athlone and Cruachain, the ritual site of the Connachta. It was

The Castlestrange Stone, Co. Roscommon, was probably the religious and ritual centre of a tribal grouping from Europe, of similar origin to those who venerated the Turoe and Killycluggin stones. The stone from Mullaghmast [National Museum, Dublin] has similar 'Celtic' ornamentation.

founded in the 8th century and the county takes its name from the saint who lived there, St Coman.

'A wall of woodland overlooks me;
A blackbird's song sings to me
Over my lined book the trilling of the birds sing to me.'

'A clear-voiced cuckoo sings to me in a cloak of bush-tops;
A lovely utterance. The Lord be good to me on judgment day!
I write well under the woodland trees'
8th century, from a manuscript in the Library of St Gall, Switzerland
[Greene and O'Connor, 1967].

To the west of the great woods was *Magh Da Cheo* [the plain of the mists] between Athleague and Ballyforan, which was 'a place of otherworldly associations'. Roscommon may also have been visited by the Romans for trade and barter, as the name of a townland near the town of Dunmore, *Roymonahan*, is probably the *Rathromanach* [fort of the Romans], granted to the canons of nearby Kilmore by Felim O'Conor, son of Cathal of the Red Hand in 1248 AD. He founded a Dominican friary near to St Coman's monastery and was buried there in 1265.

Castlestrange Stone
Celtic Ritual Stone
OS 12M.82.60

This rounded boulder, approximately 90 cm high, is one of a series of decorated stones dating to the Early Christian centuries. Its art style, showing stylised leaves and leaf-forms, is similar to the Turoe stone of Galway, Killycluggin stone in Cavan and the Mullaghmast stone of Kildare. Little is known about the significance of these stones, but the conclusion would seem to be ritual use, perhaps related to a particular place and tribe. The art displayed on these stones is also similar to some metalwork of the La Tène period between the 1st and 3rd centuries AD.

Cruachain

5th-Century Royal Burial Ground, Ritual Centre and Fortress

OS 12M.80.84

[Both sides of N5 Tulsk–Bellanagare] This complex, extensive and mysterious site covers several hundred acres across townlands in Co. Roscommon. The site was probably the residence, ritual site, royal burial ground and assembly place for the Connachta, the dominant tribe west of the Shannon. Their royal descent, from the legendary Conn of the Hundred Battles, gave them a patrimony extending over several hundred square kilometres and their probable descendants, the O'Conor Don family of [nearby] Clonalis, remain to this day. The site itself is dispersed covering a time span of several thousand years, from Neolithic burial mounds to standing stones. Its most outstanding features are the Rathcroghan Mound and several linear earthworks, broadly converging toward the mound itself. The mound is some 85 m [279 ft] in diameter and ground probing radar has detected a complex series of enclosures within its mass. In addition, the radar has revealed a surrounding trench with a diameter of about 370 m [1,214 ft] [Waddell, 2000].

Surrounding the immediate *c.* 800 ha site is a complex underlay of ancient field systems extending eastwards from the ritual complex and the major ringforts at Relignaree and Cruachain. In general, the field boundaries form a grid pattern covering several square kilometres and as mapped by Michael Herity suggest centralised planning focused on the royal site at its perimeter. This would suggest a continuously settled community with a structured management of its resources and the willingness to devote considerable energy to laying out

The Rath of Mewlaghdooey Hill, one of the many sites associated with Cruachain and close to Rathra, a triple-banked example with interior burial mounds.

The entrance to the underworld, where the shamans of Cruachain would descend and communicate with their spirit messengers, to re-emerge with visions of the future.

ringforts and eight Early Christian sites in the area, in addition to stone forts, crannógs and souterrains.

Without doubt, Cruachain was a sacred and ritual site for the ruling dynasty of Connacht and remained important into the historical period. It has features similar to other royal sites and probably had certain feasts and celebrations for the members of the tribe to become 'bound' to each other and their king. It was the residence of the legendary Queen Maeve of Connacht, and described in ancient stories as having 'halls' for visitors, being 'magnificent' and 'luxurious'.

Approximately 15 per cent of the site has been destroyed by land clearance, but this is an average figure for the country as a whole and lower than some parts of Ireland which are more viable for arable farming [Herity, 1987].

Rathra
Ritual Site
OS 12.79.72

[4.8 km (3 miles) west of Castlerea] This large fort to the side of Mewlaghadooey Hill has an external diameter of 154 m [505 ft] enclosing a habitation site of some 93 m [305 ft] across its north-west to south-east axis. It is of some importance, given it has a four-bank construction and at first sight appears as the type of ringfort one might expect at the entrance to a 'tuath', a place that the king's warriors might use as a barracks, customs post and frontier fort — the difference being that Rathra has two burial mounds within its large circumference and is on the weather side of the hill, exposed to the westerly rain-bearing winds. The presence of the burial mounds would indicate that the site was primarily ritual in purpose rather than defensive and is probably related to the Cruachain site to the east.

earth and stone banks, often extending for several kilometres in length. There are a total of 70 monuments in the area, including three megalithic tombs, ten Bronze-Age tumulii, 35 ring barrows [burial sites], six cairns, five standing stones, three avenues, five large embanked enclosures, and linear earthworks known as the Mucklaghs. In terms of the period beginning around the 1st century AD, in addition to all the foregoing, there are 134

Shad Lake
Ritual Water Site
[2 km (1.2 miles) west from N61] This small lake lies to the south of the great ritual site of Cruachain and was probably a ritual water site related to the local dynasty. Although little is known about this secluded and eerie location, its name may suggest a similar function to Loughnashade near Eamhain Mhaca, a cult site associated with the ancient centre of Ulaidh influence in the last centuries BC. Lakes such as these were often used for animal and sometimes human sacrifice, with ritual votive deposits to placate or thank the gods for their influence over animal fertility, crop maturity and opponents in war.

Sliabh Bawn
Early Celtic Habitation Site
This 260 m [853 ft] hill was, according to the *Annals*, the tribal area of a branch of the *Fir Bolg*, an early population grouping traditionally associated with trades and crafts. They were seen in a poor light by the Celts who defeated these 'noisy, contemptible, harsh and inhospitable people' upon arriving on the island of Ireland [MacNeill, 1920]. They were perhaps a mainly artisan caste, in that their name suggests 'bagmen' and the manufacture of bags from hide or leather, while not an esteemed occupation according to the Celts, was nevertheless an important and necessary trade.

The hill lies between the bogs of Mount Dillon to the east and the former great oak-woods of northern Roscommon, which stretched northwards from Lough Ree to where Strokestown now stands. The land bordering on the Scramoge River and its tributaries is particularly rich in habitation sites, with over 50 examples of ringforts in the general area west of Sliabh Bawn. There is a barrow on nearby Kilmacduagh [140 m (459 ft)] and this may have been the burial site of the tribal leaders.

Part of the rampart of Rathra, the great triple-rampart fort in the Cruachain complex.

The Province of Munster

Burial mound at Lattin, Co. Tipperary, an outlying tomb at the edge of the Barrow necropolis of the Eoghanachta Áine.

From *c.* 2500 BC miners began to arrive on the southern shores of Ireland seeking copper ore in the mountains of west Cork and Kerry. They sailed their hide boats into Roaringwater Bay and eventually established mines on Mount Gabriel and further south along the Mizen Peninsula. They used sulphite ores of copper alloyed with arsenic [Herity and Eogan, 1997] to manufacture axe heads and their metal-working skills may have applied to gold also. Their wedge-shaped tombs and the Beaker pottery found on their habitation sites suggest that they lived and worked on these peninsulas for over 500 years. They may possibly have come from Brittany, as similar tomb-types exist on that peninsula, although after time had passed a native style would have developed through innovation. Similar tombs exist in Clare on land suitable for winter grazing, suggesting farming rather than mining and probably form a later group as miners became pastoralists. The tomb style

continues northwards along the west coast and into the interior of Ulster.

Population Groups

The province of Munster, like other provinces of Ireland, was until its 'official' creation, a collection of tribal territories and independent fiefdoms [tuath]. According to the ancient annals, there were five major population groups spread across what are now the counties of Kerry, Clare, Limerick, Tipperary, Cork and Waterford. These were the different septs of the Eoghanacht, descendants of Eogan Mor, whose alleged victory at the Battle of Maynooth *c.* 123 AD forced the king, Conn of the Hundred Battles, to divide Ireland in half, with Eogan taking the southern half. The Eoghanacht, in common with other dynasties attempted to establish a pedigree in keeping with their presumed descent from an original founder, in this case Eber. Unfortunately, their propaganda was of an inferior sort and conflicting pedigrees, confused descent and a lack of ambition combined to render their particular epic a local story rather than a national tale. Perhaps their origins may have been along the River Meuse, near Namur in northern France, where the Eburones, a Belgic tribe, suffered defeat by Caesar in 54 BC [see Cashel entry].

Munster's original inhabitants who came for the copper ore of west Cork and Kerry probably survived as smaller ethnic groups and peoples such as the *Corca Baiscind*, and the *Cedrigh* may have been their descendants. The valley of the River Lee was the territory of the powerful Eoghanacht Rathlind, divided between their two septs of Uí Loegairí to the west and Cenel nAeda between Cork and Kinsale. The inhabitants of Munster who

Munster has the greatest collection of Ogham stones, coded inscriptions about fallen warriors or nobles, usually Christian but sometimes dedicated to the goddess Dovinia. These examples were originally from Smerwick, Co. Kerry.

preceded the Eoghanacht ended up paying tributes to them as overlords and this was a constant source of irritation and anger, resulting in sporadic warfare and retaliation. Iberia appears to be the likely origin for some at least of the Munster population groups, and if the Early Bronze Age miners were of Iberian origin, then a precedent had been set for travel to Ireland, much as emigrants today travel to countries with a tradition of accepting their kith and kin.

Celts of some form, perhaps the Eoghanacht, returning after perhaps three or four centuries in Britain, arrived in the last centuries BC probably landing along the River Lee and spreading through the landscape, dividing into separate groups as they did so. The Deisi of Waterford probably became their vassals. But evidence of La Tène material in the southern part of Ireland is extremely scarce and a more likely theory is that Munster remained a largely Bronze Age society with only a gradual infusion of Celtic population groups, perhaps from within Ireland itself. There is evidence within the manuscripts of the arrival of scattered groups from Ulster after the fall of Eamhain Mhaca in the early 4th century and the *Corcu Ochae*, renowned as harpists in a later era, claimed Ulaidh origins. Another possible pre-Celtic group, the *Ciarraigh*, reputed to be 'small and dark', inhabited the western peninsulas and the mountains now known as McGillicuddy's Reeks. These peoples and the *Corcu Duibne* and Uí *Cairpri Luachra* were possibly the vassals of the builders of the great hilltop forts, which date to around 1000 BC and which are more numerous in Munster than the other provinces. Although evidence is scarce, it seems reasonable to suggest that some of these hillforts were centres of continuous occupation, not merely ritual and ceremonial sites.

Stone Circles

The province also has the largest groupings of stone circles on the island and shares this geographic distinction with mid-Ulster. The largest of these in Grange townland in Limerick is 45.7 m [150 ft] in diameter and has 113 stone uprights. This site was presumed to be purely ritual as no habitation evidence was found [Ó Ríordáin, 1966]. Several of the circles contained human and animal bones and circle K near Lough Gur had exclusively the bones of children, without any grave goods. In common with many stone circles, the most prominent stone usually faced the entrance which was orientated toward the sun. The main axis of the circle at Drombeg, Co. Cork faces the midwinter sunset and adjacent to the circle was a *fulacht fiadh*, an ancient cooking site utilising hot stones in water. Perhaps feasting was an important part of the observatory ritual.

Mythology and Legend

Munster in general has always been relatively separate from its sister provinces, in that its peoples looked south to Europe rather than north or west, and from the earliest times had trading links to the continent. Munster has its own heroic sagas and its own manuscript, the *Annals of Inisfallen* whose focus is on things southerly. Munster had continuing links to the Benedictine community at Regensburg in Germany, and some of their artisans may have worked on Cormac's Chapel during 1130–1134. Their Eoghanacht kings, the MacCarthaighs, travelled to Europe becoming familiar with the court of Charlemagne and were considerably more sophisticated than either their Tara or Ulster rivals. Cu Roi, a Munster deity, was one of the gods who possessed a magic cauldron, and like the cauldron of the Dagdas, no-one who ate from it went away unsatisfied. The favourite Munster deity was, and perhaps still is, Áine, 'the sparkling one' whose hill, Cnoc Áine, is about 28.8 km [18 miles] south-west of Limerick city. South of the hill and stretching across several townlands is an extensive Bronze Age barrow cemetery containing over 200 graves from *c.* 2000 BC. They may represent burial grounds for distinctive and separate communities, with the barrow placed at the periphery of the territory, usually near a natural boundary. In this attractive, well cultivated but eerie landscape, the Morningstar River meanders between the villages of Bruff and Elton like the River Styx separating the living and the dead.

The Rock of Cashel, Munster's royal citadel, is probably the finest collection of mediaeval buildings in Ireland and was originally a seat of power for the Eoghanacht, the tribal group ultimately overtaken by the ambitious Dalcassians, ancestors of the O'Briens. Throughout the period when the northern part of the island was striven by rivalries between Ulster and Connacht, Munster enjoyed a peace and prosperity throughout much of the pre-Christian period, and this may have been due to the strong and consistent nature of its leadership. Munster was a base for the Vikings, and Norse and Danish settlements were established at Waterford, Cork and Limerick in the 9th century. They had realised by the 10th century that more money could be made from trade and commerce than the continuous raiding which ultimately destroyed the source of the wealth. A Munster king, Feidlimid mac Crimthainn was, however, quick to notice that there was no divine retribution against pillaging monasteries and he tried his hand at the same trade. He burnt the monastery of Kildare in 836 and the monastery of Clonmacnoise in 832 and 846. At that particular time, he was reputed to have murdered the vice-abbot, the vice-abbot's wife, his servant and his dog.

Munster Counties and Sites

Cork *Corcaigh*
The Swamp or Marshy Ground [County and City]

This large county was possibly populated by a tribal grouping identified as Iverni by Ptolemy, who created his [now] well-known map in the 2nd century AD. These Iverni may have been small groups of Celts from southern Europe, possibly Iberia, but the size of the county meant that other tribes, Coriondi or Coritani [Celtic tribes already in north Wales] could settle in the eastern part of the county without causing disarray. If, as seems possible, the 'Celts' of Munster had experience of dealing with imperial Rome before settling in the southern part of Ireland, it might be a reason for Munster's relative peace and prosperity, as many tribes thrived through trade with the empire, and a Scandinavian tribe, the Suiones, were reputedly wealthy through trade with and through the Roman empire. The county also has an Early Christian monastery founded by the son of a Saxon prince, St Berchert at Tullylease [3 km (1.9 miles) from Broadford on L71 Kanturk road] which contains the finest Early Christian grave slab in the country, whose 9th century inscription reads; QUICUMQUE LEGERIT HUNC TITULUM ORAT PRO BERECHTUIRE — *'whoever reads this inscription, let him pray for Berichter'* [Henry, 1940]. In the historic period, the area around Baltimore and much of coastal west Cork was the territory of the Corco Loigde, whose tradition suggested they had been the Brehons or lawyers to the ruling Eoghanacht dynasties of Munster. St Cíarán of Saighir was of the Corco Loigde as was St Declan of Ardmore, although this Christian tradition did not prevent their mediaeval descendants, the O'Driscolls, from having a thriving maritime trade in fishing and piracy [Byrne, 1973].

Cork became the destination for the early miners and their families who probably left Brittany or northern Spain around 1500 BC in pursuit of a better life. They would have travelled in open boats, probably of hide and similar to the larger currachs still operating today around Connemara. The mines they worked on Mount Gabriel are the only existing prehistoric copper mines in Europe, except for some in Austria, and so far 25 mine shafts have been found on the mountain. Archaeologists would suggest that Ireland was an exporter of copper 3,000 years ago and control over this valuable resource would have required considerable social organisation and familiarity with sea-routes and trading ports. The many stone circles and wedge-tombs in Munster have been suggested as having a connection with the 'miners' but no bronze or copper implements or artefacts have been found on these sites to correlate the sites and their possible users [Harbison, 1988].

Ancient Cooking Sites
The county also contains over 2,000 *fulacht fiadh*, possibly cooking or domestic sites, the earliest of which date from the 2nd millennium BC. These mysterious burnt mounds, generally of a crescent shape and 1 m high, occur in great numbers west of Cork city and there are dozens in the landscape between Coachford and the Boggeragh Mountains. The sheer volume of these enigmatic sites would suggest domestic use, and may have been sweat-houses, bath-houses, cooking sites or related to some form of temporary dwelling. They are usually found near standing stones and the *fulacht fiadh* which occur in profusion between Buttevant and Liscarroll in north Cork have over 50 stone

monoliths adjacent to them. Between Blarney and Macroom is a landscape of extraordinary complexity in terms of its prehistoric content. Again, we find *fulacht fiadh* in profusion and adjacent standing stones. They are also contemporary with ring barrow burials and suggest, especially in Munster, a settled society with specific areas for habitation, ritual and burial. Division of land according to tribal identity was a feature of Munster and the Claidhe Dubh, a 24 km [15 miles] earthwork which runs from north of Charleville to Carrigtwohill in east Cork, possibly separated different ethnic groups or antagonistic tribes.

War-Horns

A particular and unique Irish musical 'instrument' dating to the Bronze Age and found across Munster and Cork in particular are bronze horns usable for perhaps war, or maybe entertainment. The range of notes possible would appear to be limited, but impressive in tone and depth of sound. They are probably derived from cattle-horns in shape and function, and each tribal group may have had their own particular sound, exclusive to them. This writer feels that mediaeval *war-cries* such as 'ODonel Abu' are a rhetorical version of an acoustic threat, which the war-horns would have been capable of sending across large distances, in the electronically and mechanically silent spaces of the Bronze Age.

Ancient Farming

Ringfort settlement of *c.* 200 AD is below the national average in Munster, although there are areas, between the valley of the Lee and the River Bandon for example, that have a high density of these early farmsteads. The sites chosen, usually between 30 m [98 ft] and 120 m [394 ft] above sea-level, would correspond to well-drained and productive brown earth. It is also possible that the pattern of ringforts which appear to advance along the river valleys from the coast may suggest incomers gradually infiltrating the hinterland as these farming communities grew and took over more land. Large areas of Munster where ringforts are scarce may have retained their woodland cover or have been the territory of previous inhabitants.

Ballycrovane
Prince-Warrior's Grave
OS V.24.66.53

This is one of the most graceful Ogham stones in Munster. Instead of a lichened and crouched example, this proud monolith stretches to 5.3 m [17 ft]. Its inscription, translated from Ogham into Latin reads: MAQI-DECCEDDAS AVI TURANIAS *Of the Son of Deich Descendant of Torainn*. This was probably one of the Deisi princes who were perhaps a pre-Celtic vassal tribe, turned into tribute payers after the Eoghanacht became dominant.

Carraigcleena
Banshee Rock

The banshee Cliona has her residence at this 233 m [764 ft] outcrop, 10 km [6.3 miles] south-southwest of Mallow on the R619 and a great rock on the south-east end of the hill is reputedly the entrance to the underworld. Two standing stones stand guard at the western 'entrance' to the banshee's hill and the Munster walking route, the Avondhu Way, passes close by.

Bronze horns, for war or ceremonial use, from Antrim and Kerry, c. 700 BC.

Labbacallee,
Leaba na
Cailleach, *the bed
of the witch, a
3,500-year-old
tomb. It was
probably the
ceremonial and
burial site for a
dominant grouping
in the Fermoy area,
possibly the Fir
Maige Féne, part
of whose territory
was taken by the
Eoghanacht in the
early Christian
period.*

The Claidhe Dubh
2,200-Year-Old Frontier

OS 8.99.71

[N72 Castletownroche–Ballyhooley] Sometime in the centuries preceding Christianity, it was found necessary to create a frontier across the Cork landscape. This 24 km [15 miles] double-ditch and bank is now discontinuous, but parts of it are reasonably intact, particularly the 22 km [13.7 miles] part that runs from the Ballyhoura Hills to Nagles Mountains. The rampart is similar, if smaller, in scale to the *Black Pigs Dyke*, a frontier that was created to protect Ulster from the predatory Connachta, and the peoples who built the Claidhe Dubh may have been equally threatened by other, more aggressive tribes.

Difficulties always existed between the Eoghanacht Glendamhnach, based at Glenworth and the Fir Maige Féne of Fermoy, and the Claidhe Dubh may have been the 'border' between their territories.

Cork City

St Finbarr founded a monastery on an island in the River Lee south-west of the present city centre in the 6th century and the tower of his monastery survived until St Finbarr's Cathedral was built in 1867. His monastery suffered from Viking raids in 820, 838, 845 and several times again by the Vikings who wintered on an island in the marsh [*corcach*] in 846. These Norse Vikings returned in 917 and established a permanent base on the island thus beginning 'Corcaigh' as a centre of trade and settlement. The monastery was the setting for the 12th century *Vision of Tundale*, a popular piece of mediaeval 'vision' literature, being translated into Norse, German, French, Anglo-Norman and varieties of English.

Drombeg
Solstice Observatory
OS W.24.25.35

This fine circle is beautifully situated in gently rolling countryside in west Cork. The 17 stones are irregular and the primary stone is facing the 'entrance' which is aligned toward the mid-winter solstice on 21 December. It was probably made in the last century before the Christian era and was used for seasonal hunting. The circle may have formed part of a 'hunting camp' as a *fulacht fiadh* or ancient cooking place is situated beside the circle. These cooking sites could heat water to boiling point in 35 minutes using heated stones and were re-used over many seasons and perhaps generations.

Fermoy
Conflict Area Between Descendants of Druids
This peaceful riverside town was the centre of the tribal territory of *Fir Maige Féne*, a group claiming descent from a druid's disciple called Simon Magus. They were antagonistic toward the Eoghanacht, the dominant tribe of Munster, and fought several different branches of that dynasty at various times to maintain their independence. The ancestors of the Eoghanacht branches of Uí Fidgenti and Uí Liathain, between whose lands lay the aggressive Fir Maige Féne, were twins, Maine Munchain and Daire Cerbba, whose later genealogical tracts claimed them as cousins of the Eoghanacht ancestor, Conall Corc. This illustrious duo germinated back to back in their mother's womb with a chafer beetle, the seed of the druid Mug Roith between them, 'so that neither could come to the aid of the other'. The

reason for the Fir Maige's belligerence appears to be that they were not a 'Free State' on account of them not being of the royal blood of the Eoghanacht and were caught between two branches of that family, who to them were usurpers. They were also obliged to offer tribute to the Eoghanacht kings at Cashel during the Early Christian centuries and had to provide on a yearly basis 100 cows, 100 hogs and 100 mantles or 'great cloaks'.

Glandore
Banshee Cave
Glandore was the spot where Cliona, the banshee of south Munster, lost her mortal life while sleeping on the beach awaiting her husband's return. She was drowned by a giant wave, the 'Tonn Cliona', and at certain times the caverns under the cliffs of Glandore are believed to utter a melancholy roar, mourning her death. Cliona is the primary banshee of this area and wails for old Irish or Hiberno-Norman aristocratic families whose head of household is about to die. Most aural manifestations of the banshee take place during the time before dawn, or at dusk, times that are neither day nor night, but sometimes she is met 'on the road' and anyone meeting a fairy woman at night in west Cork would expect to be told; *Biodh an la agatsa agus an oíche againn–*, 'You have the day and we have the night'.

Part of the Claidhe Dubh, an earthen boundary that runs for 42 km from the Nagles Mountains to the Ballyhoura Hills. It may have continued further south toward Dungarvan, the limit of the Fir Maige Féne's claimed territory.

SECRET SIGHTS — *Unknown Celtic Ireland*

This beautiful and secluded spot is opposite the hard-working fishing harbour of Union Hall, transformed by local enterprise and initiative into a self-sufficient community with several modern fishing vessels and a thriving co-op.

Labbacallee

Leaba na Cailleach [The Bed of the Witch]
4,500-Year-Old Witch Burial Site
OS 22R.78.02

This 14 m [46 ft] long wedge-shaped tomb, lying on the old road between Glanworth and Fermoy, was first excavated in 1934 and found to contain, as a primary burial, the body of a woman. It would suggest that the local name was derived from very ancient times, as this tomb dates from *c.* 2500 BC. The tomb sits on a gentle slope which declines gradually toward the River Funshion, less than half a kilometre away. It was probably the burial mound of the founder of the population group whose territory was bounded by the Funshion and Blackwater River systems. As such, they were establishing their ownership of the area through placing an important tomb at the frontier of their lands.

County Limerick *Laemrich* [Norse]
Rich Soil [City and County]

The city appears first as a Danish settlement of the 9th century on the land where St Mary's Cathedral now stands. There is a possibility it was originally called *Odin's Island* [Inis Sibtond] because the Vikings made this small island a centre from which they could attack the Shannon basin and areas further north. It was Vikings from Limerick under their leader, Turgesius, who burned Clonmacnoise in 844. His fleet established a permanent base in Lough Ree, further up the Shannon. The names *Hlimerk, Allymrick* may refer to *Laemrich*, the Norse word for rich soil. Alternatively, *Luimneach* [grey marsh] is a Gaelic word applied to the mouth of the Shannon and its general estuary area. It may

be the *Regia* of Ptolemy's 2nd-century map and was probably the southern boundary of Connacht and the limit of influence of its ruling dynasties. The Vikings who established the city became rich and the more flamboyant males wore massive gold armlets, 5 kg of which [later melted down] were found on an island in the Shannon in 1836.

War Bands

The great plain that lies south of the town of Croom was a hunting ground of the Fianna, a curious rhetorical fifth-column, outside yet inside early history. In general they are seen to have been a group of unattached male hunters, who sometimes acted as bodyguards to kings and nobles but otherwise lived outside of the clans and tribal groupings, acting perhaps as a 'outlaw' band, a grouping of landless, but high-born warriors. Knockfeerina, a 288 m [945 ft] hill near Ballingarry was a favourite place for their camps and a vantage point for watching the chase across the plain below. The Fianna story of 'The Castle of the Rowan Trees' takes place in the area between Knockfeerina and the Shannon, the land of Midac, a youth who establishes a magical kingdom to revenge his father's death at the hand of Fionn, the leader of the Fianna. The townland of Cush, 3 km [1.9 miles] north of Kilfinnane [near Kilmallock], contains an elaborate and complex series of ancient fields and enclosures dating from *c.* 800 bc to 400 AD. Rotary querns, glass beads and a Bronze-Age urn were found during excavations by the late Sean P. O'Riordain in the 1930s. Presumably they cleared the trees from the fertile and drier soils before planting their crops of rye and wheat.

Grange
Ritual Henge
OS 18R.64.41

This 610 m [2,000 ft] diameter circle is impressive in its rough-hewn appearance. It was

Opposite page: Drombeg Stone Circle, a focus for hunting groups in west Cork and possibly a habitation and ritual site also.

a ritual site of importance for the Bronze Age community around Lough Gur and was probably constructed around 1800 BC [O'Riordan, 1966]. The stones reach a height of 3 m [9.8 ft] and the surrounding bank of earth is 6 m [19.6 ft] wide in places. The pottery fragments found in the circle 'floor' [raised 50 cm above ground level to achieve a level surface] were from the Beaker period beginning around 2400 BC. These pieces of ceramic ware have similarities with Beakers from other Irish sites and examples in Europe would suggest that localities had a design unique to their area. The distribution of pots from this period has suggested a movement across Europe of a Beaker culture, but folk movements are hard to prove and many new styles of pottery and manufacturing techniques may have 'travelled' through marriage and social contacts rather than widescale emigration [Waddell, 2000].

Opposite page: The massive stone of Crom, the god of the circle of Grange, Co. Limerick, dating from around 1800 BC.

Knockainey

Cnoc Áine [Áine's Hill] **Hill of the Goddess**
OS DISCOVERY SERIES 65.68.36
This graceful and rounded hill rises from a fertile plain south of Lough Gur and is about 25 km [15.6 miles] south-southeast from Limerick City. It was, in ancient pre-historic times, the sacred hill of Áine, the beautiful goddess of Munster and the 161 m [528 ft] summit was the site for festivities held through the centuries on St John's Eve, 23 June. In the Celtic period, Cnoc Áine was the centre of power of the *Eoghanacht Áine Cliach*, a subsidiary tribal grouping of the Eoghanacht dynasties of Munster whose main citadel was the Rock of Cashel. This virile and capable Celtic grouping came to power perhaps in the 5th century and may have been early arrivals sometime in the 1st century BC. They were one of the important groupings of peoples on the island in the Early Christian centuries, and traditionally held themselves to be of different stock to the *Connachta*, west of the Shannon, the *Laighen* of Leinster, the *Ulaidh* of Ulster and especially the *Féni* of the midlands.

Their goddess, Áine, was, in the tradition of celtic goddesses, of a complex nature, her character being interwoven with hunting prowess, fertility and death itself. She would have been their territorial focus and their rulers would have sworn fealty to her, in order to ensure fertility of crops, animals and the Eoghanacht themselves.

Lough Gur
Ancient Habitation Site
This was possibly the last place where the brown bear survived in Ireland, perhaps up to 1800 BC. The complex site was inhabited from the Stone Age up to the Early Christian era and has reconstructions and a comprehensive visitors site which is most explanatory. It lies to the north of Cnoc Áine, the sacred hill of the area and has hilltop cairns, stone circles, field systems, burial mounds, a crannóg, a standing stone and many others of varying degrees of preservation and access. Near the sunken trackway known as *Cladh na Leach* was found a pair of bronze chariot fittings, suitable for the end of the shafts of a light one-horse vehicle.

Mitchelstowndown North
Barrow Necropolis
[R663 Galbally–Hospital road] This area, between the hamlets of Pinkers Cross and Knocklong, contains perhaps several hundred barrow tombs from the Bronze Age and in concert with other cemeteries in the Limerick/north Cork area, constitute the largest number of ring-ditches in the country. These burial sites probably belong to different but related tribal groups who chose to bury their dead in a local sepulchre on the poorer land in their area. This ancient cemetery is not signposted and does not have any major distinguishing features but it was a major necropolis for the ruling families of a large area of productive land over 3,000 years ago. The tribal groupings based on Cnoc Áine were

SECRET SIGHTS — *Unknown Celtic Ireland*

The graceful hill of Knockainey, 'the hill of the goddess Áine', a particularly numinous site, undisturbed and rarely visited.

probably the owners of this area and the considerable area of this cemetery would suggest that they were established in this part of Limerick during the Early Bronze Age. Cooney and Grogan [Wordwell, 1994] make the interesting point that the siting of these burial mounds in less prominent places than previous societies represents a 'retreat' of the ancestors from a central position in the tribe and a downgrading of their relevance and power. Perhaps as time passed between arrival on the island and the establishment of a viable community, the reverence due to the founders decreased, with a subsequent geographic distance created between ancestor and descendant. Further data from associated and similar areas suggest a communal sense of identity related to area, with a concurrent raising in status of the individual. The rite of burial was generally inhumation, with the body being lightly covered so as to disappear without trace. This form of burial, so extensive in this part of Limerick, is well-known in Britain as *bell-barrow* and *ring-barrow* burial and are especially dominant in Wessex [O'Riordan, 1966].

County Kerry *Ciarraí*
The [Territory] Race of Ciar

Kerry is the county in Ireland that has what every other Irish county wants . . . beaches, mountains, rivers, lakes, pretty towns, a tourist industry and more besides. It holds every kind of antiquity and the Dingle Peninsula alone has Ogham stones, beehive oratories, stone forts and legend and folklore in great quantities. Up to the 17th century, the county also had great woodland, especially along the Shannon to Ballylongford, from Listowel to the Stack Mountains, to Tralee, and up the Maine Valley to Castleisland. In the Middle Ages, Dingle was a great port for exporting fish, beef, hides and tallow, with a return trade in wine, swords and firearms.

Population Groups

In the centuries preceding the Christian era, Kerry was the place where the *Fir Bolg* reputedly settled after landing in Cork. These people, the principal inhabitants of south Munster, peopled most of Kerry and parts of Cork and Limerick also. They were probably a group of the Belgae, a tribe from northern France who were described as 'small, dark and boorish' by later Celtic arrivals. The *Fir Bolg*, however, may be responsible for at least one of the great traditions of Irish mythology — The Fenian Cycle. It would appear that these particular stories were the 'soap operas' of the subject peoples, the two-thirds of the Irish race that paid rent or tribute to the ruling dynasties and tribes. The Fianna stories had three locations or origins, Tara in Meath, around parts of Leinster and among the Corcu Duibne peoples of south and west Kerry. It was therefore appropriate that Fionn, the great leader of the Fianna, should have chosen to die among them when his time came [Barrington, 1976].

The Kenmare River was reputedly the landing place for later Celtic tribes who, arriving with gifts of food and wine, were welcomed by the indigenous Belgae who dismissed their own kings! Kerry thus came to have several ancient tribal groups scattered across its headlands, mountains and river valleys; the Ciarraigh, possibly a Pictish group from Ulster, the Corcu Duibne or Belgae and the Eoghanacht Loch Leinn. This last group ultimately became rulers of Munster, imposing their will on the aforementioned Ciarraigh etc. and also levying tribute on the Uí Fearba, Alltraigh and Uí dTorna, obscure tribes whose origins are not 'inserted' into later pedigrees.

Caherconree
Druid's Fortress
OS DISCOVERY SERIES 71.73.06

This hillfort in the Sliabh Mish Mountains is reputedly the burial place of the magician Cú Roi Mac Daire, who may also have been divine, as he was supposedly the forerunner of the *Fir Bolg* or Belgae, a Celtic tribal group prominent in Belgium and the north of England. Cú Roi was also the reputed leader of a group called [according to the antiquarian O'Curry] the '*Degads*', a 3rd-century militaristic band similar to the Fianna of Leinster and the Red Branch Knights of Ulster. Cú Roi, who had absconded with a beautiful woman, Blaithnid, was pursued to Caherconree by Cú Chulainn, a warrior from Ulster, who was in love with the same girl. He hid beneath the fortress and Blaithnid signalled him to attack by pouring milk into the stream that flowed down from the fort. In the melee, Cú Roi was killed and Cú Chulainn escaped with Blaithnid. Cú Roi had a druid, however, who saw his master being killed and followed Cú Chulainn northwards. After some weeks, he seized the moment and grasping Blaithnid, flung himself and the girl over a cliff, killing both. Cú Roi's son, Lugaid, reputedly flung the spear that mortally wounded Cú Chulainn near Dundalk, where the Clochafarmore stands [see Louth entry].

Cloghane Church
Pagan God
OS DISCOVERY SERIES 70.51.11

[West of Brandon Mountain] This ruinous church contained one of the few representations of an ancient yet identifiable god, Crom Dubh. Within living memory of many people of the Dingle Peninsula, the last Sunday in July was Domhnach Chrom Dubh, the Sunday of Black Crom and a day for a pilgrimage to the top of Brandon Mountain. The return trip was by way of Cloghane Village which had a Protestant church. In the ruined chancel of the church was a pagan face, that of a Celtic god of some variety, perhaps Crom himself. The head was stolen in 1996.

Kilmalkedar
7th-Century Sundial
OS DISCOVERY SERIES 70.40.07

This ancient monastic site was established by St

Maolcethair, a noted saint who died in the year 636. It contains early Romanesque decoration in the form of blind colonnades in the nave and the decorative treatment of the chancel arch. The stone antae of the roof truss with its animal decoration is a good example of the style also. Outside, there is a sundial marked into the sections of the monastic day and an Ogham stone dedicated to Mael Inbir, son of Brocán [Harbison, 1992].

Knockanore
Battle Site
[Inland from Ballybunnion, access from R253]

This 267 m [876 ft] hill was the scene of a famous battle between the Fianna, the 'elite' soldiers of Irish kings, and a sea-borne force pursuing a princess, reputedly from Greece. This girl, fleeing her husband, begged the Fianna for help and they, being warriors, obliged. The captain of the sea-borne soldiers challenged the leader of the Fianna to single combat and this was agreed, the Fianna sending out their oldest and slowest warrior as a joke. This warrior, Conan mac Morna was old and bald and a coward by Fianna standards, but he was cute. He stumbled toward the champion of the opposition and appeared aged and weary. His opponent, Liagan, laughed at him and the manuscripts quote him as saying, 'Silly is thy visit, thou bald old man'. Conan looked up and with a look of surprise said 'Truly … thou art in more peril from him behind you, than him in front.' Liagan looked around and with one blow, Conan the Bald sliced off his head. He then threw his sword at the enemy and ran behind the ranks of the laughing Fianna. The two sides then rushed at each other and fought until exhaustion, leaving only a few standing. Among those killed was the husband of the princess who had started all the fighting. When she found that her husband had been slain, she, in true tragic fashion, died of grief. Unfortunately, her father and father-in-law arrived by boat the next day and they demanded

The remote and enigmatic fort of Staigue, similar to Aileach in Donegal and the forts of the Aran Islands. Possibly constructed by Belgae of the 1st century BC.

satisfaction from the Fianna for the deaths of princess and husband. This resulted in yet more contests, bloodshed and bodies. Eventually the mothers of the princess and her late husband arrived and their pleading succeeded in cooling the tempers of all. Over 1,000 warriors were slain during that ferocious contest and they lie buried somewhere on the side of the hill, Knockanore, the *Hill of the Slaughter*.

Naisi's Grave
3,500-Year-Old Royal Grave

Many varieties of these early tombs exist, suggesting particular arrivals brought with them a burial mode unique to their cultural group, although classes of tombs could also suggest derivatives of design according to local taste and choice of layout. Although no European tomb has been shown to be decisively a prototype for the developments in Ireland, European examples are accepted as a cultural forerunner of the Irish tomb type. The people who built these tombs had ideas about communal burial and their monuments exceed over 1,000 known examples. Curiously, a type of tomb described as *portal* and *court* tombs by their having a crescent enclosure at the entrance, are to found mainly north of a line from Dundalk to Westport, while their wedge-shaped cousins numbering over 500 or so are more common in the south and west of the country, especially in counties Sligo and Clare. Assuming the closest groupings cluster near the point of entry, it would suggest Killala Bay and the Shannon Estuary for the western examples and perhaps Carlingford Lough for the eastern. Similar burial structures exist in Scotland, south Wales and the west of England, and it is debatable as to whether they inspired the Irish examples or

vice versa, or whether all share a stylistic inheritance from the Mediterranean and Iberian passage grave culture. There are several theories that these tomb builders were miners, as their European counterparts often sited their tombs near to tin or other metal sources. The numerous Munster examples cluster near tin deposits and we could speculate that they were drawn to Ireland because of its metal deposits, establishing communities near the mother lode, working and living there for several generations only to leave when the ore was depleted.

Rossbeigh
Time Portal

[N70 10 km (6.3 miles) from Killorglin] This stunning strand juts out into Dingle Bay and is the point where the legendary 'Great Wave', *Tonn Toime* roars in from the sea every seven years. It is also the spot where the otherworld meets reality. It is the place where Oisín, the son of the Fianna's greatest warrior, Fionn, was taken to the land of Tír na nÓg by the beautiful Niamh riding her white horse. She met him while he was hunting and took him to Rossbeigh, a portal in time and space. The Fianna followed the pair as they galloped along the strand, turned toward the sea and vanished. When Oisín returned, it was three hundred years later.

Skellig Michael
Pagan and Celtic Christian Site
OS 20V.25.61

This dramatic rock soars 213 m [700 ft] above the heaving and grey Atlantic and has a collection of

Kilmalkedar sundial, possibly as early as the 7th century.

Opposite page: Skellig Michael, a 6th-century hermitage perched on a piece of slate, 4 miles off the Kerry coast.

Stone head from the chancel arch of Kilmalkedar church.

monastic cells and a small oratory. Originally a pagan site dedicated to Manannan mac Lir, the god of the sea, it was 're-baptised' as Skellig Micheal sometime in the 7th century. The monks came to this barren rock and built two small churches, a number of circular beehive dwellings and an oratory. In boats made of hide they transported enough soil for their own graves and a garden.

It was raided by the Vikings in 824, when they kidnapped the abbot, Etgal, who is later recorded in the *Annals of Ulster* as having died soon after of hunger and thirst. The monks later settled ashore at Ballinskelligs after a further Viking raid.

St Patrick's Breastplate

'Christ to shield me today
Against poison, against burning
Against drowning, against wounding.
Christ with me, Christ before me, Christ behind me

Christ in me, Christ beneath me, Christ above me
Christ on my right, Christ on my left
Christ in every eye that sees me
Christ in every ear that hears me'
[Attributed 7th century]

Staigue
Ancient Stone Citadel
OS 24V.61.63

This large stone fort is possibly a residence of the Belgae who arrived in this part of Ireland around 200 BC. It may have been used for ritual, as their god, Bolg [the god of lightning] was venerated during storms and the fort would have been a suitable amphitheatre for such observations. It has similarities to other stone forts and especially to Dún Aengus on the Aran Islands, which also may have been a *Fir Bolg* fortress. The term *Fir Bolg* is a really a 'catch-phrase' for any and every tribal group that existed on the island before the 'true' Celts. They were *probably* Belgae, who were probably a multiplicity of tribal groups originating in Gaul but perhaps travelling to Ireland via England to escape Ceasar's legions [Barrington, 1976].

County Tipperary *Tiobraid Arann*
Ara's Well

Within Tipperary existed several tribal groupings of the *Muscraighe*, a people who were established on the island long before the Christian era. Their goddess *Dovinia* is inscribed on Kerry Ogham stones of the Corcu Duibne tribal grouping and Coirpre Musc [Muscraighe] was his incestuous son. The Muscraighe Tíre of Tipperary were based around a townland called Allen Hogan and the O'Hogans are their probable descendants. The ancient primal poem, *The Cailleach Berri,* is probably a geographic hymn to the Muscraighe territories of Kerry and Tipperary and the interwoven contrast between the lonely and rugged Beara Peninsula and the fertile and prosperous plain of Femen, near Cashel [Byrne, 1973].

Cashel

Ancient Art and Architecture

OS 18S.07.41

This monument is probably the best known ecclesiastical site in Ireland and one of the most impressive in Europe. Its name may derive from the Gaelic *Cis-ail* meaning 'rent rock' as it was the residence of the Munster kings and the place where their tributes were paid. 'Cashel' is a relatively common place-name, however, and its more likely meaning is derived from the Latin *castellum* meaning a fort. Its original name as recorded in the ancient manuscripts was *sidh-dhruim* [fairy ridge] and it was changed by Conall Corc, Eoghanacht king of Munster at the beginning of the 5th century when he built a circular stone-walled citadel on the summit.

The Eoghanacht, whose sacred tree was the yew [Gaelic, *ibur*], may have been connected to the *Eburones*, a Gaulish people defeated by Caesar in the winter campaign of 55–54 BC. As a result, their king, Catuvolcus, poisoned himself with yew as an horrific penance for the defeat of his people [Byrne, 1973]. The Eoghanacht also had connections in Wales for several centuries, especially in the Gower Peninsula and it may have been returning 'emigrants' to Munster that invigorated the already-existing Eoghanacht power base. Further collaterals of the Eoghanacht were based around the Lakes of Killarney, where yew woods remain to this day. In particular, Muckross Abbey holds a large centuries-old yew with a corkscrew-shaped bark, and this writer noticed the same motif being repeated in stone on the columns of Cormac's Chapel on the Hill of Cashel, the Eoghanacht citadel.

The rock itself is a collection of early mediaeval buildings of which one in particular is unusual and quite different to the rest. In the 12th century Cormac McCarthy, king of Desmond,

caused a Romanesque chapel to be built which closely resembles Cluny in France and has a *Urnes* style, Hiberno-Scandinavian chest-tomb, that of King Cormac McCarthy.

Emly

Imleach Iber [The Plain of the Yews]

OS DISCOVERY SERIES 65.35.76

Emly, on the Tipperary–Knocklong road was, in the Early Christian centuries, the important ecclesiastical centre for Munster. Its saint, Ailbhe, was the patron saint of the Eoghanacht, the dominant tribal grouping of the south of Ireland, and the church at Emly originally had a giant yew tree, the symbol of the Eoghanacht, until its felling by the Dal Cais from Killaloe. The shrine of St Ailbhe is an 8th-century mini sarcophagus in yew wood, created to hold the relics of the saint. Although the shrine is broadly

The Rock of Cashel, seat of kings and bishops of Munster for 500 years, and one of the most majestic collections of mediaeval architecture in Ireland.

Irish in stylistic detail, the geometric pattern incised in silver on the wood, and the yellow and dark green medallions are most unusual for Irish shrines of this period and stylistically similar to examples in Tuscany [de Paor, 1958].

Glen of Aherlow
Ancient Woods
OS 18R.95.29

This Glen, stretching for about 5 km [3.1 miles] between the hills of Slievenamuck [Hill of the Pigs] and the Galtee Mountains, was originally part of the great forest of Aherlow which covered several thousand hectares until its destruction in the 17th century. The Glen was an important routeway between Tipperary and Limerick and was the scene of many battles involving the Dalcassians, later to become the O'Briens. While its woods were intact, it was shelter for many of the Irish nobility during their frequent wars against those seeking to dispossess them of their ancient lands. In the 16th century, Dr Geoffrey Keating, the historian and cleric, lived the life of an outlaw within the woods while writing his *Foras Feasa Éireann*, a history of Ireland up to the 12th century. The Glen still has an air of times past, and the road that winds its way through young woodland on the southern side is the old, 18th-century coach-road, itself replacing the original trackway through the forest.

Knockgraffon
Otherworld Music
[Off N24 from Cahir to Tipperary] This mound and its surrounding mediaeval remains are broadly 12th century, constructed as a bulwark by the English of Leinster against the O'Briens of Thomond. Its origins, however, are possibly much earlier and it is renowned as a place of otherworld music. It was widely reputed in the 19th century to be a place where *ceolsidhe*, the music of enchantment, could be heard.

In earlier times Knockgraffon was a 'dún' a residence of King Fiacha Muillethan, a Munster chieftain who fought and defeated King Cormac Mac Airt when he attempted to levy tribute. It has an ancient well, where Fiacha had placed silver cups for anyone wishing to drink, to offer hospitality and show his rule of law. A poet of the 7th century, Comgan mac da Cherda, visited the rath when it was surrounded by woodland and uttered the following verse;

'This great rath on which I stand
Wherein is a little well with a bright silver drinking
cup
Sweet was the voice of the wood of blackbirds
Round this rath of Fiacha, son of Moinche'.
[Joyce, 1913]

Longfordpass
Border Fortress
OS 18R.24.62

On a hill overlooking the Urlingford road into Tipperary sits the 'Frontier Post' at *Clar Daire Mór* [the plain of the great oak]. The terrain around this fortress would have been extremely boggy in the Early Christian period with over 100 sq. km [62.5 miles] of impassable marsh on either side of the routeway south. This massive fortress was probably constructed in the Early Christian period and is of bi-vallate [double rampart] construction, with the inner mound being approximately 50 m [164 ft] in diameter, surrounded by a deep ditch and double outer dike. In addition, its prominent siting on a hill overlooking the pass through surrounding woodland ensured those entering the territory were aware of a capability for defence or attack. This highly visible site was an important fortress defending the northern approach to Cashel and the Eoghanacht kingdom of Munster as it existed in the 8–9th century and in later times, it was the residence of a king, Donnachad mac Cellaig. It is

Opposite page: A 'new' part of the great woods of Aherlow which covered several thousand hectares up to the 17th century and provided a refuge for Geoffrey Keating, one of Gaelic Ireland's refugee scholars.

Originally
surrounded by
woods, the triple-
ramparted rath of
Longfordpass, near
Urlingford, was the
8th-century AD
'border post' of the
kingdom of
Munster.

mentioned in a manuscript in the Royal Irish Academy when King Muirchertach mac Lochlainn stayed there during his circuit of the country in the winter of 1156 AD. The document supporting his 'grand tour' was a piece of poetic propaganda, written to give his rise to power in Ulster an older pedigree by suggesting his circuit of Ireland was a repeat of his ancestors tour in the 10th century [Ó Corráin, 1972].

Rathurles

OS 18R.90.80

[Nenagh–Cloghjordan road] Rathurles is a massive tri-vallate rath which appears too large for an individual residence, but as the Muscraighe had a king to represent the different tribes from Tipperary to Kerry, he may have used this site for assemblies. Expert opinion would suggest that a fair was held here in the Early Christian era and although the interior space is cluttered by the ruins of a

15th-century church, it is walkable and atmospheric. It was probably part of O'Cinneda lands, as they were also Muscraigh and overlords of that part of Tipperary [Harbison, 1970].

St Berraherb's Kyle
A Place of Spiritual Power

OS 18R.95.29

This unknown and secret monk's arbour is one of the most hidden and sacred places of Ireland. It retains an atmosphere of almost tangible sanctity amid its lush surroundings. The monks who lived here are buried nearby and their curious circular 'church' contains many Early Christian crosses and religious symbols. It is dominated by a large oak tree, perhaps part of the original Aherlow woods, and a large high cross set into the wall and of unusual decoration. The route to the hermitage is across a boggy daffodil-filled field, and through a natural gateway of two hawthorn bushes.

County Waterford *Vedrafiordr [Norse]*

The areas around Tramore Bay and Waterford harbour have shown to be some of the earliest inhabited sites on the island of Ireland. Early hunter-gatherers of *c.* 5000 BC had their camps in these estuaries and probably fished the rich waters using arrows and harpoons made from bone and tusk [Cooney and Grogan, 1994]. Portal tombs from the second millennium BC are scattered throughout the county and their particular form is carried across the Irish Sea into south Wales. Although the county is not large, it has both scenic coastline and dramatic mountains. The Comeraghs, the Monavullaghs and the Knockmealdowns form a theatrical and rugged backdrop to the pastureland from Waterford City to Dungarvan and points further west. The many beaches form an attractive southern boundary offering clear water and a climate often some degrees warmer than the rest of the country.

The county is bounded east and west by the River Blackwater and the River Barrow, both of whom penetrate deep into the interior of Leinster. The Blackwater valley was deeply wooded from Youghal to Lismore, and remained so until Walter Raleigh clear-felled this ancient gallery forest in 1586 in order to repay his bankers in London. He had come to exploit the mussel fisheries of the estuary and through intrigue and manipulation, became the owner of the Fitzgerald of the *Decies* estate. The Decies is a name given to Waterford and it derives from the Deisi, a dominant tribal grouping who inhabited the area in the Early Christian period. The Deisi were the traditional enemies of Ossory [now Kilkenny] and sometime before the Christian period defeated the Ossory warriors in battle through the costly sacrifice of a tribal druid. It is said that the druid had the facility of shape-changing, and in this instance, had the

The spiritual oasis of Berraherb's Kyle, hidden and secret amid the woods of Aherlow.

foresight to change himself into a cow before his time came. Human sacrifice was perhaps a device of last resort to Celtic peoples and the ritual death of a sacred member of the tribe would be an expensive wager, predicated on a favourable result.

From an early period, the Deisi occupied an adjacent and related region in south-west Wales which originally was the territory of the Demetae, a Praetanic tribe who were clients [federatii] of the Roman Empire in Britain. The Deisi may also have become clients of the Romans, perhaps invited by Magnus Maximus to assist in his campaigns against the Siluri and being given an area of south-west Wales as far east as the Severn estuary. The Demetae and Deisi were in a relationship for over 500 years, contributing to the emergence of Welsh

Rathurles. A massive ringfort, reputedly the site of an ancient aonach, *or market, where hides, wool and perhaps slaves could be offered for sale and exchanged for exotic goods from abroad. It declined slowly after the Normans established Nenagh as a market-town in the 12th century.*

literature and were closely related through marriage and trading contacts. Their combined territory in Wales was known as Dyfed and the Deisi settlement there dates from *c.* 4th century. Interestingly, the relatively harmonious relationship between Dyfed and Waterford is in contrast to the mercenary and violent confrontations between the Gáileóin of north Leinster and their attempted conquest of north Wales. The same north Leinster dynasty fought the Deisi in a battle at the Hill of Tara which resulted in the slaying of Conn mac Cormack and the partial blinding of his brother in the year 265 AD [*Annals of the Four Masters*]. Their arrival in the Waterford area may date shortly after this event. The Lleyn Peninsula has over 100 Irish place-names and Ptolemy called the peninsula the 'Promontory of the Gargani' [Laing, 1975].

The Venitii

Along the coast are several promontory forts possibly of the Late Bronze Age period and these appear to form a series along the south-west Atlantic coast of Ireland. It seems possible that the forts were built by the Venetii, a Celtic population group described by Caesar as living

'on the ends of spits of headlands, difficult to reach by sea . . . impossible to attack from land' [Cunliffe, 1986]. Many such cliff castles survive along the coast of Brittany and the Venetii, being a maritime trading nation, perhaps travelled as far as Ireland for slaves, hunting dogs and hides. Their long-established homeland in Armorica [Brittany] lay between the Mediterranean and the northern seas of Ireland and England, and they were well placed to act as middlemen for trade in either direction. Waterford would have been within relatively easy sailing distance from southern Brittany and this writer has made the journey by fishing vessel in 28 hours.

Although there is no *direct* evidence of Venetii trading contacts with Ireland, the Celtic love of wine and their taste for conspicuous consumption may have attracted the Venetii to establish trading posts for the mutual exchange of goods. Trading contacts with Ireland may have gone back several millennia as Brittany has produced gold lunulae from the 3rd millennium BC which originated in Ireland, and wedge-tombs in Ireland and Brittany share many similarities. Perhaps the communities that lived adjacent to the sea from Iberia to Armorica to Dún Aengus shared an understanding based on travel and trade and a different sensibility to their neighbours inland.

In 56 BC the Venetii rebelled against Caesar but were destroyed in the great sea-battle of Quiberon when their leaders were executed and the survivors sold as slaves. Their sea-going vessels were described by Caesar as being of a large size, high out of the water, made of solid oak with decks a foot thick and held together with bronze nails. Interestingly, the Corco

Loigde, Corco Duibne, Ciarraigh and the Altraigh, of west Munster and the south-west coast in general, while sharing similar status in Early-Christian Ireland as subject tribes, appear to have controlled much of the maritime traffic along the coasts and perhaps also river access to the great monasteries founded by their kinsmen, such as Cíarán of Clonmacnoise.

Knockeen Dolmen
Dolmen and Shamanic Chamber
OS 23S.57.07

This very striking 4,000-year-old dolmen has a large chamber beneath the two capstones and a small 'entrance' on one side. This small triangular hole at the base of the two side stones appears to have been deliberately created so as to allow access to certain people, perhaps relatives paying respects to the dead, or shamans or early druids entering the chamber to commune with the supernatural.

Waterford Harbour

At the entrance to this port is the busy fishing community of Dunmore East, which also doubles as a popular holiday destination. To the south of this pretty village, on the minor road that runs along the coast, are a number of promontory forts and a standing stone. The headland fort at Rathmoylan may be the spot in legend where one of the legendary founding 'Celts' landed, *Cesair*, a goddess accompanied by 50 women. Her pilot and oarsman, Ladra, tired of rowing and being the happy sailor, took himself off with as many of the women as he could muster and was later found dead. The *Annals* record that 'it was due to an excess of women, or maybe the shaft of the oar that had penetrated his buttock' [Dames, 1992].

Ardmore
War-Gods and Christians

This striking round tower was part of a monastery founded by St Declan, perhaps as

early as the 5th century. It contains two Ogham stones, one of which has the inscription NETA-SEGAMONAS, which suggests a commemoration for the 'grandson of' Segmon [Harbison, 1992]. This individual, *Segomo*, however, is a Gaulish war-god and *Neta-Segamonas* would translate as 'Champion of Segomas'. Waterford and its tribal group, the Deisi, were connected to the Eoghanacht of Cashel and both had long associations with Roman Britain, where Ogham writing, based on Latin, began. The Deisi probably settled in south Wales in the 4th century and the later Welsh kings of Dyfed Tewdws ap Rhein were the descendants of a Deisi prince, Eochaid Allmuir mac Artchuirp who settled in Dyfed, the land of the Demetae in Roman times [Byrne, 1973].

Knockeen dolmen, constructed 4,000 years ago, with a special entrance for relatives to place gifts for the dead, or shamans to enter and commune with the supernatural.

St Declan founded the monastery here at Ardmore before St Patrick came to Ireland. The round tower is almost 30 m high. The church has beautiful c. 12th-century Romanesque arcades along an interior wall.

Béal Boru, traditionally the seat of Brian Boru, leader of the Dal Cais, *a dynasty that rose to power through defeating the Limerick Vikings in the 10th century.*

Cahermacnaghten, the Stone Fort of Neachtan, the ancient law school of the O'Davoren family.

County Clare *Clár*
The Wooden Bridge

This county is unusual in the number and extent of its megalithic tombs, with over 100 *wedge-tombs* being identified in the east of the county. These tombs, dating from around 2000 BC, were probably the 'family vault' of farming groups that came to Ireland from Brittany seeking either better land or mining prospects.

A considerable portion of the east of the county was dominated by the vast woodland known as *Suidain* of which nothing now remains. The wood extended from where the town of Ennis now stands southwards to the Shannon, thence northwards to Scariff on Lough Derg and from Gort in Co. Galway to the foothills of the Slieve Bernagh mountains west of Killaloe. Remnants

existed down to modern times, and the townland of *Cratloe Woods* between Limerick City and Shannon airport is a reminder of their importance. Local folklore suggests that timber from Cratloe supplied the roof-trusses for Westminster Cathedral but this would suggest possibly an early mediaeval date for their felling. The black oak *misericords* [seats for the clergy] in Limerick's St Mary's Cathedral were carved from the oaks of Cratloe woods between 1480 and 1500, and their depictions of imaginary animals and human figures in mediaeval costume can be seen today.

A Unique Landscape

The Burren, a limestone 'pavement' between Lisdoonvara and Ballyvaughan, is a treasure house for botanists and nature lovers alike, with over 1,100 different species of plant including rare orchids, growing in the cracks of the rocks. It has several ancient tombs on the R480 between Aillwee and Leamaneh; Poulnabrone dating from around 2500 BC and found to contain the cremated remains of 17 adults and 16 children, and Glininsheen, where a gold gorget or collar was discovered in 1930. There is reasonable evidence to suggest one of two things; either there was considerable infant mortality, or a tradition existed that saw a child 'accompany' a valued elder to the next world. The Burren Way is a right-of-way from Ballynalackan to Ballyvaughan, following the line of an ancient trackway. It connects dozens of ringforts along the pastureland between the rocky high ground and the sea. Clare also has the great tri-vallate fort of Mooghaun, sited on top of a hill and the site of a considerable community during the Bronze Age. It was populated during the Iron Age around from 500 BC to 500 AD but is now heavily overgrown. There are, however, helpful illustrations at the site to 'imagine' what things were like, but the vegetation makes it difficult. About 750 m [2,460 ft] north-west of the hillfort is Mooghaun Lough, possibly the wetland depository for the fort. In 1854, the largest find of prehistoric gold objects were found near the shore of this lake including bracelets and armbands.

Béal Boru
Royal Fortress

OS 18.69.74

This large ringfort lies at the end of a tree-lined pathway off the Killaloe–Tuamgraney road, about 1.6 km [1 mile] from Killaloe. In history, it was the site where cattle-tributes, paid to the *Dal Cais*, were forded across the Shannon to be counted and allocated. It may have been an earlier pre-historic site, as bone pins and stone axes were excavated nearby in the 1930s. It retains an atmosphere of power, suggesting the dynasty who held sway here was important. Béal Boru was probably one of a series of forts around the area, centred on Killaloe.

Cahermacnaghten

[The Stone Fort of Neachtan] **Ancient Law School**

OS 14M.19.00

This 30 m [98 ft] in diameter stone cashel was the site of a famous Mediaeval law school, run by the O'Davoren family, where the Brehon laws continued to be taught and studied down to the middle of the 17th century. The laws were also known as *Fenechas*, or laws of the 'free land-tillers'. Brehons could be male or female and were highly influential individuals who knew both the laws intimately and adjudicated on cases also. The laws when finally written down in *Berla Feini*, an obscure early Irish dialect, were divided into two volumes, *Senchus Mor*, which in general covered civil law, and the *Book of Acaill*, which dealt with criminal law and personal injuries. There was also *Cain*, which was the Brehon law that applied to all of Ireland, and *Urradus* which was local or

provincial in effect only [Joyce, 1913]. Usually Brehons were attached to a local royal family and were given land for their private use, so that legal families tended to remain within the same area for generations, serving the ruling family and the legal needs of the *tuath*, or tribal land. In cases involving property or claims for damages, Brehons were entitled to a fee, *fola*, usually one-twelfth of the value involved.

Iniscealtra

[Boat from Scariff] Founded by St Caimin in the 7th century, the monastery was burnt by Vikings in 836 and 922. The Benedictines were established on the island by the latter date and the island remained a monastery until the end of the 16th century. It is an extraordinary place, retaining an air of peace and tranquillity quite unspoiled by any development. The last witch of Lough Derg, reputedly a convert to Christianity, is buried within the nave of St Caimin's church.

Killaloe Cathedral
Christian Vikings

This 12th-century cathedral stands where a monastery was founded in the 5th century by St Fachnan. The cathedral has a unique Ogham stone with an inscription in both Ogham writing and Viking Runes, both requesting a 'prayer for Thorgrim' [Harbison, 1992]. The cathedral probably owes its scale and decoration to increased revenues when it received the dissolved see of Iniscathy and all the diocesan lands of Roscrea. It is an 'English' style of gothic cathedral and it is worth bearing in mind that Donal Mor O'Brien called in the Anglo-Normans to help maintain his territorial power in 1197, around the

The shaft of the 12th-century high-cross at Dysert O'Dea, Co. Clare, showing elaborate scrollwork, perhaps of Scottish derivation.

time the cathedral began construction. Prince John stayed at Killaloe in the same year and an English cleric was appointed bishop soon after. It has a massive east window, some 11 m [36 ft] high and 5 m [16 ft] wide. The stonework of the corbels are similar to Kilfenora and Christchurch in Dublin and perhaps the same master mason was involved, developing ideas as he travelled from site to site [Leask, 1958].

Magh Adair
Ritual Mound

OS 17R.44.77

The *Dal Cais* of Clare first appear in history around the time of the Viking settlements at Limerick. They were originally part of the Deisi Muman, the 'vassal people of Munster' and were tribute-payers to their Eoghanacht overlords. By the 10th century, however, they were powerful enough to challenge the Eoghanacht and defeat other smaller tribes such as the Uí Fidgenti. More importantly, they gained battle experience and tactical skills through fighting with and ultimately defeating the Danes of Limerick. The result of this martial activity brought to prominence two brothers, Mathgamhain mac Cennetig and Brian Borumha, later to defeat the Danes of Dublin at the famous Battle of Clontarf in 1014.

Magh Adair, disappointing in its neglected state, is nevertheless of importance. In the past, the Dalcassians were inaugurated on the central mound which forms the focal point for a complex series of earthworks. The mound itself appears to have been higher in the past and has been broken down by cattle and weather. It is partly surrounded by a semi-circular rampart which appears to have a gateway or ritual entrance beside an earthen ramp leading to the summit. The encircling rampart is higher than the mound on the eastern side and gives one the impression of a tiered viewing area, perhaps where the chieftain was brought to be 'inspected' by his peers and sub-chiefs.

Important parts of the ceremony were performed by one or more of these sub-chiefs, roles that were both honourable and hereditary. Each ancient royal family had an 'inaugurator', the O'Neills had O'Hagan and O'Cahan for that function and the O'Donnels of Tír Conaill had the O'Friel to inaugurate them. When the Dal Cais kings were brought to Magh Adair for their *ordinatio* they probably came on a white horse and followed a traditional ceremony, perhaps borrowed from another tribe. Magh Adair may have been the burial mound of a Dalcassian ancestor, and the king elect would have stood on the summit while the laws of the clan were recited by his hereditary Brehon and his lengthy obligations read out. The chief would have sworn to uphold the laws of the tribe and would then have been led around the assembly, firstly from left to right following the old pagan sun-route and then from right to left, in honour of the holy trinity. The ceremony would have concluded with the chieftain being handed perhaps a straight hazel rod, a symbol of his authority and an emblem of his conduct and honesty.

Magh Adair, the mound where the kings of Thomond were inaugurated.

Opposite page: Iniscealtra Island, Co. Clare, founded as a monastery in the 7th century and remaining under the Benedictines for almost 1,000 years.

Epilogue

This book has been about many things: the lives of people, wars, intrigue, *structure* and *space*. It has been about the archaeological remains of our history, the imaginative space therein, and, above all, the physical remains of ancient sites which are sometimes mundane yet often *romantic*. Many are pure homesteads, undulating remains of a singular farm, alone in its annual tasks and obligations. Other, perhaps earlier sites are of social and political importance, relating the tribal group to its deities and their ritual requirements of attendance and seasonal sacrifice.

A lone thorn bush, traditionally never to be cut as it 'belongs' to the fairies, the people who have gone before, the people of the past.

Sometimes the place has a deeper significance, representing an area where alyssum and earth meet, and where mortals may consort, however briefly, with gods. That ritualised encounter is often the architectural dynamic behind the form, with the veritable symbol depicting the hoped-for rendezvous. For if

mythology requires a place for its telling, then the venue chosen may give a sense of drama to its utterance. It is perhaps this *context* of discourse that fulfils an essential part of an imaginative experience. And the earlier the structure, the more likely this form to be female, a receiving earth-mother, her entombing uterine space the hub of tribal religious experience.

If we Irish have an identity that can be ascribed to any particular population group, our most dominant predecessors may turn out to be Urn-Field or Beaker Folk, European immigrants seeking opportunity and better living conditions in Ireland than their homeland. It was they who began the revolution in metal-working in Munster, over 3,500 years ago, clearing the forests to supply the voracious appetites of the Mount Gabriel mines, supplying axes in return for gold and creating the finest collection of prehistoric ornamental jewellery in Europe.

Our wishful adaptation of the word 'Celtic' for Irish people is, realistically, more romantic than factual, and this has brought with it a credulous enchantment with the past — and an unrealistic past at that. Perhaps forceful arrivals in relatively recent times left the impression that invasion was the only method by which culture could come from abroad, and that it would always be of a 'higher' form. Equally, the need for an identity separate from our dominant neighbour prompted the search through history for something 'different' and older. The reality is that, for most of pre-Christian history, the Ierni and the Praetanni of Hibernia and Albion were probably cousins in blood, language and culture.

Taking the pictures has brought me to ancient confines, both profane and hallowed, and to sites striking in their beauty yet sometimes devoid of sanctity or presence. Others are pungent with despair, neglected by current occupants oblivious to their significance and value. Researching the text has also altered the way I think about mythology. I no longer regard it as a fable, even a tale of collateral descent, but rather as a complete and perhaps logical system of thought. It is scientific in its own way, the accumulated result of generations of observation, speculation and conclusion. Our European ancestors were thoughtful and systematic in their naming of every geographical feature, and, in presuming a cause for every effect, they sought to structure their experience within a credible explanatory narrative. They lived in a world of sensory experience, frequently chaotic and often beyond explanation. But by classifying that experience through a myth, be it to generate fecundity or avert catastrophe, they arrived at the beginnings of a scientific method of analysis; for any classification, however bizarre, is superior to *no* classification.

I came to realise that the people who developed agriculture, pottery, bronze and iron-working, and who produced accomplished and beautiful works of art, were not ignorant or illiterate, in the sense of being without the tools necessary for survival or progress. They were locally organised, efficient in their use of animals and raw materials, and respectful of nature and her bounty. They used imagination and cognition to develop precepts about their world and endlessly rearranged the experiences they had accumulated within the boundaries of their mythology. They believed that by gathering memory, history, observations, discoveries and speculation together, they could account for everything that had happened and ever would happen. Their desire, their drive to be, having produced a degree of technology, law and organisation, expressed itself in their chimerical discourse, the utterance of their unconscious through mythology, it being their scientific canon, their liturgy and their method of sublimating the anarchy, libido and anxiety of that society.

The social organisation of the insular Celts as described in the ancient Irish law tracts was hierarchical and aristocratic. Elaborate fines, calculated in *cumals*, those female slaves who terrified the early monks, were levied on those who transgressed the elaborate and prescribed formalities of rank, or committed felonies against body or property. Families defended their patrimony against outsiders and eliminated internal dissent with equal ferocity, for the nobility of early Ireland defended their rights and privileges as carefully and assiduously as any latter-day politician or wealthy business-owner. As the book progressed, I realised that the arrival of Christianity brought a focus to the grouping of the Derbfine and its Tuath, and through the creation of markets, schools and a communal worship began the process of creating a sense of 'Irishness'. That society produced a quality of art in metalwork, scriptorium and stonework which suggests a highly refined, if archaic artistic sense. The Christian art of early Ireland is extraordinary, in that while the style is similar to Gaul of several centuries earlier, and contains elements of Scandinavian scrollwork and pagan symbolism, it is nevertheless unique and wonderful. It is full of beauty, colour and grace. The creatures of paganism nibble at the hem of their creator, as if eager to be remembered as those that had prepared the way, opening the consciousness of insular society to the new ideology of Christianity, an enlightened vision of humanity dispelling some of the gloom of the dark ages.

This book also owes a debt. It has relied heavily on the scholarship of other, more learned individuals who have spent decades in the fields of archaeology, mythology and early Irish history. To their credit, as new information comes to light, they have amended their theories and altered their views. Their books are listed in the bibliography. I covet their erudition and hope they find this novice historian's work of some interest.

To try and encapsulate a distant and pre-historic part of Ireland's past has not been easy. It is only when one attempts the job, on however small a scale, that the realisation dawns how large, unknown and academically demanding the centuries before the written word can be. It is *then* that the work done by scholars is appreciated. Some of this book is therefore, conjecture, but reasonably accurate within available facts and information. The convolutions of early Ireland between the tribal groupings and their somewhat bewildering changes of name and location have sometimes led to frustration and confusion. I hope this book does not add to the complex puzzle that 'Celtic' Ireland offers its students.

Ireland's lack of industrialisation, low population and respect for antiquity enabled many of our ancient sites to remain undisturbed for centuries, but inevitably this is now changing. Perhaps a negative dynamic exists between knowledge of the past and the ability to tolerate its presence.

But the past has a captivating quality: it is a text wherein we may become trapped, forever believing that whatever happened then, was better than what is happening now.

But *now* is all we have.

Bibliography

Ballymun Public Library
The Journal of the Royal Society of Antiquaries
The Library of the Royal Society of Antiquaries
The Library at Saor-Ollscoil na h-Éireann
The Rooney Library at the American College Dublin

Arnold, Bruce, *A Concise History of Irish Art*, Thames & Hudson, 1969.

Barrington, T. J., *Discovering Kerry*, Blackwater Press, 1976.
Barry, Terry, *A History of Settlement in Ireland*, Routledge, 2000.
Brennan, Martin, *The Stones of Time*, Inner Teaching Press, 1983.
Burnbaum H. & Puhvel, J., *Ancient Indo-European Dialects*, UCLA Press, 1966.
Byrne, Francis J., *Irish Kings and High-Kings*, Four Courts Press, 2001.

Campbell, Joseph, *Primitive Mythology*, Penguin, 1976.
Carney, James, *Mediaeval Irish Lyrics*, Dolmen Press, 1967.
Chadwick, Nora, *The Celts*, Pelican Books, 1979.
Connolly, S.J., *The Oxford Companion to Irish History*, Oxford University Press, 1998.
Connors, Sean, *Mapping Ireland*, Mercier Press, 2001.
Cooney, G. & Grogan, E., *Irish Pre-History*, Wordwell, 1994.
Cunliffe, Barry, *The Celtic World*, Greenwich House, 1986.
Cunliffe, Barry, *Facing the Ocean*, Oxford, 2001.
Cunningham, Bernadette, *The World of Geoffrey Keating*, Four Courts Press, 2000.
Curtiss, Edmund, *A History of Ireland*, Methuen, 1950.

Dames, Michael, *Mythic Ireland*, Thames & Hudson, 1992.
Davies, John, *The Celts*, Cassell & Co., 2000.
Delaney, Frank, *The Celts*, BBC Publications, 1986.
De Paor, Liam & Máire, *Early Christian Ireland*, Thames & Hudson, 1958.
Dillon, Myles, *Early Irish Literature*, University of Chicago Press, 1948.

Dudley-Edwards, Ruth, *Atlas of Irish History*, Routledge, 1973.

Edel, Doris, *The Celtic West and Europe*, Four Courts Press, 2001.
Elliott, Marianne, *The Catholics of Ulster*, Penguin Press, 2000.

Flower, Robin, *The Irish Tradition*, Lilliput Press, 1994.
Fréine, Seán de, *The Great Silence*, Mercier Press, 1965.

Glob, P.V., *The Bog People*, Book Club Associates, 1965.
Goodeneough, Simon, *Celtic Mythology*, Todtri Press, 1997.
Green, Miranda, *Gods of the Celts*, Barnes & Noble, 1986.
Green, Miranda, *Symbol and Image in Celtic Religious Art*, Routledge,1989.
Green, Miranda, *Animals in Celtic Life & Myth*, Routledge, 1992.
Green, Miranda, *The Celtic World*, Routledge, 1995.
Green, Miranda, *Celtic Goddesses*, George Braziller, 1996.
Greene, D. & O'Connor, F., *Irish Poetry, AD 600 to 1200*, Macmillan, 1967.

Harbison, Peter, *Pre-Christian Ireland*, Thames & Hudson, 1988.
Harbison, Peter, *Guide to National and Historic Monuments of Ireland*, Gill & Macmillan, 1992.
Haverty, Martin, *The History of Ireland*, Duffy & Co., [Dublin], 1860.
Healy, Elizabeth, *Ireland's Holy Wells*, Wolfhound Press, 2001.
Henry, Francois, *Irish Art in the Early Christian Period*, Methuen & Co., 1940.
Herity, M. & Eogan, G., *Ireland in Prehistory*, Routledge, 1997.
Hutton, Ronald, *Pagan Religions of the Ancient British Isles*, Blackwell, 1991.
Hyde, Douglas, *Early Gaelic Literature*, Fisher & Unwin, 1923.

James, Simon, *The World of the Celts*, Thames & Hudson, 1993.

Joyce, P.W., *Irish Names of Places*, Vols 1–3, Gill & Co., 1883.

Joyce, P.W., *Social History of Ancient Ireland*, Vols 1–2, Gill & Co., 1913.

Joyce, W.St J., *The Neighbourhood of Dublin*, Skellig Press, 1988 [reprint].

Kelly, Fergus, *Early Irish Farming*, Dublin Institute for Advanced Studies, 2000.

Kinsella, Thomas, *The Táin*, Oxford University Press, 1988.

Knopf, A., *Treasures of Irish Art*, Metropolitan Museum of Art, 1999.

Laing, Lloyd, *Late Celtic Ireland and Britain*, Methuen, 1975.

Leask, Harold, *Irish Churches and Monastic Buildings*, Dundalgan Press, 1955–60.

Lysaght, Patricia, *The Banshee*, Glendale Press, 1993.

MacCana, Proinseas, *Celtic Mythology*, Chancellor Press, 1997.

McDonagh, Thomas, *Literature in Ireland*, Talbot Press, 1914.

MacGeoghegan, Abbe, *The History of Ireland*, James Duffy, 1844.

MacNeill, Eoin, *Phases of Irish History*, Gill & Co., 1920.

Mac Niocaill, G., *Ireland before the Vikings*, Gill & Macmillan, 1972.

Mallory, J.P., *In Search of the Indo-Europeans*, Thames & Hudson, 1989.

Maxwell, C., *Irish History from Contemporary Sources*, Allen & Unwin, 1923.

Megaw, R. & V., *Celtic Art*, Thames & Hudson, 1989.

Mitchell, Frank, *The Landscape of Ireland*, Collins Press, 1976.

Mongan, Norman, *Menapia Quest*, Herodotus Press, 1994.

Moody, T.W., *The Londonderry Plantation*, 1609–1641. Mullan & Son, 1939.

Neeson, Eoin, *Deirdre and Other Stories*, Mainstream Publishing, 1997.

Neumann, Eric, *The Great Mother*, Princeton University Press, 1974.

Nicholls, Kenneth, *Gaelic and Gaelicised Ireland in the Middle Ages*, Gill & Macmillan, 1973.

O'Connor, F. & Greene, D., *Treasury of Irish Poetry*, Macmillan, 1967.

O'Connor, Fr Tom, *Turoe and Athenry*, Kieran Jordan, 2003.

Ó Corráin, D., *Ireland before the Vikings*, Gill & Macmillan, 1972.

Ó Croinin, Daibhi, *Early Medieval Ireland*, Longman, 1995.

O'Farrell, Padraic, *Ancient Irish Legends*, Gill & Macmillan, 1995.

O'Grady, Standish, *Essays and Passages*, Talbot Press, 1918.

Ó hÓgáin, Dáithí, *The Sacred Isle*, Boydell Press, 1999.

O'Neill, Timothy, *The Irish Hand*, Dolmen Press, 1984.

Ó Ríordáin, Sean P., *Antiquities of the Irish Countryside*, Methuen, 1966.

Pochin-Mould, Daphne, *The Mountains of Ireland*, Batsford, 1955.

Raftery, Barry, *La Tène in Ireland*, Thames & Hudson, 1984.

Raftery, Barry, *Pagan Celtic Ireland*, Thames & Hudson, 1994.

Rees, E., *Celtic Saints in their Landscape*, Sutton Publishing, 2001.

Rhys, John, *Celtic Literature*, SPCK, 1904.

Rhys, John, *Celtic Britain*, Senate Press, 1996.

Richardson, H. & Scarry, J., *Irish High Crosses*, Mercier Press, 1990.

Ross, Anne, *Pagan Celtic Britain*, Routledge, 1974.

Roy, James Charles, *The Road Wet, The Wind Close*, Gill & Macmillan, 1986.

Sjoestedt, Marie-Louise, *Gods and Heroes of the Celts*, Turtle Island, 1982.

Slavin, Michael, *The Book of Tara*, Wolfhound Press, 1996.

Smyth, Alfred P. (ed.), *Seanchas, Essays in honour of Francis Byrne*, Four Courts Press, 2000.

Spellissy, Seán, *Limerick, The Rich Land*, Spellissy and O'Brien, 1989.

Stephens, James, *Irish Fairy Tales*, Macmillan & Co., 1923.

Stephens, James, *In the Land of Youth*, Macmillan & Co., 1924.

Stopford-Green, Alice, *The Making of Ireland and its Undoing*, Macmillan & Co., 1908.

Stout, Matthew, *The Irish Ringfort*, Dolmen Press, 1997.

Waddell, John, *A Prehistoric Archaeology of Ireland*, Wordwell, 2000.

Wallace, P.F., *The Architecture of Mediaeval Dublin* [Comparative History of Urban Organisation in non-Roman Europe], Oxford, 1995.

Wallace, P.F. & Ó Floinn, R., *Treasures of the National Museum*, Gill & Macmillan, 2002.

Walsh, Paul, *The Placenames of Westmeath*, Dublin Institute for Advanced Studies, 1957.

Winnecott, D.W., *Transitional Objects and Potential Spaces*, Columbia University Press, 1993.

Zaczek, Iain, *Art of the Celts*, Parkgate Books, 1997

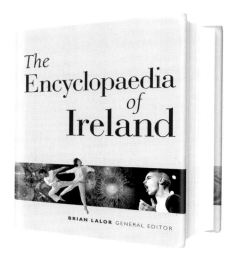